URBAN RHYTHMS AND TRAVEL BEHAVIOUR

Urban Rhythms and Travel Behaviour

Spatial and Temporal Phenomena of Daily Travel

STEFAN SCHÖNFELDER
WIFO, Austrian Institute of Economic Research, Austria

KAY W. AXHAUSEN
Swiss Federal Institute of Technology Zurich, Switzerland

LONDON AND NEW YORK

First published 2010 by Ashgate Publishing

2 Park Square, Milton Park, Abingdon, Oxon OX14 4RN
711 Third Avenue, New York, NY 10017, USA

Routledge is an imprint of the Taylor & Francis Group, an informa business

First issued in paperback 2016

British Library Cataloguing in Publication Data
Schönfelder, Stefan.
Urban rhythms and travel behaviour : spatial and temporal
phenomena of daily travel. -- (Transport and society)
1. Origin and destination traffic surveys. 2. Travel--
Statistics.
I. Title II. Series III. Axhausen, K. W., 1958-
306.4'819-dc22

Library of Congress Cataloging-in-Publication Data
Schönfelder, Stefan.
Urban rhythms and travel behaviour : spatial and temporal phenomena of daily travel / by Stefan Schönfelder and Kay W. Axhausen.
p. cm. -- (Transport and society)
Includes index.
ISBN 978-0-7546-7515-0 (hbk.)
1. Choice of transportation. 2. Route choice. 3. Travel time (Traffic engineering) 4. Trip length. 5. Migration, Internal--Social aspects. 6. Transportation--Planning. I. Axhausen, K. W., 1958- II. Title.

HE336.C5S36 2009
303.48'32--dc22

2009031267

ISBN 978-0-7546-7515-0 (hbk)
ISBN 978-1-138-27441-9 (pbk)

Transfered to Digital Printing in 2012

Contents

List of Figures

List of Tables

List of Abbreviations

ABA	Acivity-Based Analysis
AKTA	Forsøg med Kørselsafgifter i København (Copenhagen road pricing trial)
CATI	Computer-Added Telephone Interview
CHASE	Computerized Household Scheduling Survey
DPPA	Daily Potential Path Area
ETH	Eidgenössische Technische Hochschule (Zürich) (Swiss Federal Institute of Technology (Zurich)
FHWA	Federal Highway Administration
GDOT	Georgia Department of Transportation
GIS	Geographical Information System
GLM	General Linear Model
GPS	Global Positioning System
GSM	Global System for Mobile (Communications)
IIA	Independence of Irrelevant Alternatives
ISA	Intelligent Speed Adaptation
IVT	Institut für Verkehrsplanung und Transportsysteme (Institute of Transport Planning and Systems)
KTS	Osaka-Kobe-Kyoto travel survey
LRT	Light rail transit
LSE	Least-square estimation
MID	Mobilität in Deutschland (German national travel survey)
MIF	Mean Information Field
MNL	Multi-Nominal Logit (Model)
MZ	Mikrozensus Verkehr Schweiz (Swiss national travel survey)
NHTS	US National Household Travel Survey

OD	Origin-Destination (Relationship)
OECD	Organisation for Economic Co-operation and Development
PAPI	Paper-Added Personal Interview
PC	Personal Computer
PDA	Personal Digital Assistant
PROGRESS	Pricing ROad use for Greater Responsibility, Efficiency and Sustainability in citieS
SMS	Short-Message Service
SPN	Shortest-Path Network
Std.	Standard deviation
SVI	Vereinigung Schweizerischer Verkehrsingenieure (Swiss Association of Transport Engineers)
UHTS	Uppsala Household Travel Survey
UMOT	Unified Mechanism of Travel
VATS	Victory Activity and Travel Survey
WHO	World Health Organization

Notes on Authors

Dr Stefan Schönfelder is researcher at the Österreichisches Instititut für Wirtschaftsforschung (WIFO) in Vienna where he is in charge of transportation economics and policy. He is a trained regional and transport planner with a special interest in the analysis and forecasting of individual travel behaviour. He holds a PhD from the Eidgenössische Technische Hochschule (ETH) Zürich and an Engineering degree from the University of Dortmund.

Dr Kay W. Axhausen is professor of transport planning at the ETH Zürich. He holds his post in the Institute for Transport Planning and Systems of the Department of Civil, Environmental and Geomatic Engineering. Before his appointment at ETH he worked at the Leopold-Franzens Universität, Innsbruck, Imperial College London and the University of Oxford. He holds a PhD in civil engineering from the Universität Karlsruhe and an MSc from the University of Wisconsin – Madison.

He has been involved in the measurement and modelling of travel behaviour for the last 25 years contributing especially to the literature on stated preferences, micro-simulation of travel behaviour, valuation of travel time and its components, parking behaviour, activity scheduling and travel diary data collection. His current work focuses on the micro-simulation of daily travel behaviour and long-term mobility choices and the response of the land-use system to those choices. This work is supported by analyses of human activity spaces and their dependence on the traveller's personal social network.

He was the chair of the International Association of Travel Behaviour Research (IATBR) until December 2005 and is an editor of *Transportation.*

Acknowledgements

The book *Urban Rhythms and Travel Behaviour* is the outcome of a fruitful period of research on temporal and geographical routines and regularities in travel behaviour. It provides both a theoretical approach to long-term decision making in time and space and an explorative analysis of recently collected, unique data sets to reveal the structures and behavioural mechanisms involved.

This book was substantially based on the data collection efforts, methodological developments and investigations of three research projects: "Mobi*drive*" (1999–2002), "Structure and Use of Human Activity Spaces" (2002–2004) and "*Stabilität des Verkehrsverhaltens*" (2003–2004). These projects were conducted at the *Institut für Verkehrsplanung und Transportsysteme* (Institute for Transport Planning and Systems) (IVT) of the Swiss Federal Institute of Technology (ETH) in Zürich, in cooperation with our German colleagues at RWTH Aachen University and at PTV AG in Karlsruhe as well as with our Swiss colleagues at *Büro Widmer* in Frauenfeld.

Our special thanks go to the Swiss Association of Transportation Engineers and all of the colleagues involved in the projects. Another important person to thank is Prof. Chandra R. Bhat (University of Texas, Austin), who provided his expertise and advice for Stefan Schönfelder's PhD thesis, from which some chapters were derived. We are also grateful to the German Federal Ministry of Education and Research, to the Department of Civil, Environmental and Geomatic Engineering at the ETH and to the ETH itself for their generous financial support.

Work on this book involved using a range of external data sources, which would not have been possible without the cooperation of many colleagues: Jeppe H. Rich, Otto A. Nielsen, Christian Würtz and others at the Technical University of Denmark (DTU), Lyngby; Hainan Li and Randall L. Guensler at the Georgia Institute of Technology, Atlanta; and Lars Åberg at Uppsala University. We thank them for their constructive collaboration. Another "Thank you!" goes to Jean Wolf and her colleagues at GeoStats, Atlanta, who helped post-processing the Borlänge GPS data. The national diary surveys analysed in Chapter 8 were provided by the respective national data archives.

Judith Diane Weston helped us enormously to improve the quality and coherence of the book with her careful and insightful text editing and her valuable suggestions. We also thank Madis Org for his support with the data analysis in Chapter 8. Finally, we are grateful to Margaret S. Grieco, the editor of this series, for her patience and to the editing team at Ashgate Publishing, especially Valerie Rose, Carolyn Court and Sarah Wardill for their constant support.

Stefan Schönfelder and Kay Axhausen

Chapter 1
Introduction

The patterns and rhythms of urban life have fascinated observers ever since urban life began (Mumford 1961; Pahl 1970; Lilley 2002). Industrialization profoundly changed the scale of urban life from the early 19th century onwards, inspiring works by Honoré de Balzac, Friedrich Engels, Charles Booth (1889)[1] and Auguste Comte, for example. The rapid growth of cities exacerbated urban problems, making it necessary to provide and manage urban infrastructure more professionally. Transport planning and traffic engineering were two allied disciplines which emerged out of these processes relatively late, in the 1930s and 1940s, but both had been concerns of municipal engineering and urban design from the start in the 1860s (see, for example, Baumeister 1876). Their purpose has always been to provide urban actors with a reasonably priced transport system for the pursuit of spatially distributed activities (see Chapter 11 for empirical evidence).

Early success in the 1950s by social-physics researchers using large-scale, computer-based models narrowed the focus of transport planning to the peak hours of the average working day (see Weiner 2008; Hutchinson 1974; Martin, Memmott, and Bone 1961; Leibbrand 1957). While this focus was understandable against the concerns of the day, it became increasingly restrictive as time progressed. Then research in the tradition of the activity-based approach to understanding travel behaviour (see Chapter 4 for an introduction) emerged as the most important tool for widening the scope of analysis for transport planning. Not the isolated trip (see Chapter 3 for definitions), but the whole activity programme with its rhythms and interdependencies became the object of analysis (see Jones et al. 1983 and the proceedings of the relevant conference series, especially: www.iatbr.org). Better knowledge of the structures and motives of longitudinal travel behaviour has enabled transport policy and planning practice to design better measures to influence travellers according to current transport policy priorities (Long 1997; Miller 1999). Since demand management, information and counselling play more important roles in transport policy today, the traveller as an individual decision maker and his or her travel habits have been receiving more attention.

The work reported here belongs to the tradition of activity-based analysis and advances it in one crucial aspect: For the first time it employs multiday geocoded[2]

1 See also booth.lse.ac.uk.

2 Geo-coded data add an exact geographical reference (coordinate) to the item observed or reported, which allows it to be mapped, to be linked with other spatially referenced data and analysed.

observations to address questions which had been raised earlier by our discipline, but never pursued for lack of data:

- What are the multiday rhythms of activity participation?
- How variable is behaviour from day to day?
- What is the size and shape of human activity space in the urban area?
- How is innovation in spatial choice mixed with well-known routines?

This is not to say that such data have never been collected or that such analyses have never been undertaken before, but either the data was much more limited in scale and scope, or the questions were different. The only early geocoded long-duration survey (the five-week Uppsala survey of 1971; see Chapter 6) was never analysed in its spatial dimension, but employed to identify the typical day or answer the reverse question of inter- and intrapersonal variability. Analyses of various two-week surveys also focused on the latter question (see, e.g., Webber 1978; Yun and O'Kelly 1997; Miller and O'Kelly 2005).

The structure of this book

This book has four main parts. Part I presents the foundations, including a discussion of theoretical perspectives on time, space and travel, an introduction to data-collection methods and terminology and a presentation of the longitudinal data sets used in our analysis. Part II focuses on the temporal aspects of day-to-day travel behaviour, which includes the concept of activity scheduling, basic results on human mobility and an analysis of the temporal rhythms of human space-time behaviour. Part III provides a framework for the analysis of spatial aspects of day-to-day mobility and presents results on the variability of human activity space. Part IV concludes with an interpretation of our findings.

PART I – Foundations

In Chapter 2 we introduce the subject of this book by sketching the interaction between social networks, activity spaces and traffic growth. These linkages influence the adoption of intelligent transport systems, particularly with respect to their management and control technologies. We then develop qualitative models of personal activity space and commercial markets. These suggest that any decoupling between economic and traffic growth will be difficult. They also suggest that any change in trends is difficult to achieve because existing travel patterns reflect the social-capital structures of society, and society is reluctant to change without good reason or external pressure.

Chapter 3 provides a consistent definition of the units of measurement for human movement. The scope of transport and activity surveys is described, and the strengths and weaknesses of the possible implementations of such surveys (stage, trip, journey and activity-based) are highlighted, as are similarities with comparable issues in time-budget surveys.

Chapter 4 provides the theoretical and empirical background for the analyses in this book, with a focus on the introduction of the *activity-based-analysis* (ABA) tradition within mobility research, the relevant terminology of the space-time travel relationship as well as concepts and findings of earlier work on the subject.

Different levels of reporting in travel and activity diaries (stage, trip, journey and daily activity chain) result in various non-reporting strategies by the respondents that interact across the sequence of contacts between the survey researcher and the respondent. Chapter 5 summarizes what is known about these non-response processes and suggests expected values for the most crucial of them: reports of staying at home.

The analyses in this book are based on a range of individual panel-data sets derived by different data-collection methods and survey areas, which provides a great range of behavioural patterns and regional peculiarities. Chapter 6 gives a synopsis of the data bases used to reveal the structures of daily mobility. It provides a detailed description of the different data sources and clarifies differences between the observation approaches, especially between travel-diary surveys and in-vehicle GPS tracking.

Part II – The temporal aspects of day-to-day travel behaviour

The authors of this book take the view that people plan and schedule their day. Chapter 7 suggests a framework for understanding this process and summarizes current knowledge about how travellers commit to trips and activities over the preceding days.

Chapter 8 frames the other results by providing an overview of current patterns of travel behaviour in its key dimensions (share of out-of-home travellers, number of journeys and trips, distances travelled and the durations involved in conjunction with the modes chosen) while addressing the temporal (day-of-week and time-of-day) and spatial (urban, suburban and rural) dimensions.

Chapter 9 is about variability and periodicity of personal day-to-day travel. We develop a conceptual framework to investigate the day-to-day variability in activity demand and a suitable modelling approach to capture the variables driving it.

Part III – Human spatial behaviour and the analysis of activity spaces

In Chapters 10 and 11 we describe the development of approaches to visualizing and measuring human activity space and we outline a (comparative) analysis. We then provide a synopsis of the results gained by the two main analytical approaches (enumerating trips and locations over time and continuously representing and measuring space usage).

Part IV – Conclusions

Chapter 12 concludes with a summary of the results and a methodological and policy-relevant review of the major findings. The analysis of the longitudinal travel data will show a distinct ambiguity between strong habits and the aspiration for variety seeking, especially in spatial behaviour.

PART I
Foundations

Chapter 2
Theoretical Framework

Travel behaviour research works with implicit theoretical assumptions which are rarely made explicit. One which is very explicit in most work is the microeconomic assumption that more travel will be consumed *ceteris paribus* when the generalized cost of its consumption falls. But note that travel is interpreted and therefore measured in any number of ways, for example: number of movements, number of kilometres travelled (person kilometres or vehicle kilometres) and number of minutes of movement (person minutes or vehicle minutes). Given that these three basic dimensions are not perfectly correlated, it is unclear whether a particular change in any of the dimensions of the generalized costs of travel will have an effect of the same sign or size. The generalized costs of travel measure only the movement part of the day, but the overarching framework of the activity approach takes interactions into account and balances them with the activities undertaken during the day. The activity approach is based on Becker's (1965) model of leisure- and work-time allocation, expanded to account for travel (de Serpa 1971; Bates 1987) without imposing the strict rationality assumptions of Becker's neo-classical formulation on every instance of observed behaviour.

The hypothesis adopted here is that travellers trade off the generalized costs of travel with the generalized costs of the activities undertaken, which in sum make up the generalized costs of their (daily) schedules. "Generalized costs" are defined as the risk- and comfort-adjusted weighted sum of time spent on travel or activity, the associated expenditure and the social content of the movements and activities. We assume that travellers try to reduce these costs on any one day, but especially from day to day. Over longer time horizons travellers have the opportunity to change the constraints under which they must operate on a given day, some of which they choose themselves, others of which are imposed by others or are the by-product of earlier choices: home and work (or educational) locations, the availability of mobility tools (driving licences, bicycles, cars, public-transport season tickets, planes and boats), the availability of telecommunication tools (land-line phones, mobile phones, fax machines, email accounts, data lines, etc.), their network of social contacts and their contacts' home locations (relatives, friends, work colleagues, members of clubs and churches, etc., to name the most important ones). With each choice a traveller has the opportunity to trade off an up-front investment against later lower generalized costs of travel and activity. Consider, for example, the acquisition of a car, which will lower the generalized costs of travel, especially by reducing time costs, but requires a substantial outlay at the time of purchase[1].

The vast literature on transport-mode choice has shown that the time needed for the different stages of a trip and for the different elements of each stage are valued differently by travellers, as they involve different levels of comfort and risk. (See Wardman 2001, for example, for a summary of British results and Hess, Erath, and Axhausen 2008 for recent Swiss experiences.) Walking stages are valued more negatively than riding the bus or driving a car. The more likely it is that a stage along a particular route will take longer than expected, the less likely it is to be chosen, i.e., its generalized costs are deemed higher due to its unreliability. Equally, the comfort of the private vehicle is judged by most travellers to be superior to travelling by bicycle, quite apart from the higher risk of accident while cycling.

Monetary expenditures for travel and activity are obvious parts of the generalized costs of a schedule. In both cases it is appropriate to assume that travellers will only consider those expenditures which they can avoid over the time horizon of the choice at hand. The streetcar entails no additional cost to a season-ticket owner deciding on the mode for the next trip. Cost is a factor when a traveller decides whether to acquire a season ticket for the year or month ahead. Equally, the next visit to the health club only involves add-on expenditures for tips, drinks afterwards, etc., but not the membership fee any more.

The social content of the elements of the schedule are both familiar and unfamiliar to travel behaviour analysts. Social content is defined here as the sum of the social signals which a traveller sends and receives by participating in a particular trip or activity – signals which position the traveller in the social space to which she or he belongs. The use of trip-purpose classifications as a proxy is and was normal. They capture the different social contexts of the activity to which a trip leads (e.g., work, home or shopping), but mix in monetary aspects (e.g., wages earned and restaurant bills) as well as more directly social aspects, such as the size and composition of the party with whom the element (travel or activity) is undertaken. It is necessary to separate these dimensions in future analyses. The expenditure aspect should be captured separately, as should the party size and composition. Still, the social content is not exhausted by these two dimensions. Issues such as the prestige associated with certain locations, whether an activity helps to keep a long-standing promise, or whether an activity is part of a long-range plan or project need to be addressed and understood. In a social context, travellers' attitudes to risk and variety overlap because the choice of a new location for a familiar activity or a new activity at a new or known location involves monetary and social risks. One would assume that the observed number of locations never previously visited will be strongly linked to a traveller's risk aversion.

1 It is no surprise then that sellers of most long-lived consumer goods lower the barrier to purchase by offering to lengthen the payment period through leasing, loans or other similar instruments.

In summary, the key variables of the daily schedule are: risk aversion and variety seeking; the generalized costs of the schedule predicated on given locations (such as home, work and school); and the traveller's social role, social network geography, income and mobility tools. Social role subsumes age, gender, household roles and other socio-demographic factors. Our a priori expectations regarding links between the key variables and travel behaviour concern their impact in the cross-sectional sense and in the dynamic case. The following discussion will address both the cross-sectional sense and the dynamic case, but will emphasize the latter through the presentation of a series of conceptual models.

Assuming that an individual aims to live a good life and wants to realize her or his potential to the fullest (Frey 2008), the individual needs to obtain the income to live a life which satisfies the need for relationships, the need for competence and the desire for autonomy (Deci and Ryan 2000). In the absence of unearned income due to inheritance or lottery winnings, travellers (or their parents) must invest in their human capital (Becker 1962; Barro 2001). The situation for persons with inherited wealth is different, but even there the need for human capital becomes binding unless the inherited wealth affords a life without additional income[2]. Travellers find themselves in the network of effects depicted in Figure 2.1. This conceptual model describes the travel-related impacts generally inherent in the desire for increased wages, if this is the life course chosen by the traveller. Wage income can be increased through increased labour (number of hours worked per week, duration of participation between entry and exit from the labour market), through a

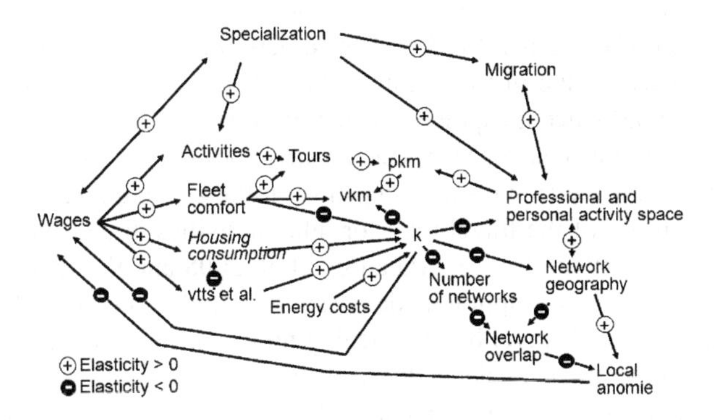

Figure 2.1 Conceptual model of the links between wages, degree of specialization and activity space

The arrows indicate the causality of the effect; the signs of the elasticity the direction of the change. k: Generalised cost of kilometre of travel; pkm: person kilometres travelled; vkm: vehicle kilometres travelled; vtts: (personal) Value of travel time savings; fleet includes the vehicles and season tickets of the persons and their households.

Source: Adapted from Axhausen 2007a.

2 Even so, a life of leisure requires an education to be able to enjoy it fully.

higher degree of specialization (human capital investment) and through residential migration at the national or international level (see Hatton and Williamson 2005 for an economic analysis of this aspect over the last two centuries).

If a person does not want to consider long-distance migration, specialization provides a secure way to increase her or his income (see Goldin and King 2008; Heckman, Lochner, and Todd 2003; Psacharopoulos and Patrinos 2004). However, specialization requires interaction across a larger activity space, understood as the geography delimited by the locations visited by the person, because the necessary training and education require some migration or commuting and because more specialized work will entail more travel, either by the person or to the person. Migration and commuting during the training phase is due to the need for efficient sizes of the training institutions. The more specialized the education, the longer the commutes or moves one would expect as the number of institutions serving this demand becomes smaller and spatially sparser. In the same vein, more specialized training makes a person more productive and *ceteris paribus* better paid, but requires more travel as work assignments will be rarer per customer and therefore more spatially dispersed. Such an increased activity space is only feasible if the gains of specialization are not consumed by the generalized costs of travel (time and money expenditures). The level of the generalized costs can be chosen by travellers through their medium-term choices, as discussed above. One would expect and can observe that travellers use increases in wage income to lower generalized travel costs by acquiring cars and season tickets (see Chapter 7), increasing the speed of travel and improving its comfort. For example, they exchange walking for bicycle travel, or second-class train travel for first-class travel. The level of the generalized costs also depends on the valuation of travel time, labelled here "value of travel-time savings", which is a function of wages (see Fosgerau 2005) since it captures the opportunity costs of travel, among other factors. Travellers consider other aspects of travel besides opportunity costs, and the value of travel-time savings also depends on these, including time pressure, trip length, usability of the travel time for other activities, travel-time reliability and safety (for recent studies, see Axhausen et al. 2008 and the literature there). Increases in housing consumption made possible by higher incomes also increase the generalized costs of travel by lengthening the distances travelled and usually by increasing the traveller's dependence on the car. The link between greater housing consumption and higher incomes has been observed worldwide since the 19th century. Larger and more comfortable accommodation is normally located on suburban land, which increases the distances travelled. Even spacious accommodation provided in central cities increases averages travel distances as it pushes out residents who can not afford the new standard (see the literature on gentrification, for example Smith 1996 or Lees, Slater, and Wyly 2007).

Higher wages increase the number of out-of-home activities because household production becomes more costly as opportunity costs increase, i.e., restaurant visits instead of home cooking or concerts instead of at-home music making. This increase is reinforced by the degree of specialization, which entails more active participants and more coordination to achieve a goal, but with a higher-quality outcome. Higher wages also increase the size of the fleet, thus reducing the need to optimize the activities of the day into time- and distance-saving tours as well as inviting the use of motorized modes, which results in more vehicle kilometres travelled. This trend is reinforced by the growth of activity spaces, which increases the average distances between locations visited.

Activity-space expansion is reinforced by the resulting growth in the social-network geography of travellers. Not only do they have more disposable resources for leisure and shopping, but their friends and relatives will be more dispersed than before. They will have formed relationships during their training or educational years and during their work-related travel, and today they will have the resources to maintain these contacts. Their contacts' knowledge about places to visit will influence travellers' location choices, especially increasing the range of places visited and their spatial spread. Joint visits will strengthen contacts between friends.

Various forms of contact, including face-to-face visits, telephone calls, email or text messaging, all maintain and build the social capital inherent in travellers' relationships. Social capital is first and foremost the property of the individuals and the persons with whom they interact. This view by Axhausen (2007a), which is based on the work of Völker, Flap, and Lindenberg (2007), Glaeser, Laibson, and Sacerdote (2002) or earlier Grieco (1987, 1996), defines social capital

> …as the stock of joint abilities, shared histories, understandings and commitments, enabling the skilled performance of joint activity, even at a distance, of a pair or larger number of persons. In contrast to discussions on human capital or teamwork, the range of activity is not limited here to gainful employment, but explicitly includes activity which is purely social, enjoyable and hedonic. The return on this social capital is the above-average enjoyment, monetary gain and speed of the joint performance in comparison to conducting the activity with a randomly selected person, even a randomly selected person trained for the specific activity. In this sense, it is a true capital, i.e., a stock of past achievement and work, stored and put to use in future activity.

Positive social phenomena such as higher levels of general trust, as discussed for example by Putnam (2000), arise from the presence of individual social capital. The increased productivity of societies with large amounts of individual social capital can be harnessed by political processes for the common benefit. Nevertheless, see Venkatesh (2006) for the limitations, maybe even pathologies, of rich social capital in the absence of reliable and sufficient legal monetary income streams and capital.

Figure 2.2 summarizes a conceptual model of the links between generalized costs of travel and social network geographies. It assumes, in line with the model above, that both the professional and the personal activity spaces of travellers increase with falling generalized costs of travel, augmented by the even more

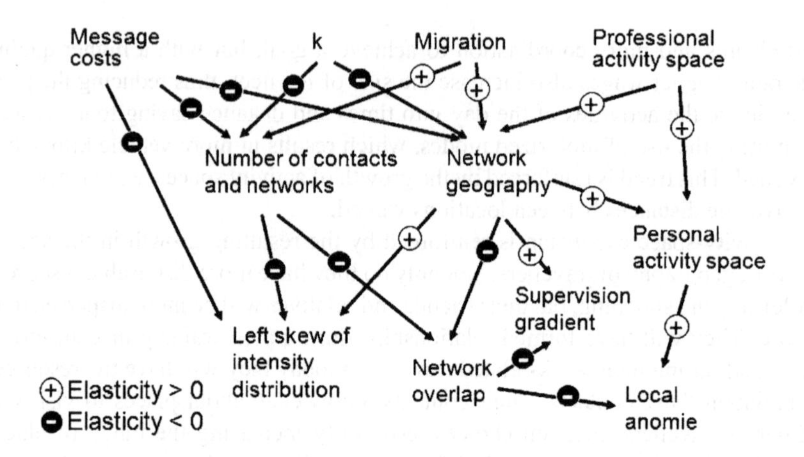

Figure 2.2 Conceptual model between the cost of contact and the structure and spatial dispersion of the social networks of the travellers

k: Generalised costs of travel.

Source: Adapted from Axhausen 2007a.

dramatic reductions in the costs of communication since the deregulation of this market[3], from SMS[4] and email to VOIP[5] (video) telephony. While the individual is now able to maintain more contacts than ever before, the lack of physical vicinity to many of them makes communication within the social networks less efficient, as they are less likely to have overlapping memberships. The work colleague is neither the cashier of the local sports club anymore, nor the member of the weekly foursome for golf, as he lives 100 km away. One can assume that the distribution of contact intensity shifts and becomes more unequal, as friends and relationships can not rely on gossip or word-of-mouth transmission of information in overlapping social networks. Each contact requires more time and effort than before for the same level of exchange, even considering the ability of some communication systems to cheaply multiply messages (such as email and photocopying letters).

We would expect these contacts maintained across longer distances than in the past to be more productive for the individuals, notwithstanding the issues discussed above. The cross-sectional travel-behaviour implications will be discussed below in conjunction with the other variables identified so far.

Interactions and face-to-face visits within the spatially widespread social network should lead to more distinct locations visited by each individual, as the joint mental map offers more alternatives. Still, variety seeking is an independent

3 Deregulation started at different points in time in different parts of the world, but generally with the construction of the first mobile (cellular) telephone networks.

4 "Short-message service" (SMS) in Europe; "texting" in North America.

5 Voice-over-Internet-protocol services, such as Skype.

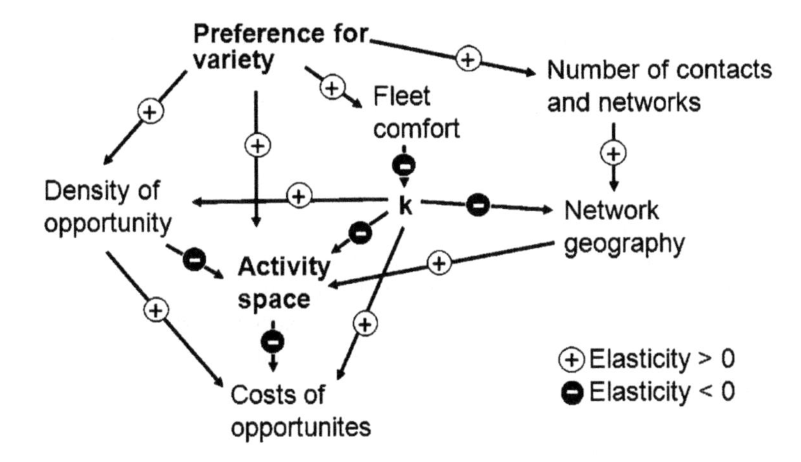

Figure 2.3 Conceptual model of variety seeking, social networks and personal activity space

attribute of the individual. The degree to which an individual can realize his or her desire for stimulation through new activities, new contents or new places depends on the available mobility tools, but also on the density of spatial opportunities; consider Berlin versus Lüneburg Heath or Manhattan versus South Dakota. Still, even after taking mobility-tool ownership into account, we would expect individuals to exercise self-selection with regard to the variety of opportunities offered by their environment. The degree of variety preferred by an individual should influence the number of social contacts maintained and the shape of the contact-intensity distribution.

In summary, we would expect to observe certain patterns in the travel behaviour of individuals in the cross-section or after an exogenous change. We assume that the daily schedule is subject to continuous improvement by individuals drawing on their *personal* (knowledge of the) *world*, i.e., their mental map, their activity repertoire and their *generalized knowledge* of the environment.

The mental map (see Gould and White 1986) is that aspect of the personal world which stores knowledge about the relative or absolute activity locations known to an individual, plus procedural knowledge about the paths between locations or, in certain areas, absolute knowledge about the network which allows the construction of new paths if and when needed. (Path knowledge includes an assessment of the required times, their reliability and their [relative] monetary costs.) Activity repertoires are based on the suitability and monetary costs of locations for certain activities at certain times and for certain groups. Finally, travellers' expectations about how places work derive from their generalized knowledge, for instance of the speeds on motorways during the peak, the presence of cash machines in airports, the presence of convenience stores around subway stops or the fringe-of-town locations of big-box retail stores.

The daily schedule defines the following dimensions of the activities of the day:

- number and type of activities;
- sequence of activities;
- starting time and duration of the activities;
- composition of the party undertaking the activity;
- expenditure and its distribution between the participants;
- secondary location choice (non-work and non-education);
- mode or vehicle choice;
- route choice;
- point of egress from the vehicle;
- composition of the party travelling together;
- travel expenditure and its distribution between the travellers.

The generalized costs of the schedules can then be assumed to incorporate the following terms for each person n:

$$k_{i,A} = f(d_{i,A}, p_i, L, d_{A,min}, d_{A,max}, sd_{1,A}) + g(s_A\, d_{i,A} + s_{A,o}\,[d_{i,A} - d_{A,max}]) + m_{i,A,L}.$$

$k_{i,A}$ Generalized costs of activity i of type A.
$f()$ Hedonic benefit of activity type A in the company of the party i of persons participating in activity i at location type L.
$d_{i,A}$ Duration of activity i of type A.
$d_{A,min}$ Minimum duration required of an activity of type A.
$d_{A,max}$ Maximum duration allowed for an activity of type A, in the case of work the maximum contracted hours for the day.
$sd_{1,A}$ Penalty for any late arrival to activity type A (non-linear in duration).
$g()$ Monetary gain from activity i of type A.
s_A (Average) hourly wage (or fee).
$s_{A,o}$ Overtime wage, if any.
$m_{i,A}$ Monetary costs of activity i of type A at location type L, which might be the result of a two-part tariff: $m^0_{i,A} + m^d_{i,A} * d_{i,A}$; here simplified as the sum of a tariff for participation ($m^0_{i,A}$) and a tariff for the duration, which is linear in activity duration ($m^d_{i,A}$).

$$k_{ir} = \sum h(d_{sm}, tp_{sm}) + r_{sm} + s_{sm} + m_{sm}.$$

k_{ir} Generalized costs across all stages s of route r between activity i-1 and activity i (i.e., origin o and destination d).
$h()$ Hedonic benefit, generally disbenefit, of stage s with duration d_{sm} with the travelling party of stage s by mode m.

The duration is a function of the length l_{sm} and the speed v_{sm} of stage s by mode m.

r_{sm} Reliability of stage s by mode m.

s_{sm} Safety level of stage s by mode m.

m_{sm} Monetary cost of stage s by mode m.

For simplicity, one can sum or average the durations, distances, monetary costs, reliabilities and speeds across stages n to obtain:

d_{imr} Duration of trip to activity i along route r and by main mode m.

m_{imr} Monetary costs of trip to activity i along route r and by main mode m.

l_{imr} Length of trip to activity i along route r and by main mode m.

r_{imr} Reliability of trip to activity i along route r and by main mode m.

v_{imr} Speed of trip to activity i along route r and by main mode m.

Note that this formulation does not allow for time-of-day dependencies of the hedonic components of the generalized costs of trips and activities (Winston 1982) due to daylight, temperature and weather generally. Neither does it allow for sequencing effects, i.e., for there to be a proper or preferred order to certain activities: shopping before cooking, leisure after work, etc., or for there to be reasonable or desired intervals between participation in the same type of activity. The social context, on the other hand, is included through the consideration of the persons participating in the activity or travelling with person n. The inclusion of the (penalty) term for late arrival captures many of the time-of-day effects which can be observed in schedules.

Given our assumption of travellers' desire to improve their schedules, we expect certain elasticities in observed behaviour.

For the total time-out-of-home (O) negative elasticities with respect to both the generalized costs of the activities $k_{i,A}$ and the generalized cost of travel $k_{i,r}$:

$$\varepsilon\,(O|k_{i,A}) \leq 0 \qquad \text{and}$$

$$\varepsilon\,(O|k_{i,r}) \leq 0.$$

For the number of tours j:

$$\varepsilon\,(j|k_{i,r}) \leq 0,$$

because the return trip home becomes less onerous, changing into the appropriate clothes for the next activity becomes less burdensome, and purposes such as picking up the appropriate kit, just resting or addressing at-home duties are less strenuous.

Therefore, the ratio of the number of trips n to tours j moves in the opposite direction:

$$\varepsilon\ (n/j|k_{i,r}) \geq 0,$$

as one can reasonably assume that

$$\varepsilon\ (n|k_{i,r}) \leq 0,$$

and especially that

$$\varepsilon\ (n|k_{i,r}) < \varepsilon\ (j|k_{i,r}).$$

The change in the number of trips implies by definition a change in the number of activities a:

$$\varepsilon\ (a|k_{i,r}) \leq 0,$$

but also:

$$\varepsilon\ (a|k_{i,A}) \leq 0,$$

and the duration responds to the monetary costs or the associated cost of travel:

$$\varepsilon\ (d_{i,A}|m_{i,A}) \leq 0 \text{ and}$$

$$\varepsilon\ (d_{i,A}|k_{i,r}) \leq 0,$$

which implies that the generalized costs of travel increase with activity duration. The minimum and maximum durations have reverse impacts on the total duration, as well as the frequency of an activity type:

$$\varepsilon\ (d_{i,A}|d_{A,min}) \geq 0 \text{ and}$$

$$\varepsilon\ (d_{i,A}|d_{A,max}) \geq 0.$$

An increase in the lower limit must increase average duration, just as raising the maximum allows those who want to extend an experience to do so. We implicitly assume that $f(d_{i,A})$ only shows a decrease in the marginal gain, but never allows the marginal gain to become negative. However, the number of activities of type A

$$\varepsilon\ (a_A|d_{A,min}) \leq 0$$

should decrease with any increase in the minimum duration and therefore generalized costs, all things kept constant.

The effect of the upper limit depends on $f(d_{i,A})$. If $f(d_{i,A})$ grows with $d_{i,A}$, then *ceteris paribus*:

$$\varepsilon\ (a_A\ |d_{A,max}) \geq 0.$$

However, in the reverse case it will depend on whether there is any other compensation or not.

Looking only at travel, we would expect trip durations and lengths to respond as follows:

$$\varepsilon\ (d_{im}\ |v_{im}) \leq 0, \qquad \varepsilon\ (l_{im}\ |v_{im}) \geq 0,$$

$$\varepsilon\ (d_{im}\ |m_{im}) \leq 0 \text{ and} \qquad \varepsilon\ (l_{imr}\ |m_{im}) \leq 0.$$

Effects on the volumes have already been discussed.

Interestingly, the constant travel-time budget proposed by Zahavi (1974) and many others adopting his arguments stipulates specific values of the elasticities:

$$\varepsilon\ (d_{im}\ |v_{im}) = -1, \qquad \varepsilon\ (l_{im}\ |v_{im}) = 1$$

and also

$$\varepsilon\ (d_A\ |d_{im}) = -1$$

for a constant out-of-home duration O. We are not aware of any empirical test of this proposition.

The framework proposed here describes a re-enforcing set of reactions of on-going growth, especially if it is linked to the responses of goods and services markets, which are driven by the same dynamics at the aggregate scale: GDP, productivity (via economics of scale and scope) and market size taking the place of income, specialization and activity space in the model above. While the upward spiral is accelerated by the responses, the downward spiral is slowed down by a whole range of mechanisms, of which the most important is the reluctance of the actors to ignore fallen costs or to write down existing investments in their home locations and mobility tools.

Chapter 3
Definitions

The analyses planned here require observations about individual behaviour which can be obtained in a number of ways: through diaries, retrospective interviews and GSM or GPS traces. In order to be consistent, the observations have to be coded into defined units. In addition, they have to be obtained from observations with a common scope, or at least the biases arising from any differences in the scope of the surveys have to be understood. The impact of differential nonresponse on the results obtained will be discussed in Chapter 5.

Capturing movement

Movement must be defined in order for observation or survey work to be amenable to measurement. Defining movement implies defining activity, as will be shown. The definitions we employed are for professional use as they frequently do not match everyday language.

The following structuring of movements into defined units is internally consistent (see also Table 3.1 for the German and French translations of the terms and Table 3.2 for an example):

- A stage is a continuous movement by one mode of transport or one vehicle. It includes any pure waiting (idle) time immediately before or during that movement.
- A trip is a continuous sequence of stages between two activities.
- A subtour is a sequence of trips starting and ending at the same location and which is part of a longer tour.
- A tour is a sequence of trips starting and ending at the same location.
- A journey is a tour starting and ending at the relevant reference location of the traveller.
- An activity is a continuous interaction with the physical environment, a service or person(s) within the same sociospatial environment that is relevant to the traveller. It includes any pure waiting (idle) time before or during the activity.
- The daily schedule is the sequence of activities undertaken between morning and the return to bed at the end of the day, but it may begin before or after midnight.

For the purposes of public transport management and statistics, it is useful to add the following unit between "stage" and "trip":

- Customer movement is a continuous sequence of (para-) transit or public transport stages of a certain type, ignoring any walking stages undertaken to reach the next point of departure due to transfers.

Customer movement can be defined according to a variety of criteria, depending on the purpose. The most important criteria are: by operator, if the purpose is to allocate revenue between multiple providers operating a revenue-sharing scheme for a large (regional) network; by type of vehicle, if the purpose is to allocate revenue within a firm operating different subnetworks, e.g., diesel buses, trolley buses, trams and cable-cars; by type of service within a firm or network, e.g., express, normal, night or shared-ride taxi services.

This is only one of many possible sets of definitions of movement, and it is based on a certain understanding of traveller behaviour and the demands of daily mobility surveys and specialized surveys, such as those on long-distance or leisure mobility. It also puts an emphasis on travel by ignoring activities undertaken while moving, for example working while on a plane, speaking on the telephone while driving, etc.

The main alternative is derived from time-budget studies, for which travel is just one more type of activity. Time-budget surveys differ in a second important aspect as well: While travel surveys have always focused on episodes of travel and activity, i.e., as coherent blocks of action, time-budget surveys tend to ask for the stream of the activity by requiring respondents to indicate their activity at regular intervals during the day, say every 10, 15 or 30 minutes. (For a review of the history of time-budget surveys, see Michelson 2005; Ås 1978;

Table 3.1 Movement defined: English, German and French

English	German	French	Other terms used as synonyms
Stage	Etappe	Trajet, Etape	Unlinked trip
Customer movement	Beförderungsfall	Voyage (Déplacement), mouvements désaggrés	
Trip	Fahrt/Weg	Déplacement, itinéraire, parcours	Linked trip
Tour	Tour	Circuit	
Journey	Reise, Ausgang	Journée	Sojourn, round trip
Activity	Aktivität	Activité	
Daily schedule	Tagesplan, Aktivitätenkette		Activity chain

and Szalai 1972 for an early international comparison.) In time-budget surveys, episodes are constructed afterwards during analysis. This roster makes it easier to ask for further aspects of the activity: group composition at the time, secondary activities such as listening to the radio or supervising children, or the beneficiary of the activity.

The definition of a stage which discounts activities performed during movement provides a clear, basic unit for discussing movement[1]. By stressing continuity while including waiting times, it ensures that the number of units does not become too large. Consider, for example, the case of a train stage which involves multiple planned and unplanned stops which would otherwise constitute separate stages. The limitation to pure idle waiting time allows one to capture any activities associated with the stages, such as purchasing a ticket, loading or unloading a car or other activities undertaken between the arrival at a station, airport or parking facility and the actual departure (e.g., shopping in an airport store, talking with someone, etc.).

While a stage is unambiguous, the definition of a trip depends on the definition of the activities to provide its starting and ending points. Depending on how an "activity" is defined, it is possible to vary the number of trips, which is the most frequently used reference unit in travel-behaviour analysis. The definition of "activity" that we propose leaves open how researchers or respondents operationalize an activity's "relevance". The socio-spatial environment is constituted by the persons involved in the interaction and by the environment in which it takes place. In the case of the environment, only the type has to remain the same. For example, a walk through a park takes place within one spatial environment. Our definition of "activity" implies that any change in the number of persons involved in an interaction constitutes a new activity, e.g., somebody leaving early from a dinner establishes a new activity of the same type; equally, visits to different stores in a shopping mall are different activities.

Importance can be assigned to one, some or all of the main dimensions by which activities and their social content can be classified:

- Kind of activity: what the person is doing: gardening, talking with someone, operating a machine, walking through a park.
- Purpose: what the person hopes to achieve in an instrumental sense: earn money, relax, get fit, grow food, get sleep, etc.
- Meaning: what the person hopes to achieve in a moral sense or be able to say about him- or herself: help someone, fulfil a promise, take care of himself or herself, etc.

---

1 Subdividing stages by the activities performed while moving is possible, but rarely done. A rail passenger could, for example, record the sequence of activities undertaken while travelling: work (reading reports), lunch, leisure (listening to music) and work (meeting colleagues).

- Project: the greater context of the activity, the framework within which it is undertaken, e.g., preparing dinner, obtaining a degree, working towards a promotion, building a house, etc.
- Duration.
- Effort accepted to be able to undertake the activity, in particular, the detour required to get to the activity location.
- Expenditure for or income from participation in the activity and the associated additional travel.
- Group size and composition.
- Urgency of the activity in terms of the possibility of (further) delay.

This list ignores further descriptive dimensions such as the number of persons involved, the location, alternative activities by which the activity could be replaced, since when the activity has been planned, the planning effort, possible time horizons for delays, the distribution of costs among participants, the distribution of costs among participants and non-participants and satisfaction with the activity in terms of goal achievement.

While the definition of a trip hinges on the definition of an activity, the definition of a journey requires a **reference location**. In daily travel this will normally be the (main) home of the respondent. Still, some travellers will have multiple reference locations (e.g., a weekend home, the family home and *pied-à-terre* of a weekly commuter, a student's dorm and parents' house, multiple homes of children living with their separated parents and stepparents). In addition, tourists on a round trip will shift their reference location between various accommodations during their holiday. In all cases, it seems reasonable to break any observed tour (from the first reference location and back to it) into smaller units for analysis. These will normally be subtours of the main tour, but in some cases they will involve a shift from one reference location to the next, e.g., a student's Friday journey from the university town to the parental home. In general, the researcher will not know the exact status of a reported location and will have to impose an external definition on the movement data obtained. For example, a reference location is any location where travellers spend at least one (or two consecutive) night(s).

At the stage level, a complete description would involve the origin, the destination (address or name of the location and its type of land use), the arrival time at the vehicle or stop, the departure time, the arrival time at the destination, the type of vehicle or type of service used, the route or public-transport line taken, the distance travelled, the size and composition of the travelling party and the expenditure for the movement, including any tolls or fares. The arrival time at the vehicle and the departure time with the vehicle are normally set to be equal, ignoring the time required to load or unload the vehicle and get it and its passengers ready for departure. This frequent lack of differentiation requires the estimation of any waiting times for public transport services. Routes taken are mostly added from network models and are not directly surveyed, which is one of the reasons for the current interest in GPS- or GSM-based movement data[2]. The distance travelled is estimated by the traveller, if required.

The following activity characteristics are common to most surveys: the type, normally precoded with a mixture of purpose and kind of activity codes; the location; the size of the party; parking fees; the arrival time at the activity location; and the starting and ending times of the activity. In most transport surveys, the actual starting time of an activity is not obtained from the respondent, so the waiting times are generally unknown. A curious omission in most surveys is the lack of information about a traveller's expenditure during and for an activity, which would be a useful indicator of its importance in social terms.

Survey practice in transport has tended to employ relatively crude classifications which mix the kind of activity with its purpose while ignoring the remaining dimensions. Typical classifications are: work, work-related activities, shopping, private business, leisure, dropping someone off or picking someone up, and escorting, as well as an open question for any other activity type. Such a rough classification communicates an interest in longer blocks of activity, mostly those involving earning or spending money, or those involving firm commitments or strong role expectations. Dropping someone off or picking someone up also falls into this category, considering the frequently lengthy detours required, sometimes involving the prior collection of other persons, e.g., the school run with children from different households. This level of detail reflects researchers' past preoccupation with the morning commute as a transport problem, but also their assessment of what level of detail respondents will accept. The level of detail will influence the number of activities and therefore trips reported. Equally, any comparison of trip numbers has to keep this priming effect of activity classification in mind: a time-budget survey with hundreds of activity codes should produce a different number of trips than the typical travel survey and its single-digit number of codes (see, for example, Hubert et al. 2008).

The problem of aggregation from stages to trips and from trips to tours or journeys is acute for those variables which can not be added together: mode and activity type. While the size of the party, the times, distances and speeds can be added or averaged, a main mode or activity type has to be determined based on predetermined rules because information about its subjective importance is generally missing. Typical rules for determining the main mode use either numerical criteria, such as the mode with the largest share of the distance travelled, of the longest duration or with the highest speed, or hierarchies of the assumed strength of the mode to shape the movement, for example: airplane–train–coach–underground–LRT–bus–car–bicycle–walking. The same types of rules are applied when the main activity type of a tour or journey needs to be determined.

---

2 Recently, web-based geocoding engines and web-hosted mapping software have been integrated into CATI interviews, which affords a much improved capture of activity locations and the routes taken; see for example Zanetti et al. 2008 or the PTV TripTracer software: http://download.ddsgeo.de/zoom/02_08/TripTracer_english.pdf).

As a result, those rules should be reported in conjunction with any results. The impact of this aggregation must be kept in mind when comparing results from different surveys. Luckily, in most cases the impacts will be small, as a single mode dominates most trips and journeys.

A related problem of aggregation occurs when counting the number of movements at different levels of social aggregation, for example: person–(family unit)–household. Joint movements, for example for leisure purposes, could mean that the number of household trips will be considerably smaller than the number of person trips: a joint car trip with three household members would count as three person trips and one household trip. The analyst must decide which type of trip is relevant for the analysis. The same attention must be given to the aggregation by vehicle used.

This section has demonstrated the link between definitions of movement and activity, in particular for the aggregates formed from the basic unit stage: the trip, the tour and the journey.

The scope of travel surveys

The totality of movement, which could be the subject of a survey, is normally not surveyed. That could only achieved by passive tracking, employing GPS or GSM units. Researchers exclude certain types of movement from each survey as irrelevant to its purpose. Some of these exclusions have become so ingrained during the seventy years of travel-survey research (see Martin, Memmott, and Bone 1961 or Axhausen 1995) that they are rarely, if ever, discussed; however, it is good practice to account properly for such exclusions by spelling out the object of a survey in detail. This also helps during the process of designing the survey, especially when choosing an overall approach to guiding the respondents' recording or recall.

The following aspects need to be defined:

- **Target movements**: Movements which are within the scope of the survey excluding the exceptions below.
- **Base unit**: Stage, customer movement, trip or journey.
- **Activity definition:** Characteristics of an activity which needs to be reported.
- **Reporting period**: Interval from a specified starting time for which movements should be reported.
- **Minimum distance**: The smallest allowable increment of distance, if any.
- **Minimum duration**: The smallest allowable length of time, if any.
- **Spatial exclusions**: Any spatial exclusions.
- **Temporal exclusions**: Any temporal exclusions.

Table 3.2 Movement defined: An example day

Episode	Stage	Trip	Subtour	Tour	Journey	Main mode trip	Main mode tour	Main activity tour
At home								
Walk	1	1	1	1	1	LRT	LRT	Work
Waiting	2	1	1	1	1			
Bus	2	1	1	1	1			
Waiting	3	1	1	1	1			
LRT	3	1	1	1	1			
Walk	4	1	1	1	1			
Work								
Walk	1	2	2	1	1	Taxi		
Taxi	2	2	2	1	1			
Walk	3	2	2	1	1			
Lunch								
Walk	1	3	2	1	1	Walk		
Work								
Walk	1	4	1	1	1	Car passenger		
Waiting	2	4	1	1	1			
Car passenger	2	4	1	1	1			
Walk	3	4	1	1	1			
Sport								
Walk	1	5	1	1	1	Walk		
At home								
Walk	1	6	3	2	2	Car	Car	Shopping
Car	2	6	3	2	2			
Walk	3	6	3	2	2			
Shopping								
Walk	1	7	3	2	2	Car		
Car	2	7	3	2	2			
Walk	3	7	3	2	2			
At home								

- **Spatial resolution**: Maximum allowable size or type of destination location.
- **Reference location**: The base or reference location.

Typical examples of such definitions are shown in Table 3.3 for three possible surveys: a survey of daily mobility, a long-distance travel survey and a tourism survey. The definitions shown are typical. Note the interaction between the target movement definition and the activity definition and the thereby accepted reduction

Table 3.3 Examples of possible survey object definitions

	Daily mobility survey	Long distance travel survey	Tourism travel survey
Target movements	All relevant stages during the reporting period	All relevant trips during the reporting period, which are part of a journey to a destination at least 100 km from the reference location	All relevant journeys, which either involve a destination more than 100 km from the reference location or at least one overnight stay
Base unit	Stage	Trip	Journey
Activity definition	Any interaction longer than five minutes, unless a "serve passenger" stop	Main activity, which has motivated the trip to the destination	Main activity, which motivated the journey to the main destination
Reporting period	One day starting at 4:00 am until ending the day at the reference location	Eight weeks, starting Monday 4:00 am of the first week	Four weeks, starting Monday 4:00 am of the first week
Minimum distance	Walks over 100m	None	None
Minimum duration	None	None	None
Spatial exclusions	Stages which are part of trips within a closed building or compound, such as factory or office campus; Stages starting or ending outside the study area during the reporting period	Trips which are part of journeys to destinations less than 100 km from the reference location; Trips within destinations	Journeys within destinations
Temporal exclusions	Stages undertaken as work while working, e.g. driving a delivery vehicle	Trips undertaken as work while working, e.g. driving a charter coach bus	None
Spatial resolution	(Building) address	Municipalities or separately identifiable settlements, e.g. resort complexes, villages, which are part of larger administrative units	Municipalities within the national boundaries, countries elsewhere
Reference location	Home address within the study area	Destinations, where the traveller spends at least two consecutive nights	Destinations, where the traveller spends at least one night

in the number of reported activities and trips. Note also that the exclusion of walking-only trips as given in the example is common, but it is not recommended practice because such short trips are important elements of the day.

The proposed definitions can structure the movements and activities of the respondents into units chosen by the researcher. Most of these definitions can not be used directly in survey questions. The survey designer must find a way to guide the respondents' recording and recall to obtain the desired information from the answers. In the design, the researcher must also consider that respondents limit the amount of effort they spend on surveys and that their memory limits their ability to recall certain details. Each of the different approaches uses a different dimension of the activity/movement stream to guide the respondents (Axhausen 1995) and stimulate their recall:

- Stops (destinations), the points with a particular land use where a movement ends, are highlighted in the **stage approach**. The characteristics of activities following a traveller's arrival at a destination are established in addition to the stage details. Arrival times at the activity location and the activity duration (including any unidentified waiting times) are derived from the stage times.
- The movement to the next activity is stressed by the **trip approach**, in which stages are not necessarily identified by sequence, although it is usual to ask for all modes used and possibly for their travel time. The coding of an activity is normally restricted to seven to ten categories, but open categories for "other" and for leisure are well accepted by respondents and allow more detailed coding during analysis. Arrival times at activity locations and activity durations (including any unidentified waiting times) are derived from the trip times.
- The sequence of activity episodes is at the centre of the **activity approach**, which inverts the trip approach but does not necessarily offer a more detailed coding of activities. This approach can cover activities at destinations, in particular at home, by appropriately prompting the respondents. The movement details are covered by a special set of items, when relevant. The starting times of trips and trip durations (including any unknown waiting times) are established from the activity times. Stages can be established if the respondents are suitably prompted.
- The flow of activities is covered by the **time-budget approach**, which invites the respondent to classify each 10-, 15- or 30-minute interval of the day by the activity undertaken (Szalai 1972; Ås 1978). The coding is open and the respondents refer to detailed coding lists for this purpose. The activity and movement episodes addressed in the first three approaches are recovered in post-processing. This approach does not normally establish the movement details required for transport modelling, but it is not impossible to do so in principle, especially with modern computer-based survey instruments. Very short trips can get lost if longer intervals are chosen for the roster.

In each case, the higher-level movement concepts – (trips), tours and journeys – have to be established during the post-processing of the data. Equally, the stages have to be constructed in all but the stage-based approach according to the information available from the answers of the respondents and external information, e.g., network models. These post-processing steps must be documented in the reports to allow a better comparison of the different surveys.

This chapter has outlined a coherent set of definitions for the measurement of movements. Each of the elements of that definition (stage, trip, activity and journey) can be the starting point of a travel survey. It is clear that their ability to prompt the recall of the respondents will vary and will therefore produce systematically different numbers. Unfortunately, there is not enough evidence to give firm guidance. The other factors favouring non-response (see Chapter 5) are too varied to allow a simple conclusion, and a proper meta-analysis is still outstanding.

Chapter 4
Time, Space and Travel Analysis: An Overview

Two dimensions of travel have become principal guidelines for human mobility analysis. First, travel is defined as a transition through time and space. Time and space are indivisible elements of physical movement (Hägerstrand 1970). Second, travel is (mostly) done not for its own sake but for the benefit derived at the destination. That is why trip making needs to be understood as a *derived demand*[1]. The spatial separation of functions such as living (home), work or leisure initiates travel as a prerequisite of having relationships with others, taking part in economic processes or generally being embedded in modern society.

This chapter connects the time, space and travel framework with the concepts and developments of the *activity-based* approach of mobility research this work refers to. Its focus, however, is on defining and explaining the temporal phenomena in individual travel behaviour which form the rhythmic structure of human life. It therefore acts as a background for the analyses to follow in Chapter 9. The spatial characteristics of travel with its destination-choice and activity-space dimensions will be conceptually explored in Chapter 10.

Time, space and the activity-based analysis (ABA)

Since the 1970s, the spatio-temporal patterns of activities and trips made by individual travellers (and households) have been the dominant focus of mobility research (Jones 1981; Beckmann 1983). The theoretical and methodological developments of the *activity-based analysis* (ABA) approach are the result of this particular interest. The conceptual foundation of ABA is the finding that the decision to change one's location – and therefore make a trip – is a consequence of a need or demand which can not be satisfied at the present place. These are commonly physiological, cultural or social needs which express themselves in a range of *activities* performed at different times and in different places. The execution of activities *in time and space* is therefore a key focus of mobility-

1 In contrast to the widely accepted concept of travel as a transition through time and space, the idea of travel as a derived demand has been discussed controversially (see, e.g., Mokhtarian and Salomon 2001). The contentious point about the latter paradigm is the assumption of travel as a disutility which is open to question in many circumstances. Trip making and travel might to some extent be an intrinsic desire.

structure investigation. This paradigm changes within travel analysis and modelling has led to the identification of complex behavioural patterns such as periodicity, variability or other temporal phenomena as central objects of investigation (see, e.g, Recker and Kitamura 1985; Kitamura 1988; Mahmassani 1988; Jones et al. 1990; Pas and Harvey 1997).

The methodology of the activity-based analysis differs fundamentally from the forecasting and planning approaches which were predominant until the 1970s. Traditional models (see Oi and Shuldiner 1962; Hutchinson 1974) consider the trip itself to be the only predictor for traffic volumes (*trip-based analysis*), neglecting the underlying activity demand as well as the individual and environmental circumstances of the trip making. The primary purpose of these (four-step) forecasting models[2], which were mainly developed in the early 1950s and are still widely used in transport planning, is the analysis of traffic flows based on a highly aggregated data base (see Ortúzar and Willumsen 2001). This has produced tools for quickly conceptualizing and assessing large infrastructure projects such as motorways. Activity-based analysis and activity-based forecasting models, in contrast, link personal mobility to the relationship between human activity patterns, needs and interactions, and forecast individual travel demand based on this complex system (Kutter 1972; Heidemann 1981; Hanson and Burnett 1981; Jones 1981; Pas 1990; McNally 2000).

The ABA framework for understanding human activities is integral to the analysis of recurrent travel patterns and the structures of destination choice discussed in this book. Therefore, the research direction is summarized in the following (see also Jones et al. 1983):

- Travel may be understood as an induced demand for (out-of-home) activities. Only in rare circumstances is travel itself a primary activity (see, e.g., Mokhtarian and Salomon 2001).
- The ABA approach (usually) considers trips and activities to be embedded in sequences. Travel is defined as a transition within a continuous pattern of daily behaviour or within a daily programme which is a sequence of activities in time and space (Figure 4.1).
- Temporal, spatial and interpersonal restrictions are explicitly considered in the development of the analysis and model. The activity-based approach refers to fundamental concepts of time-use analysis (see Bhat and Koppelman 1999) and space-time geography (Hägerstrand 1970 and others).
- Personal travel decisions need to be seen against the traveller's household context. Role models and interactions between household members are important explanatory elements for the activity-based analysis.

2 Trip-based forecasting models encompass four steps: 1) trip generation; 2) trip distribution; 3) mode choice; and 4) trip assignment.

- The analysis of activity execution needs to be combined with a detailed classification of travellers according to their similar activity demands if complex travel behaviour is to be described, analysed and predicted. Classification according to life cycle or lifestyle, which often produce similar activity behaviour, is an approach used in many studies to categorize travellers.
- Time is a key concept in the activity-based approach. Activity-based analysis goes beyond the simple consideration of time as an optimization objective or speed element. On the one hand, the timing and duration of activities are important explanatory determinants of complex behaviour; on the other hand, they are themselves of great interest when analysing dynamics, variability or periodicity within mobility patterns.

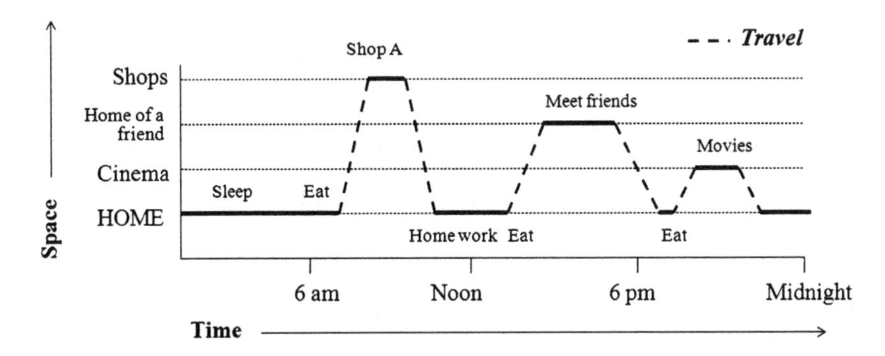

Figure 4.1 Activity and travel from the activity-based analysis standpoint
Source: Adapted from Jones et al. (1983) 37.

Temporal phenomena of travel behaviour and their determinants

The complexity of daily travel patterns is subject to several temporal patterns determined by a set of individual characteristics of the traveller (Hanson and Burnett 1981). In general, the complexity is an outcome of habitual behaviour or routines and variability, which may be described as random as well as systematic deviations from behavioural regularity. The activity-based approach has been used to focus on many of those aspects and factors affecting behavioural patterns for three decades (see Jones and Clarke 1988). The different foci of the studies are manifold (Table 4.1 provides a selective list of relevant publications), and the terminology used to describe the temporal phenomena of travel behaviour often intersects. The overview shows that a wide range of expressions are used synonymously. However, identical terms have also been chosen for different aspects. This is especially true for the term *variability*: Whereas several studies deal with behavioural variability in the context of interpersonal differences for mobility determinants such as daily travel distances or number of trips, others use variability to describe the changing behaviour of one individual over time. In general, the term *variability* is often used as a generic term for the set of phenomena described in Table 4.1.

Table 4.1 Selected studies on temporal aspects in individual and household travel

Issue	Examples
Stability	Herz 1983; Mannering et al. 1994; Schlich et al. 2000; Schwanen and Dijst 2003
Variability (intrapersonal, interpersonal, systematic)	Pas 1986, 1987, 1988; Pas and Koppelman 1986; Pas and Sundar 1995; Hanson and Huff 1982, 1988a, 1988b; Huff and Hanson 1986; Abdel-Aty et al. 1995; Muthyalagari et al. 2001; Guensler et al. 2006
Flexibility	Herz 1983; Mannering 1989; Emmerink and van Beek 1997; Saleh and Farrell 2005
Rhythmic patterns	Shapcott and Steadman 1978; Bhat et al. 2004a; Bhat et al. 2005
Repetitive behaviour	Huff and Hanson 1986, 1990; Garvill et al. 2003; Schlich 2004
Regularity	Kitamura and van der Hoorn 1987; Jones and Clarke 1988; Harvey et al. 1997
Dynamics (especially departure-time choice and trip chaining)	Chang and Mahmassani 1989; Mahmassani 1997; Mahmassani et al. 1997; Mannering and Hamed 1990; Bhat 1998; Goulias 1999; Mahmassani and Liu 1999; Steed and Bhat 2000; Bhat and Steed 2002; Pendyala and Bhat 2004
Variety seeking	Borgers et al. 1989; Timmermans 1990; Kempermann et al. 2000; Kempermann et al. 2002; Zängler and Karg 2004; Arentze and Timmermans 2005

Some definitions of the most important phenomena together with what has been discovered about their structures and determinants shall now be given.

Habits and routines in (travel) behaviour

Habitual or routine travel behaviour is the reuse of behavioural segments, sequences or – more generally – *solutions* in identical or similar decision situations. An approved behavioural pattern with known costs which has satisfied similar needs in the past is reused or reapplied. The motive behind the reapplication of known alternatives is to avoid costs for the potentially new or additional acquisition of information for the new decision. In the particular context of travel, this becomes obvious in the minimization or even avoidance of information acquisition on how to e.g., get efficiently from A to B (Goodwin, Kitamura, and Meurs 1990).

Rhythmic patterns[3]

Rhythmic patterns of travel may be observed periodically over prolonged periods of time such as weeks or over the course of a year. These may include complete daily patterns with identical attributes, activity sequences or single main activities or trips. Rhythmic patterns occur on a predictable basis and may therefore be explained "historically", i.e., they are determined by fixed external timetables, circumstances or events (Shapcott and Steadman 1978). Rhythmic patterns are fundamental consequences of habitual behaviour.

Variability: Interpersonal and intrapersonal variability

As briefly mentioned above, the phenomenon of behavioural variability may be discussed from two perspectives: First, the behaviour of two persons almost always differs due to differences in their socio-economic backgrounds or attitudes. This aspect of variability is often defined as *interpersonal variability* (Pas 1987) and may be described as the deviation of individual behaviour from the mean behaviour of the respective sample or socio-economic group that the traveller belongs to. In contrast, the behaviour of an individual or a household varies considerably if observed over periods of time which exceed a pre-defined time span such as one day (= *intrapersonal variability*). Here, variability is the deviation of behaviour from the customary individual routines and habits which have been developed over longer time periods.

Both categories of variability usually contain a systematic component which is explainable or predictable, e.g., by personal traits, together with a remaining random component (Figure 4.2). Predictable as well as random elements of variability are inherent in models of human behaviour and have implications for the reliability or explanatory power of our models.

The variability within a person's or household's behaviour expresses needs and aspirations which are not constant from day to day, as well as unforeseen events and circumstances which make short-term adaptations of behaviour necessary (Pas and Sundar 1995). In the context of the activity-based approach, intrapersonal variability of travel behaviour is given when behaviour deviates from routine activity sequences or from activity and trip attributes such as mode of travel, departure time or size of the company.

Intrapersonal variability is an underlying theme of this book, which concerns the analysis of recurrent behavioural elements as well as the stability of spatial choice. However, interpersonal comparisons will be also made systematically in order to reveal the extent of periodicity in daily activity behaviour.

3 More on rhythmic patterns may be found in Chapter 9.

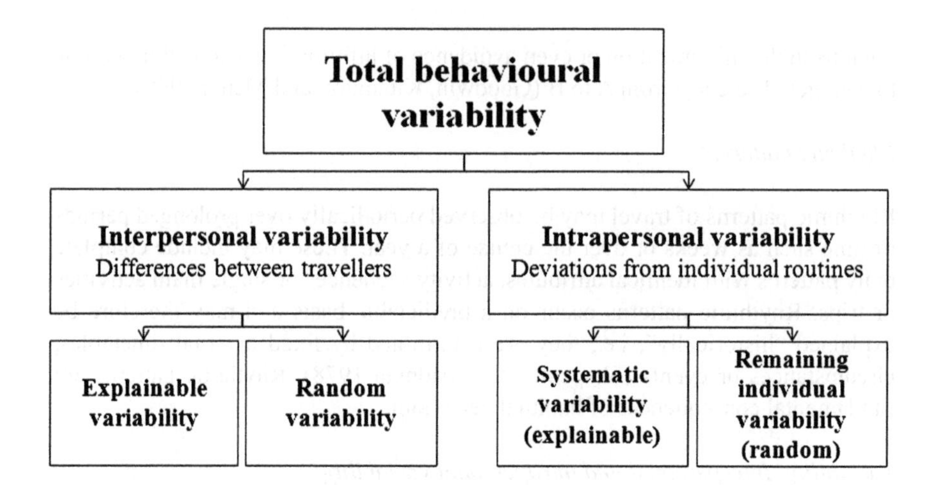

Figure 4.2 Variability in travel behaviour: Components
Source: Adapted from Pas (1987) 432.

Equilibrium of behaviour

Behavioural equilibrium is achieved when all details which determine travel behaviour have remained constant over a sufficiently long period of time and the behaviour has been completely adjusted to environmental factors (Goodwin, Kitamura, and Meurs 1990). An environmental factor is, for example, the household composition, which greatly structures daily activity patterns and the induced travel demand. Behavioural equilibrium is a long-term phenomenon which must be distinguished from random or unexpected short-term adjustments of behaviour which are not systematic.

An interesting question is if there is only one instance of behavioural equilibrium in a given set of factors. It is certainly possible for states of equilibrium to differ even if particular situations and events have been experienced by a traveller in the past.

It should be noted here that complete behavioural equilibrium over time is hardly ever observable. Most of the environmental factors are themselves subject to permanent change (seasonal rhythms, political developments, etc.). Even substantially stable determinants of travel such as household-related details like home location, life cycle and occupational status can not be defined as entirely constant. They change over longer periods with notable implications for individual mobility. Behavioural equilibrium therefore remains a theoretical construct–at least from a long-term perspective.

Dynamics

Behavioural dynamics describes the systematic adaptation of decisions to changing circumstances and to the situative context of travel, i.e., mode, departure, destination and route choice (Kitamura 1988). Those may involve a traveller's short-term reactions to traffic conditions (e.g., congestion or bad weather) or a long-term and structural fine-tuning of behaviour towards behaviour-influencing variables such as working hours, household composition or a change of workplace. Although some of the structural characteristics in a traveller's life occur in periodic intervals (e.g., change of workplace), the term rhythm is in this book used only to describe the periodicity of behaviour at the daily, weekly or monthly level. The development of rhythms of travel behaviour is a reaction by the traveller towards his or her dynamic and social environment. In other words, fundamental socio-economic alterations in life foster the development of habitual behaviour and rhythms.

Variety seeking

Variety seeking stresses the context and in particular the motivation behind varied behaviour. The phenomenon has been extensively explored in psychology and consumer-choice analysis for decades. However, geography and transportation research still face problems in incorporating aspects of variety seeking in their models of choice. A good (early) overview of variety seeking in consumer-choice analysis was provided by McAlister and Pessemier (1982). Others, for example Timmermans (1990), tried to relate the fundamental conceptual concepts to spatial-choice behaviour.

In general, variety seeking stems from two streams of motives which may be summarized as *derived* and *direct* motivations (McAlister and Pessemier 1982; see also Table 4.2). First, variety seeking may be described as *derived*, as it is often initiated by external factors. Derived variety-seeking behaviour is therefore not originally implied by taste variations of the individual decision maker, but by changes in the choice situation. Such surrounding factors may include an altered set of choice alternatives or individually perceived or actually imposed constraints. From an economist's point of view, an altered choice situation is often caused by changing prices or incomes. In addition, the varied consumption of a particular product may be influenced by *multiple needs*, i.e., the altered use of a product by different household members, as an outcome of a different usage situation (e.g., different location or different usage convenience), or simply when a product is used for a different purpose. Second, varied behaviour may be implied *directly*, i.e., by changes in an individual's personal preferences. Direct motivations for variety seeking may be categorized as (a) intrapersonal and (b) interpersonal. Intrapersonal motives may include *sensation seeking* and the desire for the unfamiliar as well as the alteration among alternatives of a perceived choice set.

Table 4.2 Variety seeking: Motives

Derived variation (due to external factors)	Direct variation (preference-related)
Changes in the choice situation	Intrapersonal motivations
Changes in the feasible choice set	Sensation seeking – desire for the unfamiliar
Changing constraints	Alteration among familiar alternatives
Multiple needs	Acquisition of (new) information
Multiple users	Interpersonal motivations (exclusive choices)
Multiple situations	
Multiple uses	

Source: Adapted from McAlister and Pessemier (1982).

Finally, interpersonal motivations for variety seeking are often manifestations of uniqueness by satisfying an individual's demand for products which are potentially unavailable to other individuals (of the same peer group).

According to these general motives for variety seeking, Timmermans (1990) identified two types of behavioural models of consumption: "non-inventory-based models" and "inventory-based models". The first group of models usually excludes the particular properties of the choice alternatives as a potential determinant for choice. These models instead predict switching probabilities according to the individual's past experiences with known alternatives. Consequently, typologies of decision makers are defined which categorize individuals into variety seekers and variety avoiders. In contrast, inventory-based models assume that there is an ideal point of consumption of the attributes of a choice alternative.

> When consuming alternatives, the marginal utility first increases, but then decreases beyond the ideal points, which reflect satiation (Timmermans 1990, 105).

According to the concept of a direct motivation for variety seeking, inventory-based models allow for a preference for new experiences as well as intrapersonal and interpersonal variety.

However, Timmermans argued that neither of the two types may act as a satisfactory explanatory model for destination choice. Whereas the non-inventory model does not allow for the integration of modifications to the choice set or to the single alternatives as a result of e.g., a transport-policy measure, in inventory models the assumption of a stable choice process would be queried, "as policy decisions will almost invariably influence the process" (Timmermans 1990, 111). Timmermans and his colleagues therefore formulated a model in which (a) choices are dependent on previous choices; (b) variety-seeking behaviour is alternative-specific; and (c) a sophisticated approach to comparing and valuing similarities as well as dissimilarities of attributes of alternatives is integrated (Borgers, van der Heijden, and Timmermans 1989).

Determinants of habitual and rhythmic patterns of travel behaviour

If travel is defined as a means to satisfy the demand for out-of-home activities, which factors influence decisions to execute those activities and to combine them in larger patterns? The development of habitual behaviour needs to be seen as a consequence of different psychological processes as well as environmental and social factors. Regularities in travel are predominantly produced by the temporal aspects of a person's social environment (such as fixed working hours, household obligations, appointments, etc.) and the psychological aspects underlying the decision processes. The latter factor refers to a range of situations in daily life (and travel) when approved behavioural alternatives promise a relief from having to make further or new decisions.

In the following, *selected generic models of time use and travel* as well as *specific determinants of periodic behaviour* will be discussed. Time-budget or time-use research offers a range of explanatory approaches to travel, having originated in various scientific disciplines[4]. These primarily include space-time geography and behavioural psychology as well as economics.

Micro-economic theory of time-use and utility maximization

The starting point for the micro-economic approach to explaining time-use allocation is the fundamental assumption that households, like firms, need to be seen as production units (Becker 1965; 1978). According to their potentials, they produce commodities such as household-related services which absorb financial and temporal resources.

Analogous to theories about the market behaviour of firms, it may be assumed that private households also follow principles of cost minimization on the one hand and utility or profit maximization on the other hand while producing their commodities. This implies that all activities underlie a (fictive) cost-benefit analysis, which influences human behaviour as well as the scheduling and execution of daily activity patterns. Activities which yield greater benefits or "utility" are therefore rated as more valuable and receive higher priority in personal time and activity planning.

A monetary aspect of time use was introduced with the assumption that the disposable income of households is a combination of the two components: income earned (time offered to the labour market) and income lost as a consequence of time used for household production, leisure or consumption. Hence, disposable time budgets may be divided into two blocks: *productive* (wage-earning) time and household-related *reproductive* time. This theory is the basis for behavioural models which may, for example, quantify the impact of a pay increase on the

4 An overview of conceptual and methodological intersections between time-use research and travel-behaviour analysis may be found in Bhat and Koppelman 1999.

allocation of time or calculate the relationship between rising prices for goods and services and their substitution by reproductive work.

Recognizing the straightforward approach, which imposes a monetary assessment on activities, time-use research itself has questioned the underlying assumptions (see, e.g., Juster and Stafford 1991; Pollak 1999), including:

- the definition and the observability of commodities (what about household-related activities that do not produce measurable outputs?);
- the assumption that activities benefit a household in a general way (rather than there being various individual benefits to different activities); or
- the assumption that every household-related activity generates the same utility for every person and that people have no individual preferences for different types of housework.

Space-time geography and related approaches

Most of the explanatory approaches to analysing and forecasting personal time budgets are based on classical theories of *space-time geography* developed by the *Lund School* (Hägerstrand 1970; Carlstein, Parkes, and Thrift 1978)[5]. There are also related concepts which try to describe the development of human activity patterns (Chapin 1965, 1974, 1978; Heidemann 1981; Beckmann 1983; see also below in this chapter). The fundamental principle linking the approaches is the idea that human behaviour is embedded in a complex system of personal as well as external restrictions. The set of restrictions or *constraints* which travellers are exposed to therefore shapes their individual *decision space* for time use and activity execution.

The constraints originate from a range of needs and requirements for human interaction as well as from cultural, legal and organizational conventions and rules. Hägerstrand (1970) defined three main categories of constraints which are embedded in a close network of interactions and which together shape the personal activity potential of travellers:

- **capability constraints**: individual biological and physiological needs such as to sleep or to eat; the physiological possibility to move or restrictions to movement; the availability of and access to mobility tools; temporal and financial resources for conducting activities and making trips;
- **coupling constraints**: restrictions to an autonomous allocation of time due to the need to coordinate with institutional logistics (schedules or given locations); interactions with other individuals (appointments or meetings with other household members, relatives, friends, business partners, etc.);

5 (Space-)time geography (*chronogeography*) emerged out of research undertaken in the late 1960s and 1970s by Torsten Hägerstrand and his colleagues Tommy Carlstein, Bo Lenntorp and Solveig Mårtensson, a group of Swedish geographers based at Lund University who became known as the "Lund School".

- **authority constraints**: formal and informal economic or legal rules or norms such as opening times, etc.

Furthermore, the Lund School associates each activity with a space and a time aspect which are intrinsically tied to each other. The model represents space and time graphically as a three-dimensional system in which space opens up a two-dimensional plane and time forms a vertical axis on this plane (Figure 4.3). The sequence of activities of a traveller over a defined period of time (a day, a week, a lifetime, etc.) may be visualized as a path through the system with movement implying a change of coordinates in space and time.

Constraints may be seen as concentric tubes if the set of described restrictions is added to this graphical concept (Shapcott and Steadman 1978). The tubes narrow the temporal and spatial degree of freedom, for example through the allocation of certain obligations (such as the activity *work*) in fixed time and/or space bandwidths (Figure 4.4). In addition to inflexible or fixed activities there is also disposable time, which is represented as a prism in the model (see also Chapter 10). The prism sizes or characteristics are predominantly determined by the individual's travel potential, which may include his or her physical fitness, mobility tool availability and household and workplace locations.

In the context of urban planning, Chapin developed a multistage model to represent activity systems in cities, particularly in his 1974 book *Human Activity Patterns in the City*. Chapin paid particular attention to interactions between the activity patterns of persons or households and the aggregate processes within (urban) institutions such as firms, public authorities or schools.

Chapin described the decision process of activity scheduling and execution as a three-component system involving:

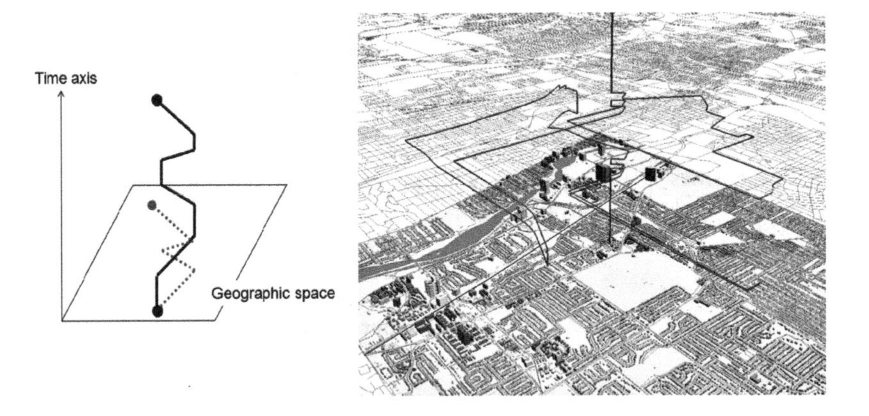

Figure 4.3 Time geography: Concept and application (right: example of a 3-D space-time path)

Source: Modified from Keßler (2006) (left); Kwan 2006 (right), with permission.

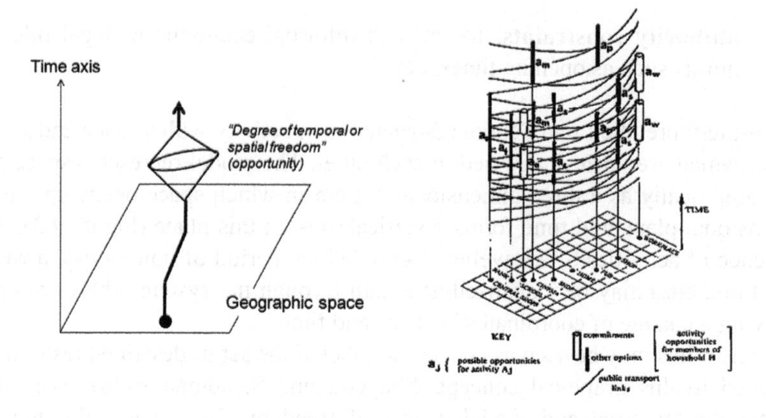

Figure 4.4 Degree of spatial and temporal freedom in travel represented by a prism and the impact of constraints on the space-time path

Source: Modified from Keßler (2006) (left); Adapted from Jones et al. (1983), with permission (right).

- the motivation to execute an activity;
- the choice of a potential option to satisfy demand; and
- the result of the decision process (Chapin 1978).

The probability of choosing and executing a particular activity is determined by *personal propensities*, the situative temporal framework or background of the decision and the perceived spatial *opportunities* connected with the activity.

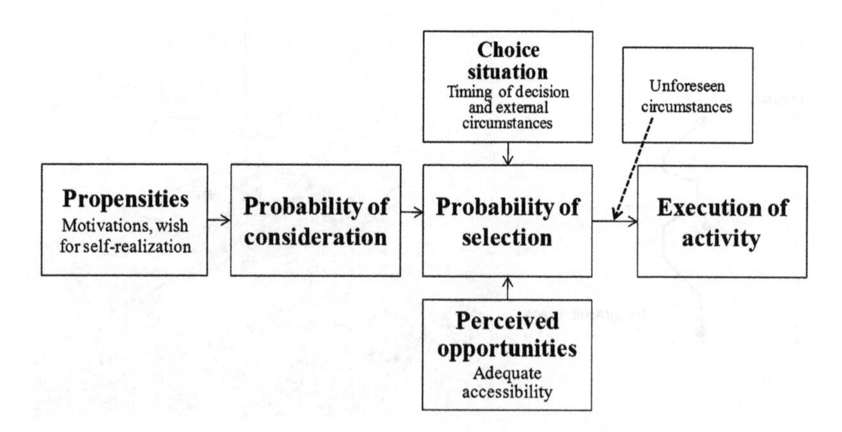

Figure 4.5 Human activity patterns in the city: Model of decision-making processes

Source: Adapted from Chapin (1978) 15.

Individuals develop propensities based on their motivations and attitudes, whereby they assess spatial opportunities according to their perceptions of accessibility and the characteristics of given locations. In contrast to the Lund School, Chapin put a stronger emphasis on the individual's perception of his or her environment. He considered the evaluation of the situative context of the activity or travel choice to be equally important.

Socio-ecological approaches

Heidemann developed his *socio-ecological approach* to explaining activity and travel behaviour based on theories from research into ecosystems (Heidemann 1981). The approach defines human behaviour as a result of the interaction between individuals (and households) with their environment, in particular with technical and social infrastructure. Interaction between the demand side (individuals and households) and the supply of opportunities (built environment and infrastructure) lead to decision or choice situations which relate the needs of an individual to the opportunities and potentials in his or her surrounding environment. The outcome of this decision process is individual spatial behaviour, which leads to movement and therefore travel.

Similar to the Lund School, it is assumed that different restrictions have a regulative impact on spatio-temporal behaviour. Heidemann introduced the terms *regimes* and *budgets*. Regimes capture general rules and laws and their effects on societal organization. Budgets are defined as personal and/or group-specific potentials and capacities to maximize utility. Societal and personal constraints are categorized as *time constraints*, *means constraints* and *information or knowledge constraints*–which is similar to the structure proposed by Hägerstrand.

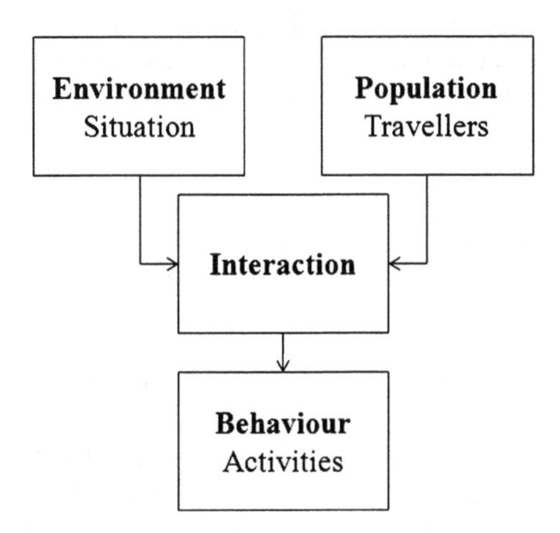

Figure 4.6 Socio-ecological model of space-time behaviour (basic approach)
Source: Adapted from Heidemann (1981) 292.

Homogenous groups of behaviour

Kutter stressed the socio-economic attributes of travellers as explanatory determinants for their time use and travel behaviour (Kutter 1972, 1973). This categorization of persons into homogenous groups is one of the predominant approaches to explaining complex activity patterns and is widely applied in forecasting models (see also Lammers and Herz 1979; Schmiedel 1984; Schlich 2004). A similar concept was developed by Harvey (1982).

Kutter referred to *role theory*[6], which has strong roots in psychology and sociology. Role theory explains behaviour as an outcome of social learning processes. Individual behaviour is believed to be embedded in fixed and predefined structures which are imposed by institutions such as school or the family. People tend to adapt to these structures with a high probability. Based on these assumptions and in consideration of so-called key roles, Kutter categorized the population according to different homogenous groups of behaviour with a high degree of socioeconomic similarity. The groups are mainly defined using the attributes occupation (status), gender and the availability of a personal vehicle.

Again, the concept of roles or group affiliation is methodologically closely connected to the theories of space-time geography. The *main activity* (such as work) associated with the respective group has a dominant impact on time use and activity scheduling, as it widely determines the travel demand of daily life. This approach, which is highly pragmatic in terms of predefining travellers mainly by their occupational status, has since been critically discussed in many travel behaviour studies (see Volkmar 1984; Schlich 2004). One of the implications which was discussed most critically is the question as to whether behaviour remains constant and/or consistent just because a traveller is assigned a main obligatory activity such as work or education. Finally, Schlich (2004) was able to show that from a longitudinal perspective–which is the premise of this book–travel behaviour and time use within pre-defined homogeneous groups is far more variable than the underlying assumption based on cross-sectional data analysis would allow for.

Social network approaches

Social networks, as an expression of the embeddedness of people in a network of personal contacts and surrounding societal settings, have long been examined by social scientists from a range of perspectives (Larsen, Urry, and Axhausen 2006), including

- a community approach which stresses how people belong to a group of peers defined by geographical propinquity, systematic social interrelationship or close personal ties such as friendship or family (Bell and Newby 1976);
- the Social Network Analysis (SNA) approach, which focuses on the "structural properties that connect people in webs of friendship, mutual

6 For an overview see Wiswede 1977; Biddle 1979.

support and sociality through face-to-face talk, phone conversations and emailing" (Larsen, Urry, and Axhausen 2006, 23; see, e.g., Scott 2000 for a UK-focused review); and
- the "small world phenomenon" approach (see Urry 2004 for an overview), which postulates that everybody in this world is separated by a few degrees of separation from anybody else due to a small number of links which bridge large physical or otherwise large social distances.

Social networks were introduced only recently as a new possible predictor of travel behaviour and movement. Researchers such as Urry and others (see, e.g., Sheller and Urry 2006) argue that flows and meetings of objects, technologies and especially people produce small worlds which require connections and meeting places. A new social network (analysis) approach called "mobilities" discusses and investigates how traffic between those places is organized on the one hand by traditional *mobility tools* such as cars or aeroplanes and on the other hand by network tools such as letters, email or the internet.

> Central to networks are the forms and character of the meetings and hence of travel in order both to establish and to nourish links or at least temporally cement them. Instead of focusing upon the formal structures of the networks themselves, this mobility approach analyses the embodied making of networks, performances and practices of networking. Social networks come to life and are sustained through various practices of networking [...] (Larsen, Urry, and Axhausen 2006, 20 ff.).

With this understanding of social networks as a facilitator of virtual as well as physical networks and the movement within them, travel–as one means of satisfying movement requirements–becomes a result of human networking. All forms of travel demand (especially work, business, leisure, etc.) therefore mirror the embeddedness of people in professional and private communities which generate the need to meet at various close or far-off places.

Specific determinants of habitual travel behaviour and periodic elements of activity demand

Habitual travel behaviour, or the reuse of behavioural alternatives in similar choice situations, is widely seen as a human strategy for coping with the complexity of the urban travel environment (Gärling and Axhausen 2003). As Cullen stated,

> The point is that the process of adaptive routinization may be viewed as an entirely rational response to a highly complex situation. It is a way of negotiating a tortuous path through a difficult environment and a wealth of commitments. Repetitive deliberation and choice are impossible luxuries then it comes to day to day living in a post-industrial city (Cullen 1978, 33).

Equally important regarding the routinization of daily life is how travellers process and use the growing amount of information about the temporal and spatial contexts of trip making. Having the possibility to decide about (new) options, for example an alternative route or mode choice, is essential to escape the boredom of quasi-mechanical behaviour. However, this requires operationalizing acquired knowledge and information of temporal and spatial circumstances (Huff and Hanson 1986).

Two of the most frequently mentioned psychological concepts with respect to the development of behavioural routines are *bounded rationality* and *cognitive maps* (see Chapter 2 for the wider concept of the *personal world*).

Despite the assumption that people tend to act in utility-maximizing ways when using their resources (time, income, etc.), the "best alternative" (from an objective point of view) is only rarely chosen. This especially applies when decisions need to be made quickly or if a decision has little priority. In most cases, the chosen alternative deviates from the optimum relative to the cost-benefit expectation attached to the choice or its importance. This behavioural strategy is known as *bounded rationality* (see Simon 1957 for an introduction to the terminology of rational choice). In a more general context of economic behaviour, travellers often seek satisfactory solutions instead of being entirely rational and searching for an optimal solution.

Accepting satisfactory solutions has the consequence that behavioural elements which have proven to be adequately successful in the past (routines) are chosen to avoid further complexity in the decision-making process, such as having to search for, organize or evaluate additional relevant information.

Further reasons for preferring known behavioural alternatives are the often insufficient availability of additional information which would be necessary to solve problems optimally, and restrictions on individual cognitive processing capacities. The quality of information of travel options such as accessibility, network structure or capacities has an important impact on the discrete choice of modes, routes, departure times, etc. (Schofer, Khattak, and Koppelman 1993). A traveller's decision space as well as the probability that he or she will deviate from a known (satisfactory) alternative will increase in proportion to the greater availability of exact, up-to-date and understandable information.

In addition, people usually apply simple rules (heuristics) to making decisions and combining their (passively) memorized experiences and their actual knowledge to decide on options, whether long-term (e.g., car purchase) or short-term (e.g., departure time of a trip) (Schofer, Khattak, and Koppelman 1993). As the combination of available knowledge and additional information may complicate the decision situation, human beings try to simplify the substance of information in order to make many decisions in the shortest time (see Kahnemann, Slovic, and Tversky 1982). The result of such heuristics is often the reapplication of previously successful behavioural solutions.

Habitual travel behaviour is finally determined by imperfect knowledge about the spatial environment and the limited set of known alternatives in space, both for destination as well as route choices. Travellers usually face mental capacity restrictions. The perception and the operationalization of spatial information within cognitive processes obviously restrict the capacity of mental representation as well as the resolution of networks or the built environment (see Downs and Stea 1977; Lynch 1960). As Lynch showed in several experiments, the representation of a person's surrounding environment is biased and therefore not entirely complete. The physical environment seems to be memorized and processed in *mental* or *cognitive maps* which are neither scale accurate, comprehensive nor errorless (see Downs and Stea 1977; Lynch 1960; Gould and White 1986).

Cognitive maps have a considerable impact on travel choices as they supply the set of alternatives for both day-to-day and long-term mobility-related decisions. For example, congested roads or areas can only be avoided if there is sufficient spatial knowledge and representation to positively evaluate alternative routes which are potentially less or not at all congested. It has been demonstrated by Lynch that there are great differences between travellers in their understanding and implementation of spatial information. This has implications for the extent to which people behave in a routinized manner or with a higher degree of variability.

Earlier investigations on variability and stability in travel behaviour

The analysis of regular structures in individual travel behaviour is not new; however, it has been limited by the scarcity of multiday mobility data which would permit the detection of periodic structures. Clearly, cross-sectional data can also be used and have in fact already been used to provide insights into the regularity of (overall) mobility patterns (e.g., Herz 1983). However, as most of the analysis in this book focuses on the variability of individual behaviour over time, the cross-sectional perspective will not be considered.

Previous investigations on intrapersonal variability have been based on the few existing multiday data sets such as the Cedar Rapids movement study (Garrison et al. 1959), the Uppsala Household Travel Survey (Marble, Hanson, and Hanson 1972; see also Chapter 6), the Hamilton-Wentworth two-week travel diary (Webber 1978), the seven-day Reading activity data set (see, e.g., Pas 1980) or the Austin area ten-day commuter-data set collected in 1989 (Hatcher and Mahmassani 1992). A more recent analysis approach to revealing regularities in travel behaviour was based on the Lexington 1996 GPS-feasibility study (data from six consecutive days) (Batelle Transport Division 1997).

The Cedar Rapids movement study covered a sample of 262 households in Cedar Rapids, Iowa, USA and surrounding areas (Garrison et al. 1959). The travel diary (all modes) was designed for a reporting period of thirty consecutive days for all household members aged ten and older. The later analysis was based on smaller subsamples and focused on the spatial regularity and extent of travel behaviour, especially for shopping (Marble and Nystuen 1963; Marble and Bowlby 1968). The investigation revealed considerable spatial stability with about three quarters of all destinations being frequented repeatedly. Additionally, the intensity of chaining trips was found to be great for city-centre shopping and weak for grocery shopping.

Susan Hanson and her colleagues focused their analysis of the Uppsala Household Travel Survey (UHTS) on the habitual characteristics of travel behaviour (see, e.g., Hanson and Huff 1982, 1986, 1988a, 1988b; Hanson and Burnett 1981; Burnett and Hanson 1982; Huff and Hanson 1986, 1990). They found that isolated elements of travel behaviour can be found on a distinct periodic basis if individuals are observed over prolonged periods such as several weeks (Hanson and Huff 1986; Huff and Hanson 1986). In addition, the researchers developed means to measure the extent of day-to-day variability for single travellers as well as the stability of individual behaviour over the entire survey period of the UHTS, using selected features of activity demand and trip making (e.g., a combination of purpose, time of day, mode, etc.) (Hanson and Huff 1986; Huff and Hanson 1986). The analysis of these indicators, which were interpreted as *similarity indices* for regular trips and *representative days*, led to the conclusion that on average there is little similarity in the behaviour of a single traveller on different days, even if the five most representative daily patterns for each person are considered (Hanson and Huff 1988b). The work prompted a discussion about the usefulness of the representative day assumption for transport-modelling approaches based on cross-sectional travel-survey data. As mentioned, the non-existence of typical days for individuals calls into question the postulate of a behavioural equilibrium for single travellers, which had been implied in most of the common models.

In his early work, Pas developed indicators for classifying daily travel behaviour according to similarities using the 1973 Reading seven-day activity-data set (Pas 1980, 1983), in analogy to the studies by Hanson and her colleagues. Koppelman and Pas later provided support for Hanson's sceptical view of trip-generation models which rely entirely on one-day travel data (Koppelman and Pas 1984; Pas 1986). They found a considerable bias between trip rates that were predicted based on regression models using cross-sectional and longitudinal data. Pas (1987) investigated the variance in daily trip rates of single travellers and used the outcome as a measure of day-to-day variability in travel behaviour. He found that about half of the observed total variability in samples could be explained by *intrapersonal variability*; this needs to be conceptually separated from *interpersonal variability*, which describes differences between travellers, e.g., their trip rates.

Pas and Sundar (1995) employed a three-day travel-data set from Seattle (1989) to analyse a range of mobility indicators such as trip chaining and daily travel budgets. Similar to the Reading results, it was found that a substantial share of the overall variability observed within the sample was caused by intrapersonal variability.

Bhat (2000a, 2001) investigated the intrapersonal variability of mode-choice and stop-making behaviour for commute trips, using the three- to five-day "San Francisco Bay Area Household Travel Survey" data (White and Company 1991).

Among other findings, Bhat strongly recommended incorporating heterogeneity aspects in mode-choice models for consecutive panel data. Only this allows behavioural variations to be captured, as they may not otherwise be explained sufficiently, even by the best systematic specifications of the models.

Mahmassani and his colleagues focused on the day-to-day dynamics of travel behaviour (Chang and Mahmassani 1989; Hatcher and Mahmassani 1992; Mahmassani 1997; Mahmassani, Hatcher, and Caplice 1997). The researchers analysed departure-time choice, trip chaining and route choice for morning as well as evening commute trips (Mannering and Hamed 1990) based on laboratory experiments and the Austin, Texas multiday survey. An interesting result of their work was that there are stronger propensities or elasticities for changing behaviour regarding route choice compared to departure-time choice.

The Lexington GPS study featured the first multiday travel-data sources not entirely based on traditional PAPI (paper-and-pencil interview) or CATI (computer-assisted telephone) survey design, but augmented by (in-vehicle) global-positioning-system (GPS) devices and geographic-information systems (GIS) (Batelle Transport Division 1997; Pendyala 1999; see also Chapter 6). The study yielded (car) travel behaviour information for up to seven days. The studies based on that data source focused on variability issues such as repetitive behaviour (Pendyala 1999), reapplying methods such as Pas' to reveal the share of intra- and interpersonal variability during day-to-day comparisons or when comparing one day of the week to another (Zhou and Golledge 2000; Muthyalagari, Parashar, and Pendyala 2001). The results were in line with earlier findings on variance in individual mobility (such as Pas 1987), but also stressed the importance of the weekday as a determinant for trip distance, frequency, purpose, direction and the type and temporal characteristics of activities.

The Mobidrive study (Axhausen et al. 2002), one of the main data sets that will be investigated in the following chapters, received considerable attention regarding the analysis of behavioural regularity, rhythms and their determinants. The econometric investigation differed in the selection and the complexity of the model approaches as well as in the objective of the analysis. Schönfelder and Axhausen (2000, 2001a) as well as Fraschini and Axhausen (2001) focused on general daily rhythms (see also Chapter 9), using survival and time-series analysis methodologies. Bhat, Sivakumar, and Axhausen (2003) analysed the impact of information and communication technologies on long-term shopping intervals by an advanced hazard-based model that incorporated sample selection, random coefficients and unobserved heterogeneity issues. Bhat et al. (2004a) had a look at the temporal structure of grocery shopping by applying a latent segmentation method. And finally, Bhat, Srinivasan, and Axhausen (2005) highlighted the structure of weekly interactivity performance using a hazard model covering several complex modelling aspects such as a flexible duration-dynamics structure and variation in inter-episode duration due to unobserved individual-specific factors. All of the models yielded interesting findings on the structure of activity demand, which differed considerably for individual travellers due to their socio-economic backgrounds and preference structures, although the weekly periodicity dominated. The most recent paper (Chikaraishi et al. [forthcoming]) analysed variance in the departure time using a multilevel approach to demonstrate again that the relative majority is due to interpersonal variations of behaviour.

Many of the analyses applied to the Mobidrive data were repeated within the framework of the Swiss SVI *Stabilität* research project with a comparable six-week travel diary (Thurgau data, see Chapter 6). The results can be found in Löchl et al. 2005.

Chapter 5
A Conceptual Model of Non-Response

Surveys require the cooperation and commitment of respondents: to win them and then maintain them is the central social process involved in survey research. In this chapter we will not review the enormous literature on that issue (for such reviews see, for example, Dillman 2000; Edwards et al. 2002; or Zimowski et al. 1997). Rather, we wish to present a conceptual model of what a researcher can expect. Our model was designed for travel behaviour research, but the discussion should apply to other research contexts as well. We shall focus primarily on non-response during the survey process. Other errors and biases, such as those arising from coverage or sampling errors, will not be addressed.

Non-response in travel behaviour surveys can be usefully structured at more levels than usual in general survey research. This structure applies to all surveys which ask respondents for events, episodes or objects whose number is unknown to the survey researcher in advance:

- "Non-participation" is the refusal to provide any information about the person(s), mobility tools and movements of interest to the researcher. This is normally labelled "unit non-response", which is not a usage adopted here.
- "Unit non-response" is the refusal to provide information about one or more of the logical units of related items in the survey, here:
  - A person and his or her attributes
  - A mobility tool and its attributes
  - A daily schedule chain or any of its subunits: activity and its associated tours, subtours, trips or stages (see Chapter 3).
- "Item non-response" is a missing or refused answer to a specific question item about any of the units above, for instance a person's age, brand of car or the starting time of a trip.

There are multiple tools and approaches used to correct for non-participation and item non-response, depending on whether the non-response is a random or a non-random process (see Rubin 1978; Little and Rubin 1987; and Rubin 2004). Item non-response can generally be treated as having happened at random, with the exception perhaps of any income-related question. The bias arising from elements (items, units or non-participation) missing at random can at least be corrected by reweighting them.

Randomness can not generally be assumed for unit non-response. In spite of this, the literature is sparse for unit non-response correction as defined here, which is interesting in its own right, as the number of movements and their characteristics is the central object of interest in travel behaviour research. The current correction methods are generally ad hoc and only work at the level of the derived aggregate statistics, e.g., at the level of the number of missing trips, but not at the level of the characteristics of the missing trips or individual units. They are also generally based on data from respondents who took part in special protocols, raising questions about the comparability of the results given the inherent biases of any element of the protocols. (For a sophisticated example, see Polak and Han 1997).

To win the commitment of the respondents, the survey must:

- have a sponsor who is entitled by his or her tasks to ask the questions at hand;
- come from a competent and trustworthy researcher and fieldwork firm;
- express the seriousness and commitment to the survey of the sponsor, the researcher and the fieldwork firm;
- involve a response burden and complexity which is proportional to the problem addressed;
- ask questions relevant to the problem addressed.

The fulfilment of these requirements determines whether a survey suits its purpose, both socially as well substantially. The respondents, whom we assume to be generally willing to answer, judge whether their time and effort will result in worthwhile answers and whether they will have a chance to contribute to the sponsor's decision making. This requires a match between the sponsor and the problem studied, for instance a road authority asking about travel but not about sleeping patterns. Questions which are likely to be perceived as off-topic for the sponsor require special justification, which is difficult to provide in many cases. The competence of the researcher and fieldwork firm in the study area must be established, which favours large or local fieldwork firms and well-known institutions such as universities or consultancies. The renown of the sponsor can balance a fieldwork firm's lack of prominence, but only to some extent.

Seriousness and commitment to the survey are communicated through the survey protocol and survey materials. The protocol, i.e., the sequence of contacts and their content, have to communicate interest in obtaining the answers. Announcement letters, cover letters, motivational calls, incentives, reminders, etc. all help to convey that message. The literature shows that each type of contact increases response, but their joint effect is sublinear; we observe decreasing returns. Survey materials (letters, reminder postcards, emails, websites, printed questionnaires, thank-you notes, etc.) must be error-free, easy to read and easy to use throughout, as one lapse might jeopardize the ongoing commitment of a respondent to the survey. They should also be proportional to the sponsor: the respondent will not expect a survey undertaken as part of a MSc project to be properly printed and bound, but a government-sponsored survey should not arrive as a set of badly copied and carelessly stapled pages. On the other hand, publicly funded research in particular should avoid the impression of unnecessary luxury, e.g., overly expensive materials and design. This especially applies to incentives. While they reliably increase response, particularly when provided upfront, they should not attempt to pay for the respondents' time. This would be financially impossible for just about all surveys and would defeat the purpose of signalling the seriousness of the interest. The incentive should acknowledge the extra effort made by the respondents, but not insult them by paying them too little or too much.

The response burden is a function of the number of questions, but also the number of movements undertaken and the questions about each movement. For household surveys, the number of household members increases the response burden further as all members above a certain age have to participate to generate a complete and valid record for household-level analysis.

The effect of the response burden interacts with the channels for asking the questions and the channels provided for the response. Today's survey protocols rarely rely on just one channel, but mix them in multimethod or multimodal protocols. Channels for the questions are as follows:

- Written: on a paper form.
- Written: on a computer display (all possible platforms and form factors, including: wall displays, desktops, laptops, web terminals, personal digital assistants (PDAs), mobile phones and special-purpose devices).
- Oral: by pre-recorded messages played over the phone or another device controlled by touch-phone input or voice recognition.
- Oral: by an interviewer over the phone.
- Oral: by an interviewer face to face.

The respondents can answer:

- In writing without an interviewer present (in writing on a paper form or to a data terminal).
- In writing (on a paper form or to a data terminal) in the presence of an interviewer who provides help.
- Orally to a automatic recording device.
- Orally to an interviewer.

It is clear that each channel excludes certain groups: written channels exclude the functionally illiterate depending on the reading level of the questions and the degree of the respondent's illiteracy. They also exclude the blind. Oral channels exclude the deaf, but include the substantial share of the population which is functionally illiterate. They also exclude those who are under time pressure at the time of contact unless they can reschedule the interview. Computer-based channels exclude those without access to the tool unless it is provided with the survey, and it discourages those with little computer practice.

The respondent can easily assess the likely response burden of a written paper form: its length is immediately clear, and the complexity of the questions is apparent after a bit of browsing. Computer-displayed forms do not allow such an assessment. While the researcher can provide guidance in the announcement letter or through an on-line countdown device, the true complexity of the questions is only revealed when they are displayed. This similarly applies to oral channels. In addition, computer-based channels may give rise to technical problems (such as browser incompatibility, server availability, server speed, operating-system incompatibility and screen-resolution mismatch) and are generally not as easy to handle as paper-and-pencil forms. (For a general discussion of web-based surveys, see Wyatt 2000; Van Selm and Jankowski 2006; and Weis et al. 2008.)

The respondents then have to weigh the perceived response burden (on their time, as well as their memory and search effort), the availability of time in their schedule, the seriousness of the survey (the issue, the sponsor, the researcher, the fieldwork firm, the incentive, the quality of the materials) and their own interest in the topic of the survey to decide if they want to participate, and if so, to what extent. Note that the response burden of travel surveys depends on the number of movements undertaken during the specified reporting period. Respondents can reduce their response burden by not reporting all movements or even by reporting none, claiming to have stayed at home the whole reporting day.

We assume that participation falls as the response burden increases. This view is supported by evidence from a natural experiment carried out in Zürich. A series of self-administered paper-based surveys with vastly different response burdens were conducted over a number of years by the Institute for Transport Planning and Systems (IVT) for purposes of basic and applied research. A point scheme used by a local research firm for budgeting face-to-face interviews was applied to the written forms, resulting in the trend shown in Figure 5.1. One must be careful about generalizing from so few cases, but the clear trend is consistent with our expectations.

Prior contact with the respondents through telephone-based recruiting or a timely motivational call improved their participation, but only by an additive share. This demonstrates that (prior) commitment given to the issue or to the fieldwork team naturally has a positive effect. Note also the striking difference in response behaviour (Figure 5.2) between employees and students of the ETH and the University of Zürich who were approached by an ETH institute with a web-based survey of interest to both institutions.

Beyond the response burden and the respondents' commitment we would expect their time availability at the time of contact to interact both with the channels used for the answers and responses and with their degree of literacy. Functional illiteracy has been the subject of a series of large-scale surveys in the 1990s (OECD and Statistics Canada 2000; OECD and Human Resources Development Canada 1997; and for an assessment of the methods, see: Blum, Goldstein, and Guérin-Pace 2001; Barro and Lee 2001; and Boudard and Jones 2003). They indicate that a substantial share of the population will be unable to handle a survey of the

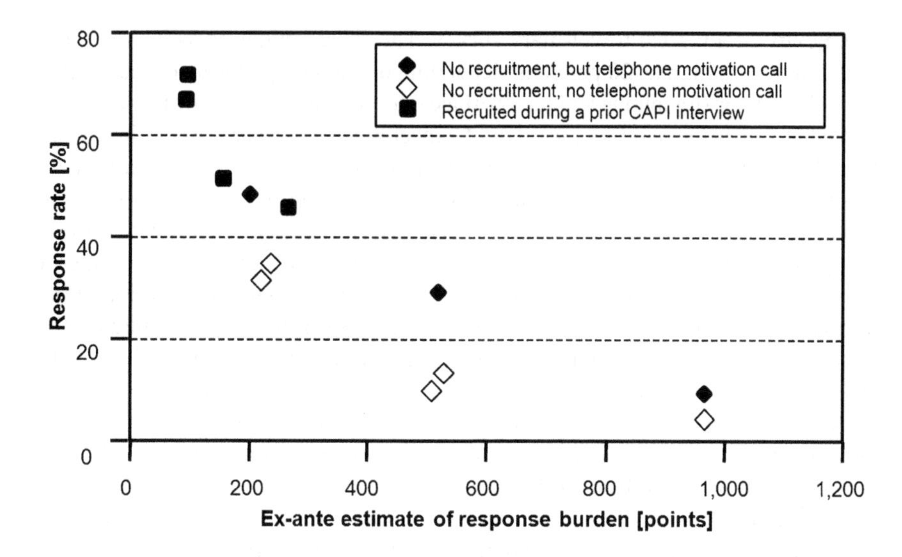

Figure 5.1 Participation versus response burden in recent self-administrated paper-and-pencil surveys

Source: Axhausen 2007. See source for details of the point system and the underlying studies.

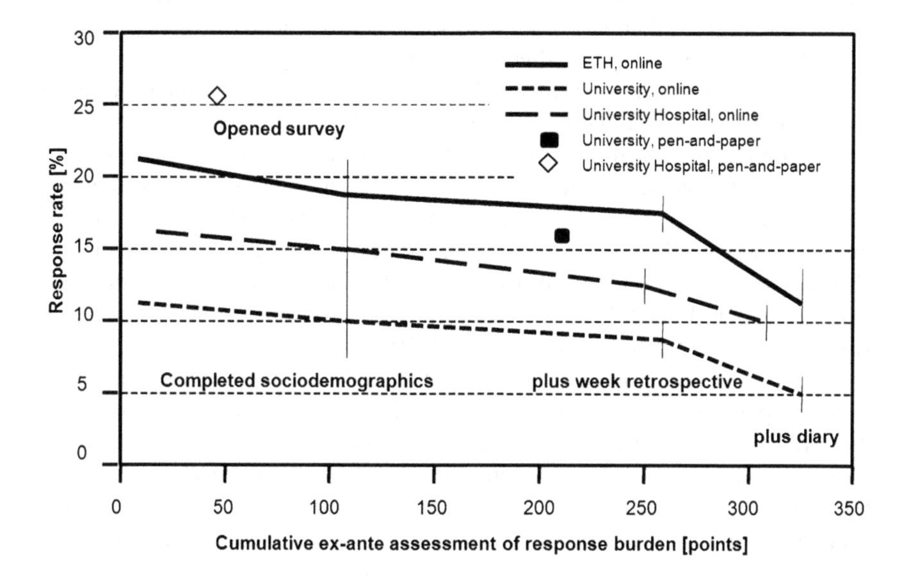

Figure 5.2 Web versus self-administered paper-and-pencil surveys

Source: Weis et al. 2008.

complexity of a typical travel-diary survey. The shares might be as low as 5 per cent, but also as high as 20 per cent, depending on the interpretation of the results. As oral channels (telephone and face-to-face interviewing) require the respondents' immediate attention and time, we would expect those who spend much time away from home, travel a lot, or have a large family to be less likely to participate in such a survey. Oral channels also exclude those who do not understand the language of the survey well enough, especially recent immigrants. All of these groups would be better served by a written instrument which leaves the time of answering up to the respondents, but the instrument has to gain the attention of the respondents among many advertisement mailings. (See Edwards et al. 2002 for the effectiveness of various design elements to increase attention to the mailing.) Still, the functionally illiterate would be excluded, as pointed out above.

We also expect "soft refusal" through unit non-response, i.e., omitted movements, especially when the number of items per movement is high. The pervasiveness of soft refusal has been documented by Richardson (2003a), Madre, Axhausen, and Brög (2007) or Hubert et al. (2008). They show that the share of immobiles, i.e., those who report no movement for the reporting day, is generally far greater than the correct share of about 7–8 per cent on working days for the general population.

We also assume that the average number of reported movements is below the true value, as persons with a larger than normal number of trips on the reporting day are *ceteris paribus* less likely to participate and more likely to suppress the reporting of individual units (stages, trips and tours). This is borne out by the comparison of the GPS traces of travellers who also provided a diary record of the same day (see Table 5.1). The alternative explanation for forgotten trips has been investigated many times, but the result reported by Richardson (2003a) of about 5 per cent trips forgotten during reporting is typical[1].

The remaining difference is due to the respondents' choice of accepting the response burden on the day they were approached. This interpretation is supported by the reported trip making of persons who were approached orally a second or third time, who rescheduled their interview, or who answered only after reminders. They consistently reported lower trip rates with underreporting rates comparable to those given in Table 5.1. The results in Table 5.2 are typical of the literature (see Brög and Meyburg 1980, 1981 or Wermuth 1985).

In summary, patterns of non-participation and unit non-response are linked to the response burden of the number of units to be reported for the reporting day. We have seen that even the number of trips reported by respondents at first contact is low compared to the number identified through independent GPS traces. Considering different levels of interest in travel and transport, the random availability of a time window, different levels of commitment to the public good and the effect of any incentive offered, we still observe the full range of trip

1 The result was gained by intensive, personal face-to-face checking with the respondents.

Table 5.1 Underreporting of car driver trips: Comparison of travel diary versus GPS traces

Location	Year	Number of households for comparison	Rate of trip under-reporting
Laredo [1b]	2002	87	81%
Los Angeles [1c]	2001/2	293	35%
Austin[1a]	1997	200	31%
Pittsburgh[1]	2001/2	46	31%
Ohio[1c]	2002	230	30%
California[1]	2001	292	23%
St. Louis[1]	2002	150	11%
Kansas City[1]	2004	228	10%
Zürich, Winterthur, Geneve[2d]			13%

[a] 120 sec dwell time threshold for activity; [b] Excluding trips outside the study area; [c] Driver and car passenger underreporting; [d] Driver and passenger underreporting, but only based on aggregates from two separate and strictly contemporary studies; based on 4,800 person-weeks of GPS data.
Source: [1] Bricka and Bhat 2006; [2] Schüssler and Axhausen 2008.

Table 5.2 Underreporting in the Melbourne metropolitan VATS[1] survey 1994–1996 (%)

Response to the	Relative to answers to the first mailing			Relative to face-to-face interviews of persistent non-responders		
	1994	1995	1996	1994	1995	1996
First reminder	16.0	8.0	12.1	17.6	8.6	19.3
Second reminder	16.7	20.6	17.6	18.3	21.1	24.3
Second mailing	33.4	26.8	27.9	34.7	27.3	33.7
Third reminder	27.7	27.7	24.5	29.0	28.2	30.6

[1] VATS is a self-administered written survey.
Source: Adapted from Richardson 2003a.

numbers in spite of the response burden, but the distribution is shifted to the left (see Schüssler and Axhausen 2008). This shift is also visible in lower trip rates for those respondents who answered later during the protocol, i.e., for a day of their choice. In addition, we can expect omitted units of movement once a respondent experiences the work involved in reporting them. Omissions are easier to make on written forms. Respondents can go to the extreme of claiming to have been immobile. Such soft refusal is pervasive in travel-diary surveys and needs special attention, as its share directly affects the average rate of movement calculated from the survey.

Given the inherent and unavoidable downward bias of survey-based methods, it comes as no surprise that passive GPS- or GSM-based tracking will become very prominent in the near future. Still, errors and omissions are possible even with these devices, requiring careful attention to the biases, which will hopefully be smaller than those in survey-based methods.

Chapter 6

The Multi-Day Data Sets Employed

The analysis of the multiday aspects of travel behaviour in Chapters 9 and 11 is based on a range of recently collected travel-data sets which will be presented in this chapter. Before getting into the details of the respective survey designs and data availability, the challenges and advantages of using longitudinal (panel) data will be discussed, particularly as regards the study of timing in transportation and travel behaviour. Another focus of this chapter is the description of the data-collection and processing methodology applied to the three GPS-data sets used. By nature, the GPS approach differs considerably from the ordinary travel survey methods introduced in Chapter 3.

Characteristics and merits of longitudinal (panel) data

Statistics define the similarities and especially the differences between cross-sectional or regression data, time-series data and longitudinal (panel) data. Table 6.1 gives a synopsis of the discriminating characteristics of the data categories based on Frees (2004). The two main advantages of longitudinal data are the possibility to study both the *dynamics* of a selected variable, i.e., its change over time, as well as common cross-sectional issues (comparison of individuals). In addition, heterogeneity effects may be analysed and tested for, such as all omitted and immeasurable variables in people's choice process, including different tastes or preferences, routines or socio-economic attributes.

Table 6.1 Cross-sectional, time-series, and longitudinal data in comparison

	Time scale	Population	Frequency of measurement	Suitability
Cross-sectional or regression data	Point of time	Cross-section of subjects	One observation per individual	Cross-sectional aspects
Time-series data	Over time	One subject	Repeated measurements	Dynamics of a single issue
Longitudinal data	Over time	Cross-section of subjects	Repeated measurements	Dynamics *as well as* cross-sectional aspects Heterogeneity effects

Given these benefits, longitudinal data are believed to be an appropriate and effective basis for studying stability and variability in travel behaviour. Further functional and statistical merits of longitudinal data analysis (see Diggle, Liang, and Zeger 1994) are as follows:

- When individuals' behavioural changes over time are analysed based on cross-sectional data, there is a certain risk that the parameters which represent the expected change for one individual will be estimated wrongly. This often occurs because the effects of unmeasured individual attributes (such as personal habits) which influence variability persist over time and are not captured when comparing one person's response to others with different values. In longitudinal studies, by contrast, each observation of a person can be thought of as serving as his or her own control.
- The use of longitudinal data offers the possibility to distinguish the degree of variation across time for one person from the variation among people. This is particularly important if the variation is large, which is true for many phenomena in travel behaviour due to differences in travellers' socio-economic backgrounds and tastes.

In transportation and especially in travel-behaviour analysis, researchers and planners are often interested in how travellers react to changing travel contexts or environments, irrespective of whether the external reason for change is strategic, i.e., a planning measure, or whether it has a natural cause such as a certain weather condition. The objects of interest are twofold. On the one hand, knowledge about the magnitude or power of a reaction is a crucial prerequisite for estimating its impact on the system. On the other hand, it is essential to know when the feedback started.

Being aware of the *timing of change* "contributes to the accuracy of a prediction at a point in the future" (Hensher 1997, 305). In this context, longitudinal panel-data play an important role if their potential to capture *timing*, *duration* and *event histories* is explored. There is a wide range of applications of this kind, e.g., in the analysis of delays, in accident analysis, or – as in this book – the analysis of temporal aspects of activity participation (Bhat 2000b).

Miller (1999) gave three further important arguments for the collection and analysis of multiday surveys. First, weekend travel – which has often been entirely neglected in cross-sectional travel surveys due to the predominant interest in commuting – has developed into an important demand factor and has a considerable impact on capacities, congestion and emission levels. Second, a realistic representation of travel behaviour requires understanding household interactions over more than a day or two. Inner-household time-use planning and travel decisions often exceed one-day periods and often have implications for the availability of mobility tools (person A took the train for his weekend trip because person B needed the household car to get child C to an event on Saturday). And finally, sampling and therefore cost efficiency support the decision to implement multiday surveys because fewer households need to be interviewed for a given number of travel days (Stopher et al. 2008; Stopher and Greaves 2007; or Richardson 2003b).

Data types

Table 6.2 provides an overview of the data sets used in the analysis of Chapters 9 and 11. These data sets span the range from rural villages and small towns (in the Swiss canton of Thurgau) to metropolitan environments (Copenhagen, Denmark and Atlanta, USA). The possible impacts of these scale differences will be traced in the analysis of human activity spaces in particular. A first insight into the differences between the levels of personal mobility is provided in Table 6.3.

The data sources differ substantially with regard to their style of data acquisition, their structure and the amount of information available. Whereas the Uppsala survey, Mobidrive and the two Swiss studies were conducted as ordinary paper-and-pencil self-completion (PAPI) travel diaries, the Borlänge, Copenhagen and Atlanta data were collected by in-vehicle GPS devices. The differences are not only visible in terms of the width and depth of the travel-related and socio-economic attributes, but also in terms of the resolution of their geocoding, which is an important issue in the analysis of human activity spaces. Moreover, the definition of a *unique location* – which is a main methodological issue – needs to accommodate the different sources given the different sets of available information and geographical resolutions of trip-destination coding. A unique location is here defined as the product of the geocode and the trip purpose (see also Schönfelder and Axhausen 2004b). For this study, the unique locations for GPS data had to be created by clustering trip-end positions (see below in this chapter for the respective approach). Trip purposes, however, were not imputed for the GPS-data sets used.

GPS observations

Before describing the data-collection procedures of the various surveys in detail, some remarks about GPS data collection are necessary:

Researchers have long been interested in acquiring multiday travel data which capture even seasonalities in travel demand. One obvious technical possibility is the collection of travel-behaviour data by GPS devices in connection with GIS mapping. This innovative data-collection methodology looks promising, especially in the field of route-choice analysis, in which exact-choice data from longer periods are practically non-existent. In travel-behaviour research, the methodology has been discussed and tested since the mid-1990s (see Wolf, Guensler, and Bachman 2001 for an overview of feasibility studies). The existing data-collection approaches may be categorized as follows (Lee-Gosselin 2002; Wolf 2003):

- GPS-based data collection as an enhancement of traditional travel diaries: In most of the feasibility studies, the portable or in-vehicle GPS or GIS device acts as a supplementary means of collecting data on exact times, locations and route choices. Hence, the technique replaces corresponding parts of the ordinary travel-diary survey and reduces the survey respondents' reporting task. The remaining trip-related information such as the trip purpose, the number of people travelling together or activity expenses are collected separately, either by means of ordinary travel-diary forms or electronic data-collection devices such as personal digital assistants (PDAs).
- Passive monitoring: Within a passive monitoring framework, travellers are observed automatically without being requested to provide any additional information on their trip making (no driver-device interaction). Most of the studies which used passive monitoring were traffic safety driven. The focus of the analysis may be the style of driving or the behavioural reaction of the drivers towards external conditions. The reason for the drive and the activity related to the movement were of minor interest.

The use of *passive-monitoring* GPS vehicle data represents an innovative approach to broadening the analytical base in activity-based analysis. The fully automatically collected data of the various studies contain movement information on single travellers over a span of two years or more (e.g., the Atlanta study).

All three data sets used here are passive-monitoring data sets and stem from instrumented vehicle setups. The technology used was mainly a combination of mobile GPS data loggers and a geographical information system (GIS) (see Draijer, Kalfs, and Perdok 2000 for an example). Vehicles were equipped with on-board data-collection systems consisting of a GPS receiver, a data-storage device with a GIS for mapping all movements and a mobile power supply. For each trip, the recruited drivers switched on the system. This started data transmission to the computer (for storage) in short (e.g., second-by-second) intervals. After data collection (i.e., tracking the travellers), the highly exact spatial and temporal information was transferred to a conventional computer for processing.

The motivation for the studies arose from different concerns (traffic safety in Borlänge; road-pricing experiments in Copenhagen and Atlanta), which creates problems with regard to data analysis and comparability. This includes, for example, insufficient identification of the drivers, their incomplete socio-economic descriptions or the lack of trip- and activity-purpose information.

Cleaning and imputing the GPS-data sets (Borlänge, Copenhagen and Atlanta)

As GPS data-collection methodology differs greatly from ordinary travel-diary approaches, vehicle-movement information needs to be cleaned and enriched to obtain better comprehensiveness and quality. This cleaning and enriching process will be described briefly:

Because only vehicle activity was monitored, there was a systematic omission of other travel modes such as walking, bicycling and transit use. Positive driver identification was also not provided by the system, which appears to increase weekend travel for shared vehicles significantly (see for comparison Guensler, Ogle, and Li 2006). The most important information that was not directly collected for each trip is trip purpose. While approximately 60–70 per cent of travel is fairly routine and trip purposes can be identified based upon physical location (home, work, school, day care and basic shopping), significant additional data processing and imputation is required (georeferencing routine locations based upon travel-diary data). However, given that the objectives of this analysis are both to demonstrate how data can be used and to demonstrate the ad hoc analysis of location-choice structures over time, the data used here have been not processed to code trip purposes, as has been done in other studies (Schönfelder and Samaga 2003; Wolf et al. 2004). Such coding work was ongoing in all three projects (Borlänge, Copenhagen and Atlanta). To meet the minimal requirements of a straightforward investigation, post-processing involved an initial filtering of the raw data as well as identifying trip-end positions.

Initial filtering and cleaning

The GPS data were pre-processed to remove vehicle activities that did not contribute to travel demand. Vehicle engines are often started, stopped and then restarted before a real trip begins (perhaps to go back into the residence for a forgotten item). Vehicles are moved in and out of driveways and are often idled for extended periods. While such information is useful in vehicle-emissions analysis, these activities do not constitute vehicle trips. Criteria established in previous studies (Wolf 2000; Pearson 2001; Wolf, Guensler, and Bachman 2001) were applied here. To remain consistent with these previous studies, trips with engine-operating durations of less than 30 seconds or activity durations of less than three minutes were screened from the travel data[1]. In addition, trips were eliminated for which GPS data were not available (or a previous trip's destination did not match the next trip's location of origin) due to satellite data drops. Filtering the database by applying a threshold approach does not mean that all erroneous trips are systematically detected and erased. Rather, it guarantees a minimum of quality, especially when dealing with large data sets like all of the data sets used here (see also the discussion in the final chapter).

1 More recent analysis of the Commute Atlanta data indicates that these criteria are probably a bit too stringent. Drop-off trips to video stores, stops at automatic teller machines and passenger drop-offs often have a very short activity duration. The Atlanta research team is currently analysing short-duration trips to enhance screening criteria and methods.

Identifying trip-end positions

All three studies established trip starts and ends through engine operation. Trip recording began when the engine was turned on, and stopped when the engine was turned off[2]. For repeated trips to the same location, the final resting position of the vehicle can vary significantly. Parking location depends upon parking availability. To identify and categorize unique destinations, a straightforward statistical clustering approach was applied. All trip-end positions within a radius of 200 metres were grouped to one unique location using the highly efficient *nearest-centroid sorting* cluster method (Anderberg 1973). In principle, all trip ends within the given radius were assigned to a calculated cluster, which obviously reduced the number of locations (Figure 6.1).

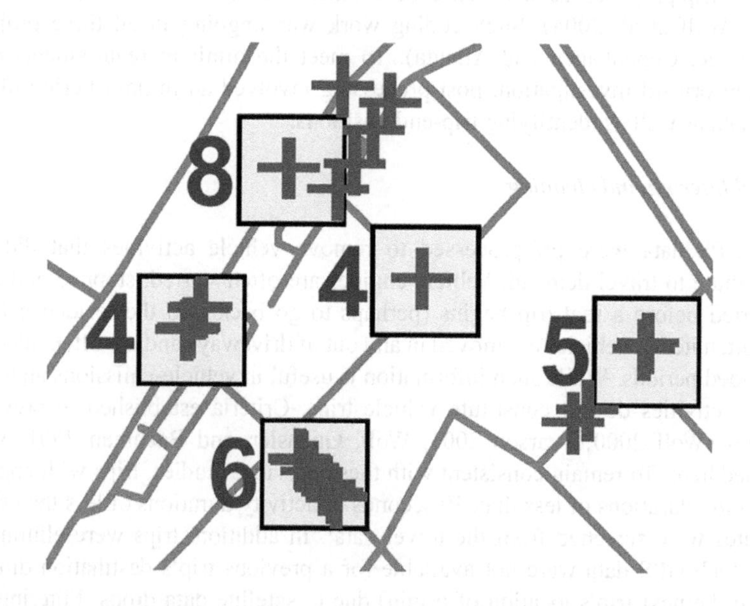

Figure 6.1 Schematic overview: Clustering observed trip ends (crosses) to unique activity locations (boxes)

2 Chained trips that do not include turning the engine off (for example, approximately 15 per cent of all trips made during the travel-diary comparison period in the *Commute Atlanta* study) must be identified through post-processing in a GIS system (see Wolf, Oliveira, and Thompson 2003; Ogle et al. 2006). However, this imputation exercise was not conducted for the data used in this study.

Applying the threshold approach: Implications

Figure 6.2 shows for the Borlänge GPS data how the threshold approach deals with the issue of unique locations and filters potentially irrelevant trips. The size of the chosen cluster radius considerably affects the number of unique locations generated. The number of total places falls by a half when the radius is merely increased from a 50 m to a 200 m beeline distance from the cluster seed. This strong response indicates the need for a more sophisticated search strategy. In addition, by applying the threshold cleaning approach (which is independent of the clustering), the total number of observed trips is reduced tremendously from about 85,000 to 52,000 trips. Again, this shows that more certainty about trip attributes is guaranteed only when a more advanced way of complementing and correcting the GPS traces is applied (such as in Wolf et al. 2004; Chung and Shalaby 2005; Tsui and Shalaby 2006; Du and Aultman-Hall 2007).

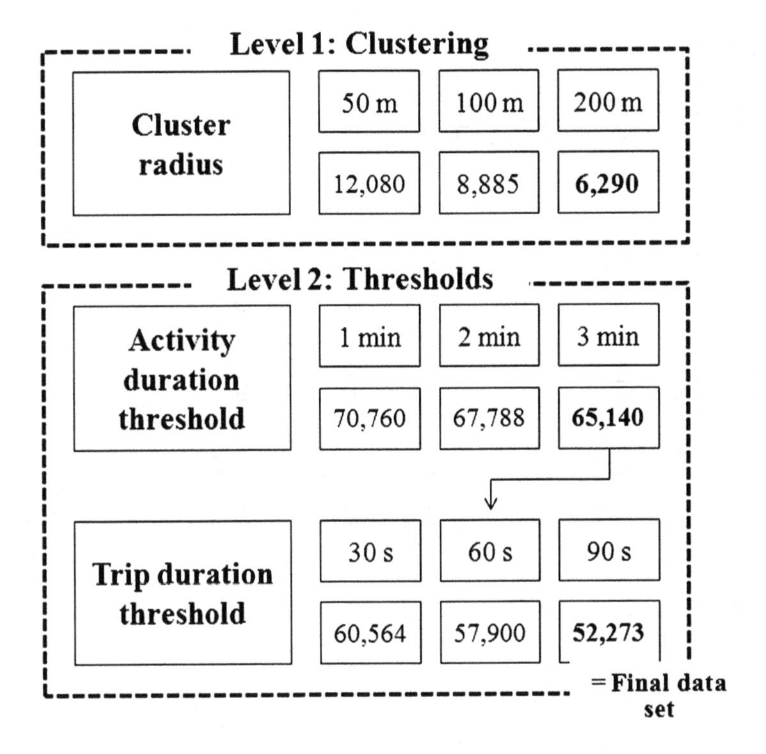

Figure 6.2 Sensitivity analysis of the Borlänge GPS data: Effects of varying clustering and cleaning thresholds for GPS data

Table 6.2 Overview of the data sources

Name of the survey*	Year	Original focus	Location(s)	Period	Resolution: geocoding	Resolution: purposes	Persons	Trips
Uppsala Household Travel Survey	1971	Travel behaviour	Uppsala, Sweden	35 days	Building	All purposes	144	23,000
Mobidrive: Dynamics and routines of travel behaviour	1999	Stability of temporal patterns	Karlsruhe and Halle, Germany	42 days	Street block	All purposes	361	52,000
Borlänge GPS study (ISA Rätt Fart)	2000-2002	Speeding behaviour	Borlänge, Sweden	Up to 80 weeks	Trip ends: GPS; unique locations: pre-defined clusters of trip ends	Unknown, potentially all	189 veh.**	240,000 car trips
Leisure study (SVI Gesetz-mässigkeiten des Wochenend-Freizeit-verkehrs)	2002	Leisure travel behaviour and activities	Zürich, Switzerland	84 days	Post-code level	31 leisure purposes	75	9,900 leisure activities
Thurgau diary (SVI Study of the stability of transport behaviour)	2003	Stability of temporal patterns	Frauenfeld and villages in the Swiss canton of Thurgau	42 days	Building	All purposes	230	37,000
Copenhagen GPS study (AKTA Road Pricing Experiment in Copenhagen)	2001-2003	Route choice under road pricing	Copenhagen, Denmark	18-24 weeks	Trip ends: GPS; unique locations: pre-defined clusters of trip ends	Unknown, potentially all	500 veh.	250,000 car trips
Atlanta GPS study (Commute Atlanta Study)	2004-2006	Travel behaviour; test of policy measures such as pricing	Atlanta, USA	Up to two years	Trip ends: GPS; unique locations: pre-defined clusters of trip ends	Unknown, potentially all	Approx. 500 veh.	Approx. 1,000,000 car trips

* In the following, the data sets are simply titled Mobidrive, Thurgau, Uppsala, Borlänge, Copenhagen and Atlanta for better readability.

** Private cars only.

Table 6.3 Selected comparative characteristics of the data sets (mobile days only; GPS: after 'cleaning')

	Mobidrive main study	Thurgau*	Uppsala	Zürich 12-week leisure study**	Borlänge GPS***	Copen-hagen GPS****	Commute Atlanta GPS
N respondents (GPS: cars with a positive number of trips)	317	230	144	71	66	200	418
Male (GPS: main user)	158	117	63	34	25	140	175
Full-time (GPS: main user)	120	143	75	37	21	+200	225
Mean daily trip rate [hours] (Std.)	3.9 (2)	4.3 (2.3)	4.5 (2.5)	1.6 0.9	3.8 (1.0)	4.2 (1.2)	4.1 (1.5)
Mean daily distance [km] (Std.)	31 (58)	47 (63)	20 (5)	n/a	20 (7)	34 (13)	49 (24)
Mean daily trip duration [hours] (Std.)	77 (62)	111 (211)	68 (65)	n/a	27 (8)	54 (17)	74 (72)

* includes few long-distance or long-duration trips. ** leisure activities only.
*** socio-economic data incomplete for Borlänge. + commuters.
**** control period only.
° means calculated for mobile survey respondents.

Data sets and data-usage concepts

The different data sets are used according to their particular features and qualities. The analysis of the temporal phenomena of individual travel (see Chapter 9) is based on the travel-diary data of the Mobidrive and Thurgau surveys. They offer a rich description of the respondents' socio-economic situations, a detailed activity-purpose categorization and comparable data structures. The analyses of destination choice as well as activity spaces rely on a wider range of data sets and make use of the GPS data, which are much less detailed in their socio-economic attributes.

Table 6.4 Data-use and analysis concept

	Mobi-drive	Thur-gau	Uppsala	Leisure study	Borlänge GPS	Copen-hagen GPS	Atlanta GPS
Temporal regularities and rhythms (all subcategories)							
Descriptive	X	X					
Hazard models							
Non-parametric	X	X					
Semi-parametric (Han and Hausman)	X	X					
Fully parametric (Weibull)	X	X					
Destination choice / activity spaces (all subcategories or only partial)							
Enumeration and listing of places visited	X	X	X	X	X	X	X
Continuous space representation and measurement							
Confidence ellipses	X	X	X		X	X	
Kernel densities	X	X	X		X	X	
Shortest-path networks	X				X		
Activity spaces and socio-economic attributes	X	X	X		X	X	(X)*

* Atlanta where available.

Uppsala Household Travel Survey ("Uppsala")

The *Uppsala Household Travel Survey* (Marble, Hanson, and Hanson 1972) covers a period of five continuous weeks. The survey was conducted in 1971 and is the basis of a series of publications by Hanson and colleagues concerning the stability of travel behaviour.

The city of Uppsala is located approximately 70 kilometres northwest of Stockholm and had a population of about 130,000 at the time of the study. A random sample of 20 per cent of the total population was drawn. The persons who agreed to participate were classified as belonging to six different life-cycle groups. The respondents began to fill in the diary on five sequential days. The final sample size was 488 persons in 278 households, of which 92 households (comprising 144 persons) were chosen for further analysis by Hanson and colleagues[3]. This group was roughly representative of Uppsala's population. A detailed description of the sampling procedure and the survey instruments is given in Marble, Hanson, and Hanson (1972). As part of the survey design, the interviewed persons were contacted frequently. Due to this, the number of participants who dropped out of the survey was below 15 per cent. No signs of significant fatigue effects could be detected (Burnett and Hanson 1982).

The manual geocoding of the trip destinations for the available sample of 144 persons was successful for 17,138 of the 17,147 trips reported.

Mobidrive: Dynamics and routines of travel behaviour ("Mobidrive")

Like the earlier Uppsala survey, the 1999–2001 Mobidrive research project proved that fears of losing information in multiweek travel-diary surveys were unfounded (see Axhausen et al. 2002; Zimmermann et al. 2001). A continuous 6-week travel diary formed the core of the project.

The travel-diary survey itself was conducted in the German cities of Halle and Karlsruhe in the autumn of 1999. A total of 317 persons aged 6 years and older in 139 households participated in the main phase of the survey, after the survey instruments were tested with a smaller sample in the spring of 1999 (44 persons)[4]. The PAPI travel-diary instrument was supplemented by further survey elements covering the socio-demographic characteristics of the households and their members, details of the households' car fleets, the number of transit season tickets owned, household members' personal values as well as their attitudes towards the different modes of transport.

One objective of the Mobidrive researchers was to provide exact location data in order to facilitate the analysis of variability in spatial behaviour over time (e.g., destination, route and mode choices). The precise location data were obtained by geocoding the trip destination addresses of all the trips collected in the main study (approximately 40,000 trips). The addresses, including home and workplace locations, were transformed into Gauss-Krüger coordinates in the World Geodetic System (WGS 84) geodetic reference system. The geocoding was positive for about 95 per cent of the reported trips. Due to incomplete addresses and the limited availability of digital address information outside of the urban cores in the case-study regions, the geocodes of the addresses have different degrees of resolution

3 That subsample is used in this analysis as well.

4 The analyses in this book are based on the main study data only.

for the different spatial units. For the City of Karlsruhe and the City of Halle, street addresses could be geocoded on the basis of (small) building blocks (more than 90 per cent of all geocoded trips), whereas addresses outside of urban boundaries were only geocoded to the centres of the relevant municipality.

Twelve-week leisure study (SVI Regularities of weekend leisure travel) ("Leisure Study")

The Swiss leisure study *Gesetzmässigkeiten des Wochenend-Freizeitverkehrs*, which was initiated by the Swiss Association of Transport Engineers (SVI), aimed to collect long-duration travel data, focusing especially on leisure activities (Schlich et al. 2002a; 2002b). The 12-week travel-diary survey at the centre of the study was conducted in the canton of Zürich, Switzerland (including the City of Zürich and two smaller suburbs) at the beginning of 2002. The sample size comprised 71 respondents who did not show any significant fatigue effects in reporting. A pre-test in the autumn of 2001 with 16 respondents helped to finalize the structure of the main study survey.

The survey instrument focused on leisure travel, requesting information from the respondents about the start and end times of each out-of-home leisure activity trip, the detailed purpose of each trip, the modes of travel, the places of destination, accompanying travellers, trip expenses and the frequency of recent trips. In addition, a simple time-budget survey (by one-hour resolution) was added to place the leisure activities into context. The usual socio-economic data were collected to frame the travel-diary data.

A total of 5,600 separate leisure activities could be collected. The geocoding was limited to the postcode level only. The very detailed coding of the leisure purposes balances this aggregation only to a limited extent. Due to the special focus on leisure travel and its limited geocoding, these data will not be analysed as intensely as the other sets in this book.

One interesting and new feature of the survey design was the question in the trip-diary instrument of whether the trip destination belonged to the set of regularly or at least sometimes frequented places, or whether the destination was entirely new to the respondent. The item yields interesting insights into the characteristics of variety-seeking in location choice (see Chapter 11). The same information is available from the Thurgau travel-diary data, too.

2003 Thurgau travel-diary data (SVI Stability of Transport Behaviour) ("Thurgau")

The Thurgau travel-diary survey (Buhl and Widmer 2004; Löchl et al. 2005) is a Swiss attempt to: 1) collect up-to-date panel data analogous to the Mobidrive study, and 2) develop approaches to exploring the stability of travel over the course of one day, within households and groups of travellers, as well as explore the stability of mode choice. The survey, which was also commissioned by the SVI, was performed in the canton of Thurgau (eastern Switzerland) in 2003 and covered a 6-week reporting period with a sample of 99 households (230 persons). The vast majority of the destination addresses and household locations were geocoded with high precision (36,454 of the 36,783 available trips; see Machguth and Löchl 2004).

Borlänge GPS data (ISA Rätt Fart study) ("Borlänge")

The GPS-data set *Rätt Fart* was made available for travel-behaviour analysis by transport psychologists from the universities of Dalarna and Uppsala (Sweden) in 2002. The traffic-safety project *Rätt Fart* ('Right Speed')[5], based in the town of Borlänge in central Sweden, was one of the subprojects of the Swedish National Road Administration's 'Intelligent Speed Adaptation' (ISA) initiative (see Biding and Lind 2002). *Rätt Fart* in Borlänge itself focused on collecting information about the drivers through GPS devices. The study was conducted from 1999 to 2001 and involved about 260 private and commercial cars, which were equipped with GPS and speed adaptation systems over a period of two years. The essential characteristics (speed, acceleration, actual time, location, etc.) were collected either every second or every 10th second, depending on the type of road link, and were stored internally for analysis in logs.

The original movement file contains 245,000 private car trips. The area for detailed monitoring was, however, limited to the town of Borlänge plus some of the surrounding region, an area with a radius of about 20 kilometres around the town centre of Borlänge. Travel out of this boundary was not monitored, except erroneously.

The total subsample of GPS trips used in this book consists of approximately 52,000 car trips made by 66 vehicles. The period of monitoring for each of the cars ranged from 27 to 469 days involving 70 to 2,207 trips. The available survey period lasted from September 29, 2000 until March 4, 2002. Only a very limited range of socio-economic variables is available for the test drivers.

Copenhagen GPS data (AKTA Road Pricing Experiment in Copenhagen) ("Copenhagen")

The AKTA study conducted by the Centre for Traffic and Transport of the Technical University of Denmark (Nielsen and Jovicic 2003; Nielsen 2004) was part of the EU-funded project 'Pricing ROad use for Greater Responsibility, Efficiency and Sustainability in citieS' (PRoGRESS)[6]. AKTA was a real-life road-pricing experiment in the greater Copenhagen region.

5 See http://publikationswebbutik.vv.se/upload/3571/2002_96_E_results_of_the_worlds_largest_isa_trial.pdf.

6 http://www.progress-project.org/ as of 27 Sept. 2005.

In 2002 Copenhagen had 620,000 inhabitants in the city proper, about 1,800,000 in Greater Copenhagen (*Koebenhavn kommun*) and more than three million inhabitants in the Öresund region, which covers Greater Copenhagen and the neighbouring Swedish city region of Malmö.

Approximately 400 cars were equipped with a GPS-based device in three experimental rounds or waves, which differed by the starting date. Each of the rounds consisted of two periods (one control period without the simulation of a pricing scheme plus a period of pricing) of about 8 to 12 weeks in 2001 and 2002. The following three control-pricing combinations were tested:

- Control – High kilometrage charge (up to 5 Danish kroner (appr. 0.7 Euro) per km driven).
- Control – Low kilometrage charge (up to 2.5 Danish kroner (appr. 0.35 Euro) per km driven).
- Control – Cordon based charge (1 to 12 Danish kroner (appr. 0.14 to 1.7 Euro) per crossing of cordon).

Vehicle-movement data were collected every second. An onboard system simulated road pricing by providing cost information for every trip within the City of Copenhagen, which was virtually divided into cordon rings defining prizing zones. After two monitoring periods, which differed according to the pricing scheme virtually applied (high kilometrage, low kilometrage or cordon), the AKTA test drivers were paid an amount of money according to their observed route-choice behaviour. The GPS monitoring was accompanied by a telephone-based before-and-after survey consisting of attitude questions and SP instruments.

Nielsen (2004) described the sampling for the AKTA study in more detail. In brief, the participants were recruited based on a factorial design according to income groups, residence and workplace locations and pricing schemes. All drivers belonged to one-car families, which is common in Denmark due to high car taxes. All households were located within the pricing experiment area. All participants were regular or even full-time workers with associated daily travel.

The analysis of destination choice patterns in this book is based on a subsample of the total AKTA movement data. The subsample comprises 200 vehicles and drivers and contains about 43,000 trips (after post-processing). For consistency purposes, only control period trips were used for our analysis.

Atlanta GPS data (Commute Atlanta Study) ("Atlanta")

The *Commute Atlanta Study* was a long-term programme sponsored by the Federal Highway Administration (FHWA), the Georgia Department of Transportation (GDOT) and the Georgia Institute of Technology. The main objective of the multiyear *Commute Atlanta Study* has been to assess the effects of converting automotive fuel taxes, registration fees and insurance costs into variable driving costs. The project was led by Randall Guensler of the School of Civil and

Environmental Engineering at Georgia Tech and his former colleague Jennifer Ogle (now at the School of Civil Engineering, Clemson University). It has included the parallel collection of instrumented vehicle data, household socio-demographic surveys, annual two-day travel diaries and employer commute-options surveys.

The research programme spanned three phases and included multiple data-collection efforts. The first phase included one continuous year of data collection with no treatments to define baseline travel patterns. Due to seasonal variations in travel, researchers desired a full one-year baseline to develop appropriate relationships between pricing treatments and changes in travel behaviour in later years. The second research phase began in July 2005 and was designed to evaluate the effects of fixed cent-per-mile pricing. The third phase of research began in 2006 and included a real-time congestion-pricing increment of 20 cents per mile when the vehicle was operated on the freeway under congested conditions (in-vehicle data terminals displayed real-time prices). Households began with larger incentive accounts which were drawn down at a faster rate. The third phase was designed to examine the impact of such financial incentives on travel-time choice.

To establish baseline travel patterns, the research team installed 487 Georgia Tech 'Trip Data Collectors' in the vehicles of 268 participating households to collect second-by-second vehicle-activity data (vehicle speed, acceleration, position and engine-operating parameters). Monitoring began for almost all of the vehicles during the period from September to December 2003. The data used in preparing the analyses reported in this book were collected from January until December 2004. Fieldwork and recruitment were reported by Ogle, Guensler, and Elango (2005).

The resulting database for analysis (after post-processing; see above) contains trips involving 418 cars owned by 263 households comprising 655 household members (including non-drivers, children, etc.). The number of monitored days per vehicle ranges from seven to 367. The average share of usage is about 75 per cent, i.e., the vehicles were used on 75 per cent of the monitoring days on average. More than 3,600 trips per car were observed.

The subsample matches available cross-sectional information, but not in total congruity. This is logical considering the unique longitudinal structure of the *Commute Atlanta* data, the limitations given by the sample size and structure as well as the rough post-processing of the database. The average number of car trips per day (4.1) was about 20 per cent higher than the NHTS average (3.4), with the mean daily trip duration (70 minutes per day) and distance (48 kilometres per day) smaller than the national mean (88.7 and 52.8, respectively). Considerably shorter trips were monitored as a result. Similar results were found in earlier comparisons of GPS studies with ordinary cross-sectional travel-diary data (Wolf et al. 2004).

PART II
The Temporal Aspects of Day-to-Day Travel Behaviour

Chapter 7
Current Patterns of Travel Behaviour

Our expectations about travel behaviour have been formed by seventy years of one-day travel diaries; multiday diaries have been very rare in comparison (for a history, see Axhausen 1995). To contrast our results here, but also to provide a frame of reference to highlight the insights gained from multiday surveys, this chapter will employ four different large-scale, one-day diary surveys to describe travel behaviour as a function of the most important socio-demographic influences: income, age and gender, whereby income is a proxy for education and employment, and gender for household roles and responsibilities. The availability of cars and the ownership of public-transport season tickets will be treated separately, as they influence travel behaviour through the great differences in the relative expenditure levels for the relevant modes.

This chapter will furnish context for the other results by providing an overview of current patterns of travel behaviour in its key dimensions (share of out-of-home travellers, number of trips, distances travelled and the durations involved in interactions with the chosen modes). The four survey examples are: the 2001/02 US National Household Travel Survey (NHTS)[1], the 2001/02 German National Travel Survey (MID[2]), the 2005/06 Swiss National Travel Survey (MZ[3]) and the 2000 Kansai regional travel survey (KTS, Osaka-Kobe-Kyoto)[4]. All four were large-scale survey efforts backed by national or regional governments and were conducted after substantial pre-tests and by experienced fieldwork firms. The results shown are based on the official data files and were properly weighted. These four surveys span the experience of established industrialized countries. It should be noted that the Japanese data cover only working days. The first three

---

1 NHTS is a CATI-only household survey involving 1,46,500 persons based on a national sample with regional add-ons covering the whole year (persons over 6 years of age only).

2 The MID: *Mobilität in Deutschland* ("Mobility in Germany") survey was conducted as a mixed-mode survey, mostly relying on CATI interviews. The sample of 52,600 persons is representative for the country and the reported days cover all the days of the year (persons over 6 years of age only).

3 MZ: *Mikrozensus* (microcensus) is a CATI-only survey of a national representative sample with cantonal (regional) add-ons of 33,400 persons spread across the whole year (persons over 6 years of age only).

4 The Kansai survey is a paper-and-pencil survey of the workdays (Tuesday to Thursday). The weighted sample is representative of the regional population based on 400,000 person records (persons over 6 years of age only).

figures (7.1 to 7.3) address the distribution of the number of trips, durations and distances, while Table 7.1 summarizes the differences.

The US travellers reported more, faster and longer trips than the other three surveys' respondents, reflecting a more car-based society at all levels of income and age, as we shall later see. The Swiss and German data are generally comparable, which is not surprising given the strong similarities in urban structure and public transport availability. The low speeds reported from Kansai are due to the very dense settlement of the region, where both car travel and a substantial share of public transport are relatively slow.

The US figures reflect behaviour, which is nearly exclusively based on the car, leaving public transport for rather long trips and walking for short movements. The Kansai data show the opposite, with the smallest share of car travel (trips and distances) and many and long walking trips[5]. The average numbers of trips by the surveys' mobile respondents reflect the countries' different public transport shares, and in the case of Kansai, long working hours, especially for employed males. As discussed in Chapter 5, this number is very sensitive to shares of immobiles (persons reporting no trips for the reporting day). The share of immobiles was particularly high in the Kansai survey, but the pattern of immobile shares varied with the respondents' socio-economic situation, as expected (see Table 7.3). Economically

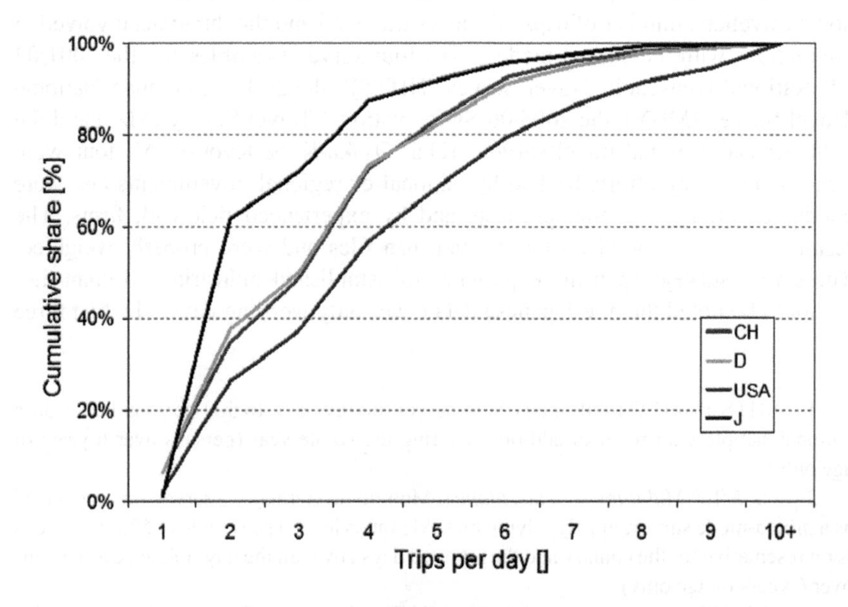

Figure 7.1 Distribution of the number of trips per day
Source: 2001/02 NHTS, 2001/02 MID, 2005/06 MZ, 2000 KTS.

---

5 Note that a zonal network model used to calculate walking distances resulted in overestimates.

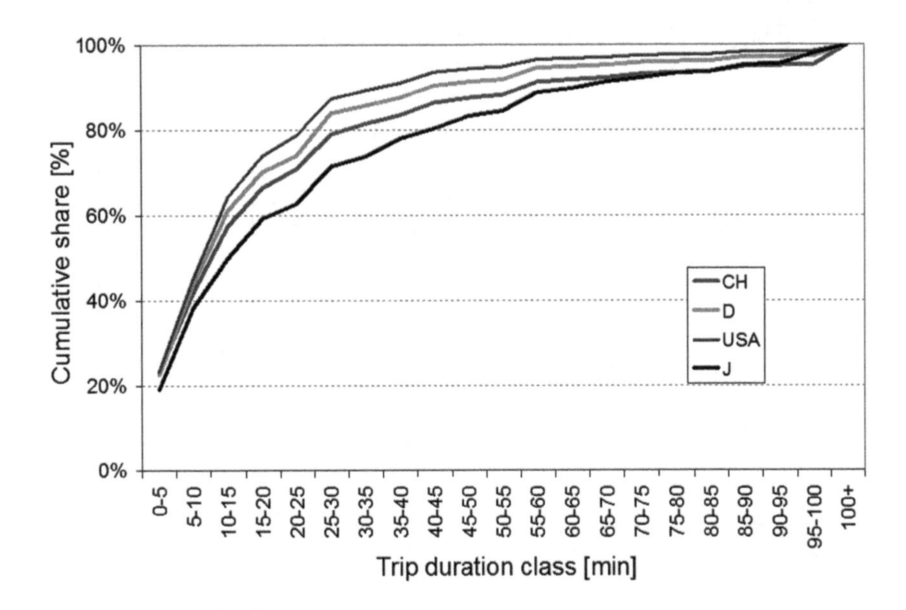

Figure 7.2 Distribution of the trip durations
Source: 2001/02 NHTS, 2001/02 MID, 2005/06 MZ, 2000 KTS.

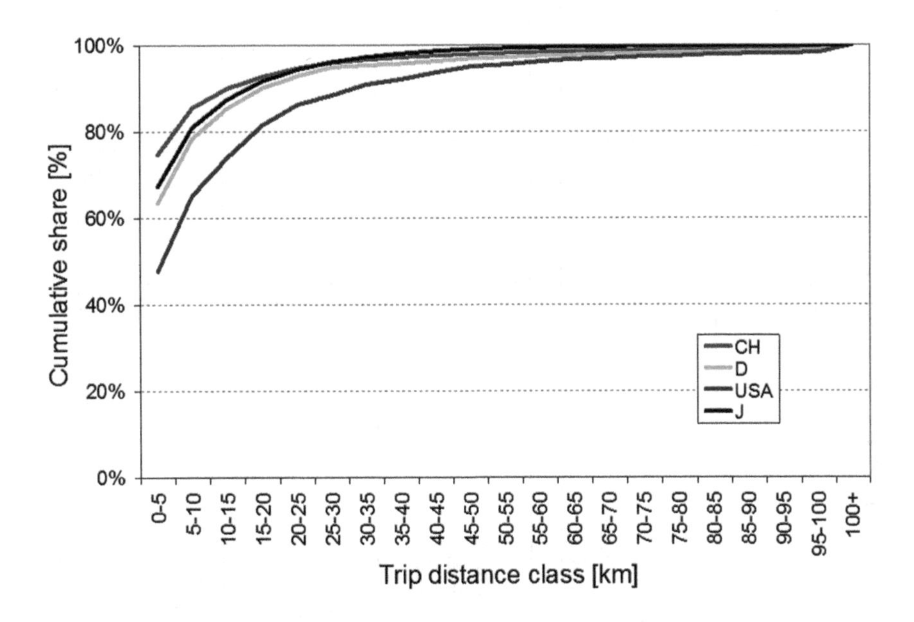

Figure 7.3 Distribution of the trip distances
Source: 2001/02 NHTS, 2001/02 MID, 2005/06 MZ, 2000 KTS.

Table 7.1 Mean characteristics of the trips

	Mean duration per trip	Standard Error of Mean	Mean distance per trip[1]	Standard Error of Mean	Number of trips/day[2]	Share of all trips	Share of all kilometres travelled
	[min]		[km]		[]	[%]	[%]
Car							
USA	19.1	0.0	16.4	0.0	4.0	86.7%	87.8%
Germany	21.5	0.1	14.7	0.1	2.1	57.9%	77.8%
Switzerland	26.3	0.2	16.7	0.2	1.9	51.6%	61.4%
Kansai[3]	26.0	0.0	8.2	0.0	1.1	37.3%	37.5%
Public transport							
USA	45.4	0.0	51.5	0.0	0.2	3.5%	11.2%
Germany	45.0	0.5	20.4	0.6	0.3	8.1%	15.3%
Switzerland	46.7	0.6	24.0	0.5	0.4	11.8%	20.2%
Kansai[3]	57.3	0.0	15.6	0.0	0.6	21.6%	39.2%
Slow modes							
USA	16.9	0.0	1.3	0.0	0.5	9.8%	0.8%
Germany	21.8	0.2	1.9	0.0	1.2	34.0%	5.8%
Switzerland	23.3	0.2	1.8	0.0	1.4	36.6%	4.5%
Kansai[3]	12.1	0.0	4.9	0.0	1.2	41.1%	22.9%
All (including other modes)							
USA	19.8	0.0	16.1	0.0	4.6		
Germany	23.6	0.1	11.0	0.1	3.7		
Switzerland	28.5	0.2	14.0	0.3	3.7		
Kansai[3]	27.1	0.0	8.4	0.0	2.9		

[1] Unless otherwise indicated, respondent estimates. [2] Without persons reporting no trips on the reporting day. [3] Distances include zonal connectors.
Source: 2001/02 NHTS, 2001/02 MID, 2005/06 MZ, 2000 KTS

Table 7.2 Trips by purpose and socio-economic status

	Trip purpose						Trips per journey	Share of leisure of non-return home trips
	Work and education	Shopping and private business	Leisure	Accompany-ing	Return home	All[1]		
	[]	[]	[]	[]	[]	[]	[]	[%]
Full time employee								
USA	1.11	0.59	1.20	0.30	1.54	4.79	3.11	37.1%
Switzerland	1.21	0.29	0.77	0.04	1.54	3.87	2.51	33.3%
Germany	0.70	0.64	0.67	0.11	1.38	2.80	2.03	47.3%
Kansai	1.26	0.31	0.11	0.00	1.05	1.47	1.40	25.5%
Part time employee (1 post)								
USA	0.83	0.72	1.41	0.39	1.74	5.14	2.95	41.4%
Switzerland	0.82	0.50	0.85	0.09	1.67	3.96	2.38	37.2%
Germany	0.59	0.87	0.68	0.30	1.57	3.43	2.18	36.7%
Kansai	1.05	0.51	0.13	0.00	1.04	1.68	1.61	21.0%
In education								
USA	0.90	0.42	1.28	0.29	1.63	4.62	2.84	42.8%
Switzerland	0.92	0.24	0.95	0.02	1.58	3.73	2.37	44.3%
Germany	0.04	1.13	0.78	0.40	1.52	3.83	2.52	33.7%
Kansai	0.78	0.47	0.17	0.00	1.01	1.65	1.63	26.4%
Homework								
USA	0.07	1.03	1.60	0.61	1.80	5.15	2.87	47.9%
Switzerland	0.24	0.62	0.82	0.16	1.67	3.57	2.14	43.2%
Germany	0.08	1.06	0.88	0.31	1.41	3.66	2.59	39.3%
Kansai	0.00	1.22	0.19	0.00	1.03	2.44	2.37	13.3%
All respondets[2]								
USA	0.73	0.71	1.37	0.32	1.59	4.79	3.01	42.9%
Switzerland	0.81	0.39	0.83	0.05	1.57	3.69	2.36	39.1%
Germany	0.43	0.85	0.77	0.15	1.41	3.19	2.26	43.2%
Kansai	0.67	0.61	0.15	0.00	0.94	1.70	1.80	19.8%

Table 7.3 Share of immobiles by socio-economic status

	USA	Switzerland	Germany	Kansai
In education	9.9%	8.3%	18.8%	11.6%
Full employee (multiple posts)	3.0%			
Full employed (one post)	6.0%	7.3%	10.3%	4.3%
Part-time employed (multiple posts)		3.2%		
Part time employed (1 post)	6.6%	6.9%	9.8%	14.7%
Less then part-time employed			10.4%	
Currently unemployed	13.9%	17.5%	10.7%	50.1%
Home work	19.0%	15.7%	17.0%	26.5%
Retired	24.5%	20.1%	22.7%	-[1]
Other	28.4%	27.7%	18.6%	
All	11.6%	11.3%	14.7%	20.7%

[1] Category not available.

Source: 2001/02 NHTS, 2001/02 MID, 2005/06 MZ, 2000 KTS.

active respondents reported low shares of days without travel, while the shares rose for those involved in out-of-home activities. Still, the shares for Germany and Japan must include a substantial share of soft refusals, as the differences between their values and the US values, and especially the Swiss values, are too large to be credible (see Madre, Axhausen, and Brög 2007).

Just as employment or any other firm commitment to out-of-home activity is a crucial influence on trip making, so are factors such as age, gender and the availability of mobility tools. Figure 7.4 provides a comparison of the four surveys. The saturation level of car availability[6] was reached early along the income axis, especially in the USA. In Germany and Switzerland, willingness to trade a (second household) car against a public-transport season ticket is visible in the more gradual growth of car availability and the generally lower car-transport values. Ownership of the various forms of season tickets (regional passes in Germany and Switzerland and a nationwide pass and discount ticket[7] in Switzerland) fell with income at first and then increased again. Note the high share of national season-ticket ownership in Switzerland despite the high share of car availability.

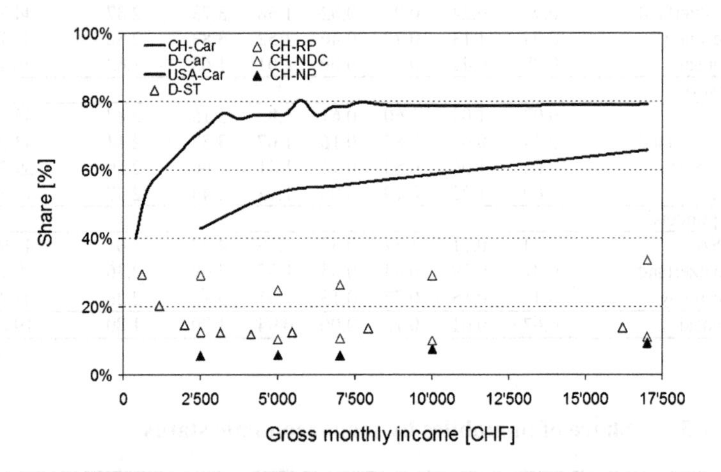

Figure 7.4 Mobility tool availability as function of gross monthly income
The German after-tax figures were scaled up to gross before tax incomes using rough assumptions; ST: Season ticket; RP: Regional pass; NDC: National discount card; NP: National pass.
Source: 2001/02 NHTS, 2001/02 MID, 2005/06 MZ, 2000 KTS.

6 Car availability is defined in the NHTS as positive when the respondent had a driving licence (NHTS); in the MID and the MZ as when the respondents stated that they always had a car available; and in the Kansai survey as when the respondents owned a car.

7 In 2009, this discount ticket (*Halbtaxabo*) costed 150 SFr and entitled the owner to a 50 per cent rebate on all heavy rail tickets and to smaller rebates for local services, including some tourist services (lake boats, cable-cars, etc.).

The impact of mobility tools on travel behaviour becomes visible when persons with and without car availability are compared. In the USA the difference is rather great, starting with a difference of one trip per day, which continues to increase with the respondents' age. In the other countries the difference is marked, but much less so: only around 0.3 trips per day, and this does not change much with the respondents' age, reflecting more alternatives. The age impact follows a common pattern: a peak during the active years, followed by a small reduction towards retirement and a small increase after retirement, then a steady decrease. The pattern remains the same if one focuses only on respondents who only had a car available or who had no mobility tool at all, as one can do for the German and Swiss data (Figure 7.6). The differences increase somewhat to about 0.5 trips per day. Gender differences are non-existent, except that younger males in Germany reported fewer trips.

The impact of the availability of different mobility tools is much stronger with regard to the travellers' mode choices. The Swiss data show the best differentiation (Figure 7.7), as the various types of public transport ticket imply rather different levels of annual monetary commitment (150 SFr for a national discount ticket; 400-800 SFr for regional season tickets; and 3,100 or 4,850 SFr per year for a second- or first-class national season ticket). Shifts from car-based travel to public transport travel clearly correlate with the travellers' degree of commitment to the public transport system. Exceptions to this were those who had no mobility tools at all or who had just the national discount card. They added about two trips per day by slow and other modes, while the rest added about one trip per day by such modes. The precommitment or inertia effect should be taken into account in every case of mode-choice modelling. This requires the inclusion of relevant questions in travel surveys, something all too frequently forgotten. The exceptions are evident in Figure 7.8, which shows that these two types of traveller traded off car-based travel against travel with slow and other modes.

The final aspect to be discussed is the interaction between trip purpose and the modes used. The dominance of the car across the board is obvious for the USA, even for the purpose of education, as parents were obliged to or chose to drive their children to school. Public transport was relevant for work-related trips in the other countries. In all of the countries, work and education formed the largest market shares for public transport, which was barely present for other purposes. Slow modes were prominent for local trips such as to school (other than in the USA) and for leisure and shopping.

This chapter has provided an overview of the current patterns of daily travel across the industrialized world. While the four examples are different, the basic impacts of mobility-tool availability, age, gender and income are comparable. The availability of mobility tools, especially motorized modes, increased travel overall. As mobility-tool ownership increased with income, so did the intensity of trip making, both in terms of the number of trips as well the kilometres travelled. Trip-making intensity also increased along with the travellers' age, up to the point when the effects of old-age infirmity hampered mobility. Gender effects were not

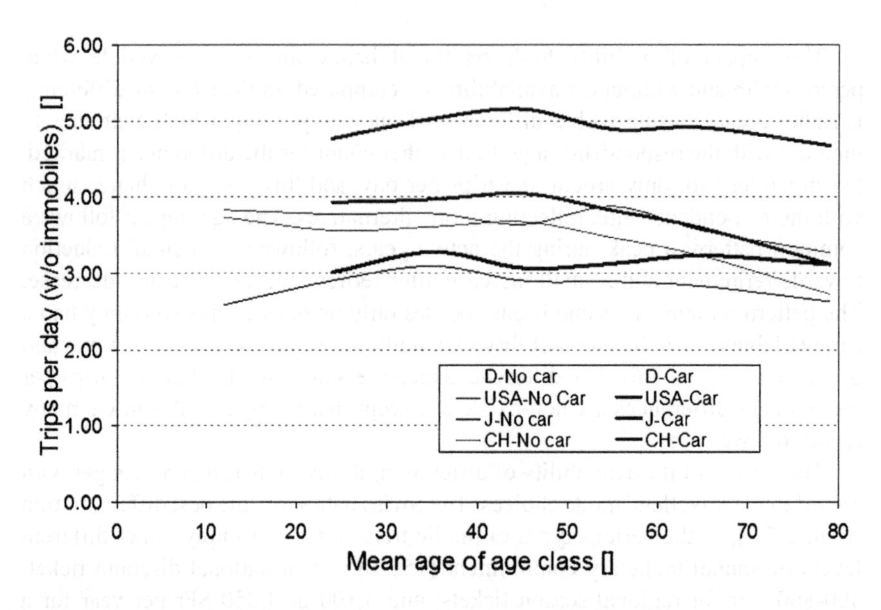

Figure 7.5 Number of trips by age and car availability (without immobiles)
Source: 2001/02 NHTS, 2001/02 MID, 2005/06 MZ, 2000 KTS.

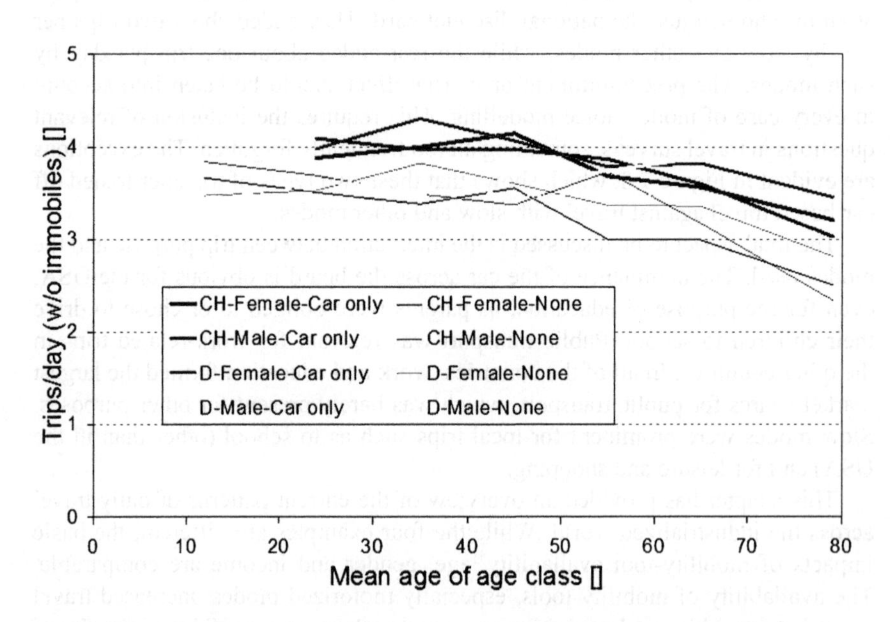

Figure 7.6 Number of trips by age, sex and mobility tool availability (without immobiles)
Source: 2001/02 MID, 2005/06 MZ.

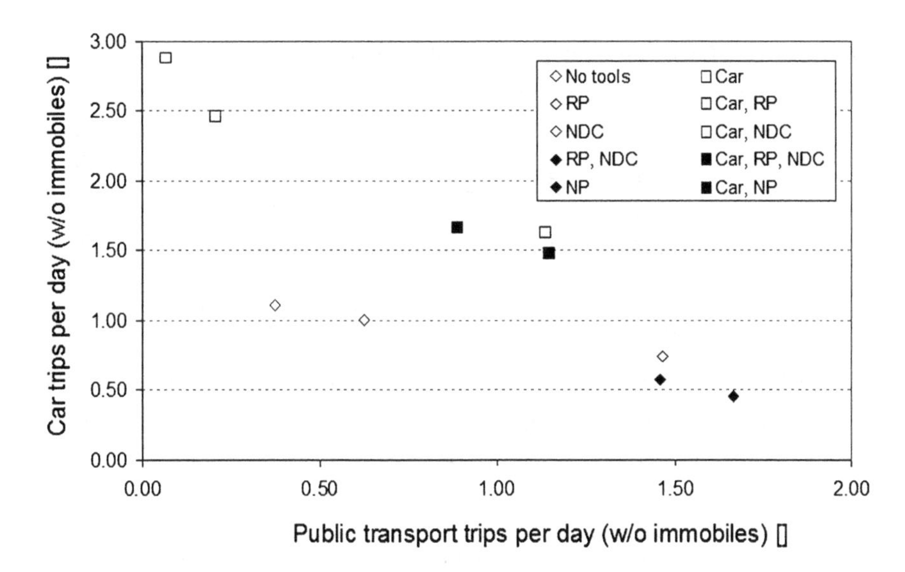

Figure 7.7 Number of trips by mode and mobility tool availability (Switzerland) (without immobiles)

RP: Regional pass; NDC: National discount card; NP: National pass.
Source: 2005/06 MZ.

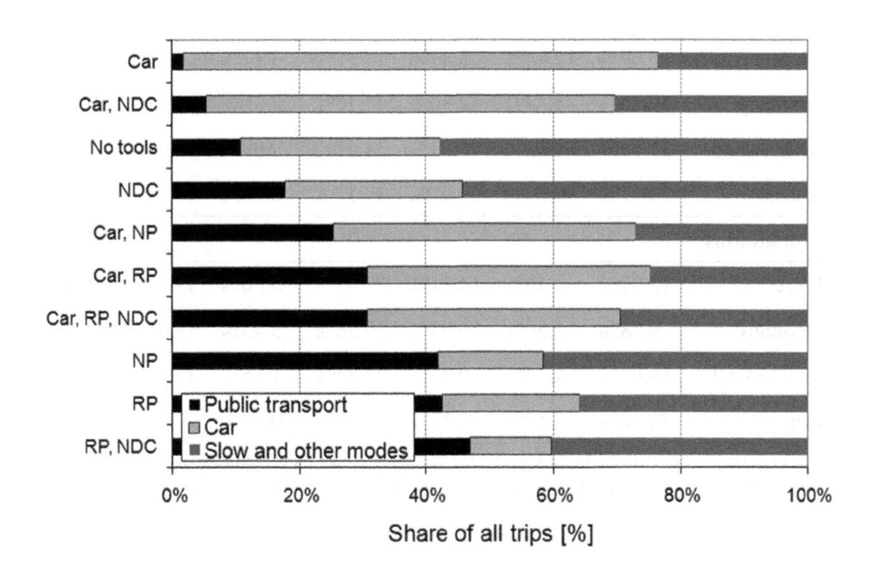

Figure 7.8 Modal shares by mobility tool availability (Switzerland) (without immobiles)

RP: Regional pass; NDC: National discount card; NP: National pass.
Source: 2005/06 MZ.

Table 7.4 Mode shares by purpose and survey

	Work and work-related	Education	Shopping and private business	Leisure	Accompanying[3]	Return home	All purposes[1]
Car							
USA	90.66%	58.48%	93.03%	83.82%	95.72%	86.44%	86.68%
Germany	70.66%	29.26%	59.52%	49.36%	74.17%	60.26%	58.22%
Switzerland	62.08%	11.82%	50.68%	54.14%	79.15%	49.51%	51.80%
Kansai	50.25%	5.36%	38.17%	35.12%		35.62%	38.46%
Public transport							
USA	3.69%	28.47%	1.26%	1.50%	0.88%	3.93%	3.50%
Germany	11.39%	29.84%	5.79%	5.61%	2.08%	8.21%	7.90%
Switzerland	13.39%	23.33%	8.98%	9.56%	1.36%	11.53%	11.50%
Kansai	26.33%	34.24%	11.23%	14.57%	0.00%	22.59%	21.09%
Slow modes							
USA	5.09%	12.84%	5.47%	13.95%	3.17%	9.20%	9.31%
Germany	17.25%	38.84%	34.30%	44.10%	23.38%	30.81%	33.14%
Switzerland	23.59%	61.63%	40.01%	34.87%	19.09%	37.58%	35.43%
Kansai	22.75%	60.36%	49.97%	49.12%	0.00%	41.20%	39.82%
Share of all trips[2]							
USA	12.07%	3.15%	14.31%	29.05%	6.50%	33.68%	100.00%
Germany	9.08%	3.50%	20.03%	20.56%	5.43%	37.63%	100.00%
Switzerland	18.03%	4.43%	9.87%	22.44%	1.35%	42.99%	100.00%
Kansai	26.28%	5.19%	23.17%	5.62%	0.00%	39.74%	100.00%

[1] Including purposes not listed. [2] Including modes not listed. [3] Not reported in Japan.

Source: 2001/02 NHTS, 2001/02 MID, 2005/06 MZ, 2000 KTS

so pronounced when one controls for the effects of age, income and mobility-tool ownership. However, car availability shows strong cohort effects, especially for women, which, like the current unequal patterns of household responsibility, will disappear only gradually.

Chapter 8
Scheduling

The traditional idea of scheduling which we discussed in Chapter 2 holds that it is dynamic during the day, but static between days. This is a massive simplification, or, less neutrally, a massive error, as the dynamics of anyone's day-to-day behaviour show. These dynamics are the topic of this book. The implicit model discussed in Chapter 2 was an optimization of an individual's daily activity participation and travel without considering his or her social context or knowledge about the world. That simplification was due to data constraints and modelling constraints of the past. The agent-based micro-simulation framework has opened up new possibilities, allowing us to consider approaches which integrate previously missing factors into a truly dynamic model. These include the social networks in which people live and the personal world which they continuously update as they experience the success of their schedules. Figure 8.1 depicts such a networked individual. Short-term choices are the result of interactions with members of one's social networks, the distribution of the networks in space and those choices which can not be reversed at short notice (home and work locations, other regularly used locations such as shops, clubs, etc. and mobility tool availability). Members of the social network and their personal worlds are both resources and constraints: Their knowledge, abilities and material resources can be drawn on within the limits of convention and the strength of the personal relationship, which gives an individual extra leverage in his or her daily life. Their locations, abilities and resources are also limiting, as they have to be considered in decision making. Consider the trivial case of a restaurant choice if one of the members of a group has particularly strong dislikes, such as an aversion to a cuisine, or is allergic, for instance, to seafood.

Such a dynamic view of the individual requires a division of the modelled processes into short-term and long(er)-term ones. This simplifies behaviour, like any translation into a modelling structure. Our proposal relaxes a number of the constraints imposed in Chapter 2. Most importantly, it is open and does not prescribe equilibrium. A possible division is suggested in Figures 8.2 and 8.3. The understanding sketched here does not require an equilibrium concept, but assumes a willingness on the part of the individual to improve his or her situation incrementally, but continuously.

The central process for the short term (Figure 8.2) is the formulation of *schedules*, such as the complete description of a day, as discussed in Chapter 2. It is assumed here that the scheduler draws from an *activity calendar* which lists the activities or, more generally, activity types to be accomplished at particular points in time due to project engagements, commitments, physiological needs or desires. This list reflects the *activity repertoire* of the person, and it can be expanded

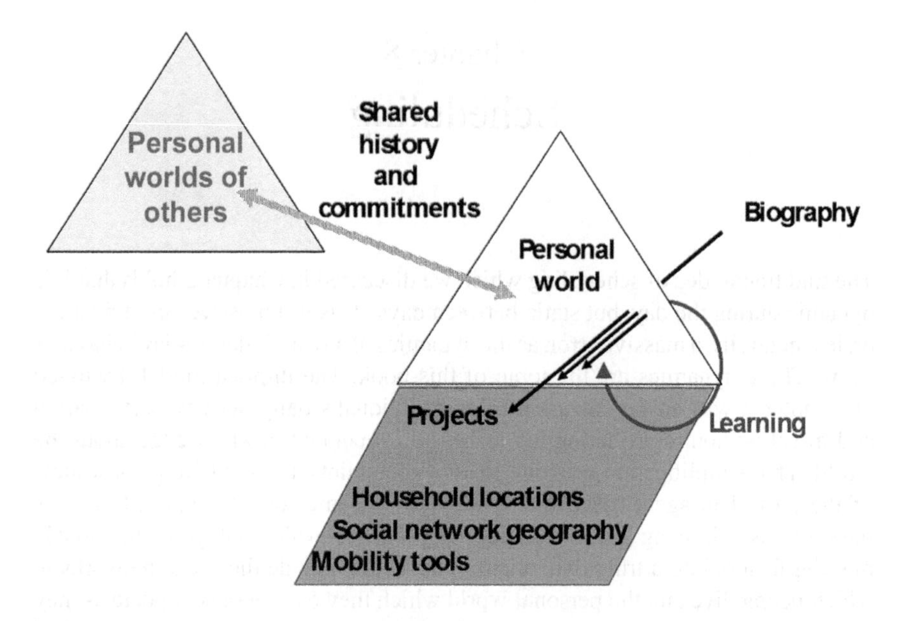

Figure 8.1 The networked traveller in the dynamic social context

through interaction with others and the environment. As people generally aim to improve and possibly even optimize their schedules, they will draw on their *mental maps* to reduce the effort and uncertainties of the day. We know that travellers, as a rule, do not fully book their days, but leave slots of time for the unexpected and the unplanned. In a simulation framework it might be necessary for the sake of computational convenience to impose the assumption that the current day had been fully allocated to activities by some arbitrary point of time in the previous night.

The execution of the schedule requires interacting with other people in the networks and during activity opportunities, such as at shops, cinemas or other persons' homes. In some cases, the resulting congestion or the failure of an activity opportunity to deliver an expected service or good forces travellers to adjust and to reschedule. At the end of the day, travellers will have updated their knowledge about the elements in their activity repertoires and mental maps. They may have developed new solutions for meeting their needs by trying new routes, modes or locations, by drawing on new information, by expanding their *expectation space* or by accepting solutions proposed by others on the basis of their knowledge.

Longer-term processes, which structure the shorter-term ones, revolve around the projects which travellers formulate to translate their life goals and their understanding of themselves into reality (Axhausen 1996; Nuttin 1984). In any one period these projects need to be sequenced to provide a reasonable load and prioritization. Such planning requires negotiation with other people, as

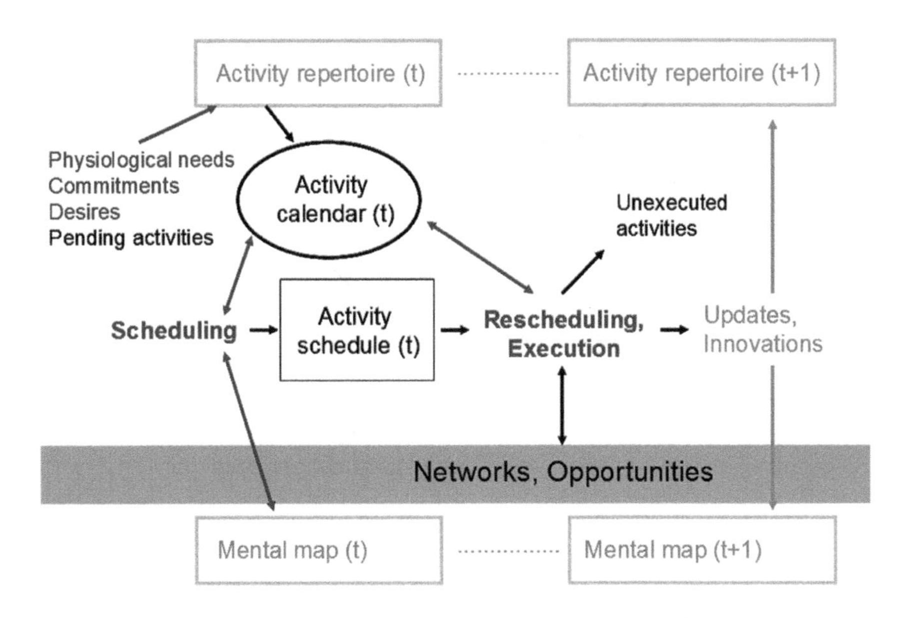

Figure 8.2 Modelling the individual's day-to-day dynamics

many projects must be synchronized or will depend on others' input, presence or permission. Interaction with even more people in the markets and networks during a project's execution may require adjustments and changes, including abandoning the project or project elements. The experience will update and expand the individual's *personal world*, but also shape the set of life goals pursued in the next time interval.

The impact on travel behaviour modelling of such a framing of its task would be profound. It would move the centre of attention away from the idea of equilibrium and towards concepts such as innovation, solution generation, life goals and commitments to people and ideas. It would also put the concept of rhythm on the stage, as we would expect the drivers behind activity participation to have their own rhythms. Physiological needs have natural daily rhythms; the desire for novelty and stimulation or the desire for company might have yet unknown weekly or longer rhythms.

While this conceptualization of the scheduling process is an improvement on the isolated traveller acting on an isolated day, it does not do full justice to the ad hoc nature of the actual experience of a day: the surprises, the new opportunities opening up, the small crises. Doherty and his colleagues made this aspect the focus of a series of dedicated surveys which were built around week-long, computer-based activity diaries of increasing sophistication and ease of use. (See Doherty and Miller 2000; Doherty 2002; Doherty et al. 2004. One of the largest of these studies was reported in Doherty 2005.) Carefully screened data for 373 respondents

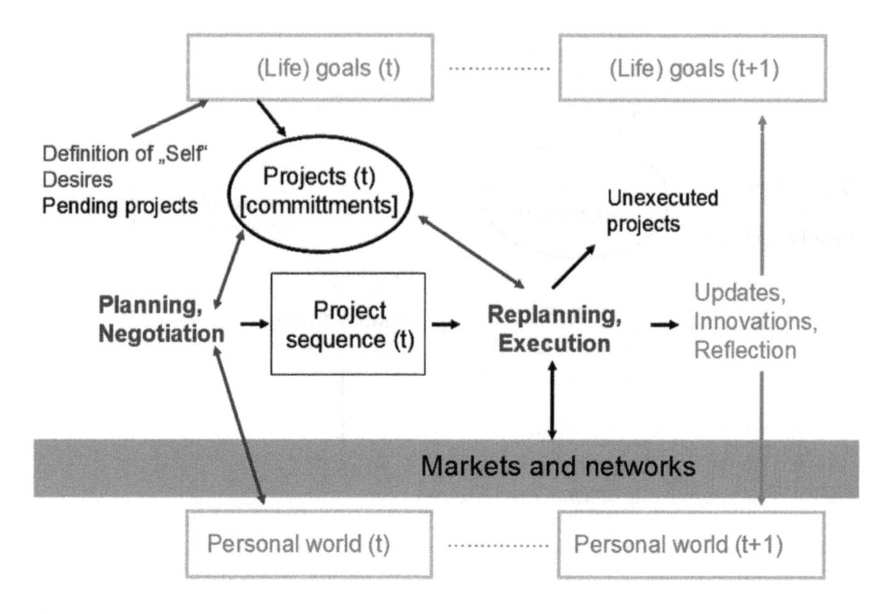

Figure 8.3 Modelling the individual's longer-term dynamics

resident in Toronto, Canada, formed the basis of the following tables. At the start of the protocol of Doherty's survey instrument CHASE (Computerized Household Scheduling Survey), the respondents were asked to fill in a detailed agenda of their planned activities for the next seven days to the best of their knowledge. Any remaining blank time slots were left by design and reflect the lack of a specific activity planned for those time slots. During those seven days, the respondents were asked to note down any changes to their schedule for the current and coming days. The respondents were requested to give reasons and time horizons for new additions and any subsequent changes. CHASE thus obtained a record of the activities and trips that were finally executed as well as their planning history.

About 9 per cent of the 31,000 recorded activities were routine, while 80 per cent involved a conscious choice by the respondents. As Table 8.1 also shows, their planning was relatively short-term. About 40 per cent of all activities and 40 per cent of activities involving travel were planned within the day they occurred. Longer time horizons were not rare, however, and matching expectations concerned substantially longer-than-average activities (ratios of 1.5 to 1.6 of the share of durations and the share of activities). Table 8.1 is based on both out-of-home and in-home activities (20 per cent to 80 per cent) captured by CHASE. These shares indicate that there was still leeway for a shift between in-home and out-of-home activities. Looking closer at the planning horizon in Figure 8.4, one can see that many activities were decided upon spontaneously or at very short notice (within one hour before they started—note the log-scale of the x-axis!). This was even true for activities which the respondents deemed routine. Only about 25 per cent of activities were planned more than a week in advance or, in the case of routine activities, at least thought about. This emphasis on the very short term was even more pronounced for changes to the already planned activities, both routine and otherwise (including cancellations or modifications in time, mode or location).

Table 8.1 Activities by planning horizon (%)

	All activities		Activities involving travel	
	Frequency	**Duration**	**Frequency**	**Duration**
Impulsive	29.1	20.0	21.2	11.0
Same day	16.4	11.6	22.8	13.4
1 - 3 days ahead	14.4	18.3	23.5	26
Several weeks ago	2.5	3.5	6.3	8.2
Months	5.5	6.3	9.1	12.5
Years ago	9.7	13.7	11.0	22.3
Routine	8.8	10.4	n/a	n/a
Cannot recall	10.8	13.5	4.1	4.4
Unknown	2.7	2.6	2.0	2.2
All []/[min]	30,971	3,563,938	6,708	969,131

Source: Adapted from Doherty 2005.

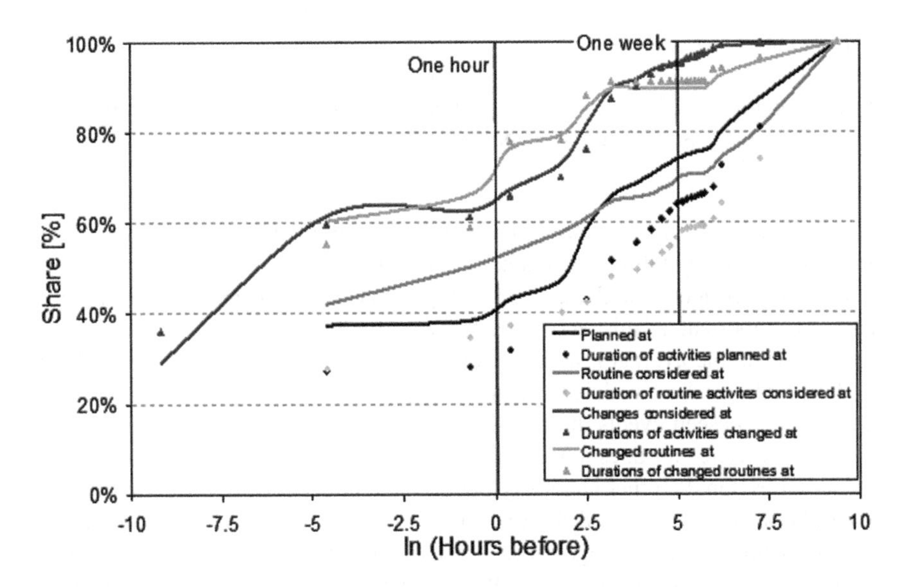

Figure 8.4 Cumulative distribution of the planning horizons by scheduling action

Source: Adapted from Doherty 2005; without the categories "Cannot recall" and "Unknown".

The planning horizon has been investigated in other contexts without CHASE-style instruments. Axhausen et al. (2007) integrated the question into the six-week Thurgau travel diary together with the question of how often the respondent had visited each address before (see above in Chapter 6 for a detailed description of the survey). The instrument offered less precision than the computerized CHASE instrument, and in particular grouped "routine" and "return home" together. Even when removing the 45 per cent share of return-home trips from the total, these Swiss respondents had somewhat longer planning horizons than Doherty's Canadian ones. Same-day and spontaneous trips made up only 20 per cent (35 per cent without return-home trips) instead of the 40 per cent share reported by Doherty. The Swiss respondents also reported more routine activities. Not surprisingly, locations never previously visited were considered the farthest in advance. These visits involved planning and probably needed to be coordinated with friends and relatives.

Table 8.2 Activities by planning horizon and frequency of previous visit (%)

Frequency of previous visit	Planning horizon				Share of all trips
	One or more days before	During the day	Spontaneous	Routine/ Return home	
Never	60.8	16.7	22.5	0.1	4.1
Once to three times	53.2	23.0	23.8	0.4	6.4
More often	14.3	8.6	9.7	67.5	89.5
Share of all trips	18.7	9.8	11.1	60.4	100.0

Source: Adapted from Axhausen et al. (2007) (Table 5).

The empirical evidence shows that our conceptual model sketched above is at best a step in the right direction, but not yet a complete solution. It is an advance by being path-dependent and dynamic. The explicit acknowledgement of the activity agenda is important, as this recognizes that activity formulation and generation do not follow simple averages, as is currently assumed, even in many agent-based models. It allows the schedule to be updated quasi-continuously as the respondent reacts to unforeseen events during its execution. Still, it does not allow for new ideas to intervene, nor does it account for the impacts of social interaction during the activities. On the other hand, any operational model of this conceptual model would be a big step forward for transport modelling. Even the most ambitious current efforts employing agent-based micro-simulations (Arentze et al. 2000; Bhat et al. 2004b; Bowman et al. 1999; Bowman 1995; Bradley and Bowman 2006; Mahmassani 2001; Miller and Roorda 2003; Nagel, Beckman, and Barrett 1998; Pendyala et al. 2005; Schnittger and Zumkeller 2004; TRANSIMS 2009; Vovsha, Petersen, and Donnelly 2002) still have some way to go.

Chapter 9
Modelling the Rhythms of Activity Demand: An Explanatory Approach, Modelling Details and Results

The rhythmic structure of time use and travel is a fundamental element of daily life. Recurrent patterns of activities or trips can be identified in anyone's life if observed over a prolonged period.

Deeper insight into the structures of and motives for behavioural periodicity is a prerequisite for understanding people's full repertoire of choices. Although the focus of this book is on the spatial behaviour of travellers and its variability over time, our analysis of the temporal structure of activity demand and trip making reflect the social dimension of time and timing as well as people's strategies for simplifying and optimizing daily life. It will be shown that the repetition of activities, trips and travel choices in general is – at least partially – a person's individual response to embeddedness in work, leisure and family structures.

As discussed in Chapter 4, numerous activity-based research studies have already focused on characterizing and analysing regularity in travel. This work adds a further methodological approach to the investigation whilst placing a special emphasis on the timing of activities and the duration of interactivity spells. We aim to reveal the (quantitative) impact of personal attributes on the regularity of travel in daily life by considering a set of life cycle and lifestyle variables from the data sets used.

An explanatory approach to regularity in activity demand

Any analysis of the character and determinants of rhythmic patterns in individual travel behaviour requires a conceptual background and an appropriate methodological approach. As many activities and trips occur on a periodic and predictable basis, they may often be explained *historically*, i.e., they are the result of coordination between the travellers' human physiology, dynamic travel environment and social networks (Shapcott and Steadman 1978). This analysis tries to identify those causal factors of the observed temporal stability and variations through a particular type of *proportional* or *parametric hazard model* (Han and Hausman 1990).

Hazard modelling (or in general: *duration analysis*) refers to the terms *event*, *duration* and *probability* or *risk* (i.e., the hazard). The approach involves modelling time to event data, i.e., it considers methods for investigating duration until some event of interest happens. As a result, it predicts the probability that the time of an event will be later than some specified time.

Transferring this concept to the analysis of the rhythmic structure of activity demand, the relevant terms may be defined as follows:

- **Event**: the occurrence of an activity of a certain type or category;
- **Duration**: the spell or interval between activities of the same type[1];
- **Probability**: the probability that an activity is performed/starts.

Hence, rhythmic patterns of activity demand may be described as a dynamic relationship between the time when an activity did not take place (a spell) and the start of the activity (an event). The degree of probability itself is shaped by the observed duration process, the external travel environment and the attributes of the travellers.

The concept of probability for executing an activity or taking a trip is not necessarily new. Campbell (1970) made an intuitive appraisal of daily life by classifying trips into a system of regular structures constituted by different probability levels. These categories were described as:

- activities scheduled regularly over time;
- activity demand gradually built up over time;
- activities evenly spaced in time; and
- time-contagious activities.

Figure 9.1 shows a graphical representation of this classification. Regularly scheduled activities such as club meetings are tied to personal commitments which produce evenly distributed probabilities over time. Activities which are described as regular over time also follow periodic demand. However, they are connected to physiological or other needs which themselves are regular. Travel of this type includes trips to purchase regularly needed items (such as groceries). Time-contagious activities "tempt" the individual to execute the same activity again soon after the last time. In other words, participation in the respective activity increases the probability of further participation (soon) – a phenomenon which might appear for "exciting" leisure activities such as playing golf (an example given in Jakle et al. 1976). Finally, some "activities" such as emergencies occur randomly and have a very low probability. In these cases, the probability development may be described as independent of time and traveller.

The analysis in this book refers to Campbell's early model. Our approach may be called the *increase-in-demand concept* as it suggests that the demand for executing most activities will naturally build up again. Figure 9.2 provides a more

1 Hazard models are more often applied to the analysis of the duration of activities (see Oh 2000 for an example).

technical description of the idea and uses the terminology *probability/risk* and *event* explicitly: The timing of the occurrence of an identified travel pattern or activity (i.e., the event) at a certain point of time *t* can be expressed as a probability function (dotted line). The probability of occurrence mainly depends on the time elapsed since the last occurrence of the behavioural pattern and will most likely increase over time.

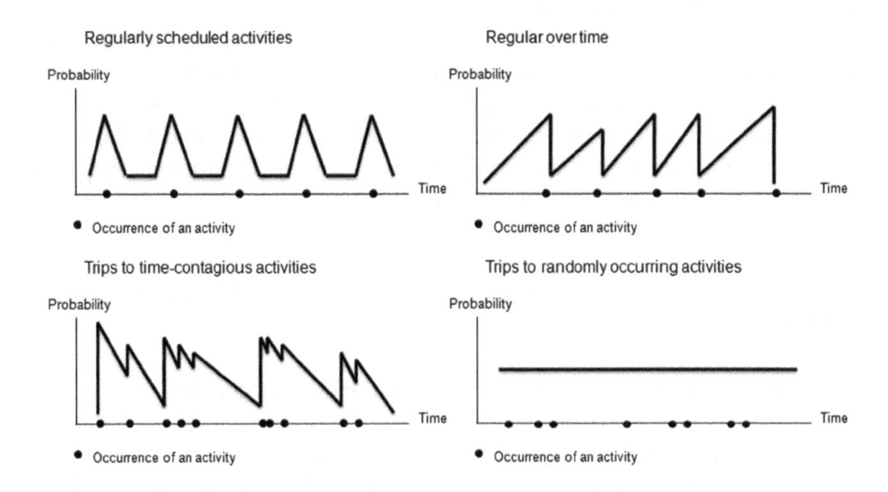

Figure 9.1 Time and the probability of trips to different activity locations
Source: Modified from Jakle et al. 1976, 96; after Campbell 1970.

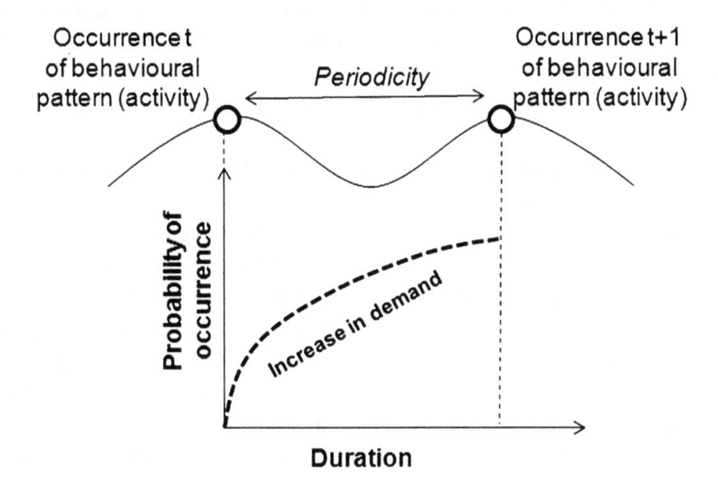

Figure 9.2 Periodicity in travel demand: An explanatory approach
Source: Modified from Schönfelder and Axhausen (2000) 134.

Without a doubt, this model contains several theoretical constraints and simplistic behavioural assumptions. Its main shortcoming is the hypothesis that the assumed increase in probability is a monotonic function of time. This implies that individual behaviour is independent of any internal or external effects such as the spontaneous modification of a person's own activity scheduling or the activity scheduling of other associated individuals (see the discussion and empirical evidence in Chapter 8). Furthermore, it remains disputable whether the model can be assigned to all activity categories in the same way, regardless of whether an activity is discretionary or compulsory and whether it is constrained by fixed societal structures (such as opening hours) or flexible in space and time.

Despite these limitations, the proposed approach offers a first explanation for the temporal form of the recurrence of activity performance over time. It allows the comparison of different socio-economic groups by considering different shapes of the probability function for different covariate values.

Analysing duration data: An introduction to survival analysis and hazard modelling

Hazard modelling deals with the analysis of timing and duration and is used extensively in other fields of technical and social sciences such as biometry, mechanical engineering and market research. (For an overview, see Kalbfleisch and Prentice 1980.) Since the end of the 1980s, hazard models have been estimated in transportation research for a wide range of issues. (See Hensher and Mannering 1994 for an overview of potential applications of this methodology in transportation.) In activity-based research, hazard models have often been used as analytic approaches to investigating activity scheduling or duration (Mannering and Hamed 1990; Hamed and Mannering 1993; Mannering, Murakami, and Kim 1992; Hamed, Kim, and Mannering 1993; Niemeier and Morita 1996; Bhat 1996a, 1996b; Ettema, Borgers, and Timmermans 1995; Reader and McNeill 1999; Oh 2000).

Analysts usually apply linear regression models as a standard approach to analysing the relationship between a response or dependent variable and a set of independent or predictor variables. However, the application of models using least-square estimation (LSE) is problematic for duration data, which are by nature limited to positive values (see Hosmer and Lemeshow 1999). This and other constraints (e.g., the existence of censored[2] durations) led to the development of techniques labelled as *survival analysis, failure time* or *hazard modelling*.

The fundamental purpose of hazard modelling is to specify the occurrence of an event within a certain time span by a probability or risk function called *hazard function* (for basic information, see Kalbfleisch and Prentice 1980; Cox

2 Duration data is sometimes only incompletely observed (e.g., duration is observed until no further information is available). This phenomenon is called "censoring".

1984; Kleinbaum 1986). The *hazard function* describes the immediate risk of an event occurring within a time span t, $t+\Delta t$, provided that the event was not observed by time t. This restriction therefore defines a limited *risk set* which only captures events which have not occurred by $t+\Delta t$, leading to the term *conditional probability*. Hazard models are therefore employed to forecast the probability of a transition from one state to another. In medicine this could be the event of having another stroke after a recovery, or in engineering the collapse of a device after a period of fault-free performance.

Mathematical basics

Hazard modelling and survival analysis are generic terms for a group of models which characterize a probability distribution of the random variable T. In other words, the time at which events occur is determined by some random process causing a certain distribution of T. In our model, the event time T defines the end of an interval between two identical patterns of behaviour and thus the start of the next activity of the same type.

It would now be useful to mathematically describe the hazard function and its corresponding functions, which are the *cumulative distribution function F(t)*, the distribution function and the survival function, as shown in Figure 9.3.

The *cumulative distribution function F(t)* and its derivative *f(t)* give the probability that an event will occur before or at least at some point in time t:

$$F(\mathrm{t}) = \Pr[T < t]$$

$$f(t) = dF(t) \,/\, d(t) = -dS(t) \,/\, dt = \lim_{dt \to 0} \frac{\Pr(t \le T < t + dt)}{dt}.$$

Usually, what is more interesting than the question as to whether T is less or equal to any value t is whether a process survives beyond a certain point, such as beyond the end of the observation period. The *survival function S(t)* expresses the related probability, i.e., survival beyond t. As *S(t)* is a probability, the function is limited to values between 0 and 1 and must be non-negative by definition. In addition, $S(0) = 1$. The function takes various shapes according to the character of the processes observed. Along with the restrictions mentioned, in most cases it decreases.

$$S(t) = \Pr[T \ge t] = 1 - F(t).$$

The most common function representing the distribution of durations is the hazard function *h(t)*, which is essential to the further modelling process. It gives the probability or the direct risk that the occurrence of an event can be expected in a (small) interval between t and dt, provided that the event has not occurred until this point in time. Thus, only individuals (processes) which belong to the actual risk set are considered, i.e., which survived until the beginning of the time interval mentioned. In contrast to the probability density function (note the similarity of the terms), the hazard function represents a conditional density which follows the restrictions of the risk set:

$$h(t) = f(t) / S(t) = \lim_{dt \to \infty} \frac{\Pr(t \leq T < t + dtT \geq t)}{dt}.$$

Due to its definition, the interpretation of the hazard rate (as part of the model output) requires some attention. Hazard rates represent "latent intensity variables" of transition from one state to another, rather than common probabilities in a narrower sense (see Schneider 1991): the higher the value, the quicker the transition from state A to state B takes place on average.

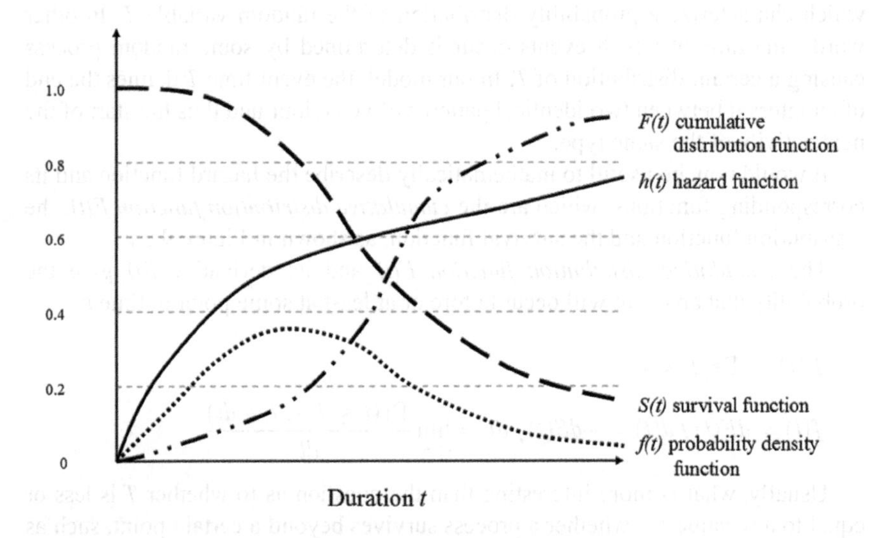

Figure 9.3 Survival analysis: Functions
Source: Modified from Hensher and Mannering (1994) 67.

Testing effects by incorporating covariates: The *parametric* or *proportional hazard model* approach

Hazard modelling not only considers durations as essential determinants for the probability of an event's occurrence, it is also able to incorporate duration-independent determinants such as socio-economic attributes or travellers' commitments. Controlling for external factors is one of the core issues of this analysis because it yields more realistic model results for the periodicity of travel behaviour as a result of the complex structure of personal and environmental factors. In the following, their impact will be investigated more closely using a *parametric* or *proportional hazard model*.

In principal, parametric hazard models treat explanatory variables as a function of a multidimensional vector X that has a multiplicative effect on an underlying *baseline* hazard. In non-parametric models which neglect covariate effects, potentially explanatory factors equal zero and do not account for any change in probability or risk. Thus, the hazard function given in the equation above is a product of two separate functions, with $h_0(t)$ as a function of survival times while $g_0(t)$ gives the potential change caused by subject covariates. In many cases, the term *proportional hazard* is used, which describes changes to the characteristics of the hazard function according to the values of the covariates. This is true to the extent that the ratio of the hazard function remains stable over time (i.e., the assumption of constant hazards $\approx h_1/h_2$). The hazard rate of an individual i is therefore defined as a fixed proportion (*ratio*) of another individual j with different personal attributes:

$$h(t|X) = h_0(t)g_0(X) = h_0(t)\exp(\beta X),$$

with X = the vector of covariates,
β = the vector of parameters, and
$h_0(t)$ = the baseline hazard without covariate effects.

Calculating the logarithm of both sides of the equation, one obtains

$$\log h_i(t) = \alpha(t) + \beta x_i + \ldots + \beta_k x_k.$$

The hazard ratio based on the proportionality definition above is given by

$$\frac{h_i(t)}{h_j(t)} = \{\exp \beta_1 (x_{i1} - x_{j1}) + \ldots + \beta_k (x_{ik} - x_{jk})\}.$$

There is a wide range of approaches to parametric hazard models which differ by their distributional assumptions for the baseline hazard. The selection of a certain distribution or the possible omission of an explicit predefinition for a distribution is usually made according to theoretical considerations for the duration process observed.

Fully parametric models are based on both an explicit distributional assumption for the baseline hazard and the incorporation of selected covariates. The shape of the hazard curve is dependent on the distribution assumptions for the processes which control the lengths of the intervals (i.e., the baseline hazard). That is because the hazard function may take several forms (Figure 9.4) such as monotonously increasing, U-shaped, monotonously decreasing or constant. Monotonously increasing hazard rates (which correspond to a Weibull distribution) are often related to decision processes of which the termination becomes more probable with increasing duration. On the other hand, processes which tend to last longer with increasing duration create a monotonously falling hazard curve (again, a

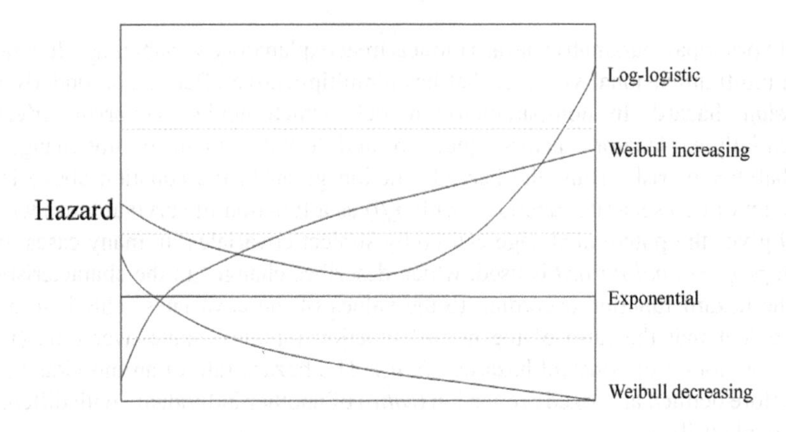

Figure 9.4 Possible shapes of hazard functions based on different distributional assumptions for the baseline

Source: Modified from Ettema et al. (1995) 102.

Weibull distribution). A constant shape of the graph (by an exponential distribution) reflects processes with no identifiable relationship between the duration and its termination. Finally, uneven shapes with no distinct direction are also possible (log-logistic distribution).

Each of the distributions shown is principally eligible to represent duration processes, although wrong assumptions may lead to an incorrect estimation of the baseline hazard (Meyer 1987). Generally, a theoretical justification of a priori postulations for the underlying processes is difficult. In some cases, it is questionable whether the progression of an increase in demand between two identical activity types – as described in Figure 9.2 – rose monotonicly and is therefore of a Weibull type. It is easily possible that the satisfaction of the demand could have been substituted by other activities or that activities were spontaneously rescheduled or cancelled if the opportunity to perform them disappeared.

The Han and Hausman semiparametric hazard model

The restrictions imposed by a stringent predefinition of the baseline distribution are bypassed by *semiparametric hazard models* developed since the 1970s (Prentice 1976; Cox 1972; Prentice and Goeckler 1978; Meyer 1987). This model type nicely allows one to estimate the interactions of covariates in the model without requiring distributional assumptions for the baseline. Several related applications in transport research have followed this methodology (see Hensher and Mannering 1994; Sueyoshi 1993).

The model developed by Han and Hausman (1990), a flexible approach to the semiparametric model family, is tested in this book. Han and Hausman proposed an *ordered-response model*. Conceptually, it belongs to the group of discrete-choice models as durations are treated as categorical. The continually measured interval durations t_i (e.g., "26 hours and 13 minutes") are transformed into an arbitrarily defined number of categories k with a suitably chosen cell or class size. Each of the discrete periods should have one or more duration completions[3].

Compared to other semiparametric approaches such as the widely applied Cox approach, which uses *partial likelihood* (see Kleinbaum 1996 for details of the likelihood estimation), the ordered-response model has the advantage that it can efficiently handle large number of ties, and it circumvents problems with unobserved heterogeneity. In addition, the cell sizes do not have any effect on the covariate parameters, which allows the classification to be adjusted according to the sample size.

Generally, the model is based on the assumption

$$y = \beta X_i + \varepsilon_i$$

$$\begin{aligned} y_i &= 0 \text{ if } y =< i_0 \\ &1 \text{ if } i_0 < y =< i_1 \\ &2 \text{ if } i_1 < y =< i_2 \\ &J \text{ if } y > i_{j-1}, \end{aligned}$$

where

β_i is the parameter estimate,
ε_i is the error estimate, and
X_i is a multiplicative vector with impact on the hazard rate (e.g., attributes of the traveller or the activity performed).

It should be mentioned that a time-constant character of the variable X is assumed, which means that it does not change during the period of observation. The error estimate ε describes unobserved effects on the interval durations. The semiparametric model uses a logistic or normal distribution of ε.

Han and Hausman started their derivation of the model with the *proportional hazard* specification by Prentice (1976):

$$h(t) = \lim_{dt \to \infty} \frac{\Pr(t \leq T < dt | T \geq t)}{dt} = h_0(t) \exp(\beta_i X).$$

3 It is clear that a categorization of the time scale contradicts the continuous processes which control the interval lengths between identical activities. However, this discretization may be seen as rounding the reported durations. In the particular case of activity demand, in which most of the activities are performed only once per reporting day, the rounding on the basis of full days (t = 1, 2, 3, …) may be accepted without any significant loss of information.

A logarithmic transformation leads to the integrated hazard function

$$\log \int_0^{Ti} h_0(t)dt = X_i\beta + \varepsilon_i,$$

with an *extreme value* distribution for ε_i

$$F(\varepsilon_i) = \exp(-\exp(\varepsilon_i)).$$

In the following, it is defined that

$$\log \int_0^{T} h_0(t)dt = \delta_T$$

which gives a probability of failure P in the period t for individual i:

$$P[B_{t-1} < T_i < B_i] = \log \int_{\delta_{T-1}}^{\delta_T} {}^{-X_i\beta}_{-X_i\beta} f(\varepsilon)d\varepsilon.$$

The logs of the integrated baseline hazards, δ_t, are treated as constants in the different periods and are estimated with the (unknown) parameters β_i.

The log-likelihood function is found by defining an indicator variable y_{it} with the values

$$y_{it} = \{^{1if \in -1;]}_{0} \text{ and}$$

$$\log L = \sum_i \sum_T y_{iT} \log \int_{\delta_{T-1}}^{\delta_T} {}^{-X_i\beta}_{-X_i\beta} f(\varepsilon)d\varepsilon.$$

The distributional assumptions for the error estimate ε determine the form of the model. A standard normal distribution results in an ordered probit form, whereas an extreme value distribution for ε yields an ordered logit form. Only the latter case actually strictly meets the proportional hazard specification of shown above. However, as there is great similarity between the distributions (normal and extreme-value distributions only differ at the edges of the curve), the ordered probit model remains a useful approximation.

Finally, the hazard rate *h(t)* may be estimated by

$$h(t) = \Pr ob[t_j < t < t_j + 1] / \Pr ob(t \geq t_j).$$

The hazard rate is calculated by using the forecast cell probabilities for the model at the means of the different variables. These probabilities are divided by the cell width if values to do so are given (Greene 1998).

Two-person household.
Top: male, 37, homemaker; bottom: female: 35, works full time:

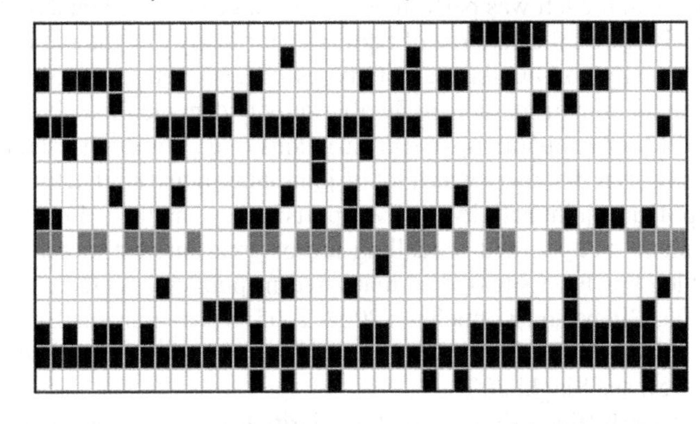

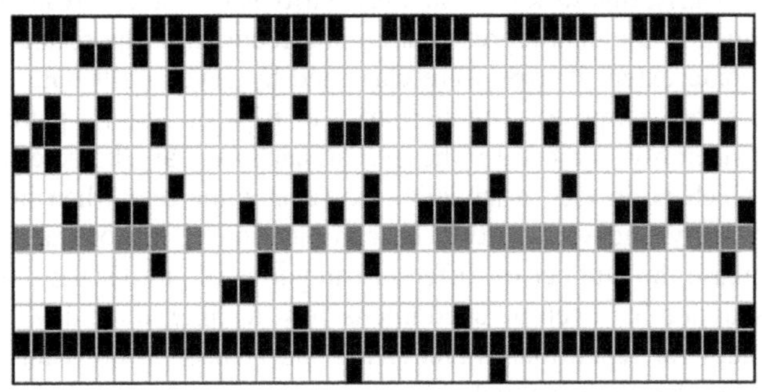

Pupil, 17:

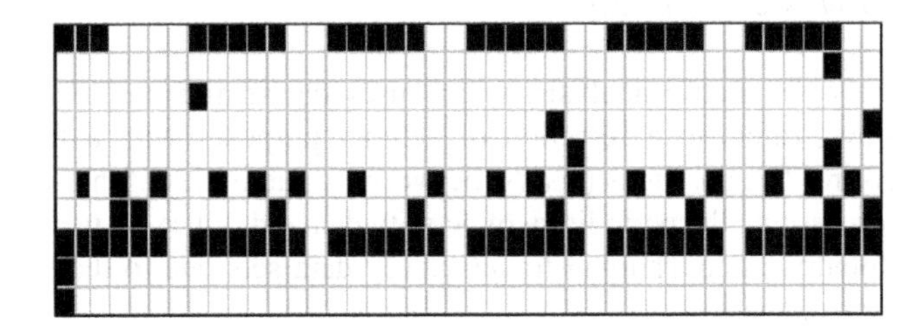

Figure 9.5 Example of activity demand over time
Source: Adapted from Löchl et al. 2005.

Applying the hazard model

Every single data set used for the analysis in this book confirms the existence of regular activity patterns in individual travel and activity behaviour. Figure 9.5 is an exemplary illustration of the strong periodicity in daily time use. It shows the activity patterns of three Thurgau survey respondents over the 42 days of reporting. Each of the dark boxes indicates that the respective activity type given on the left was performed at least once on the given day. The representation nicely shows the patterns of regularity for many obligatory activities, but also for apparently non-binding activity types such as "active sports". However, there is a large amount of sporadic or flexible activity demand for activities with less priority and fewer temporal (spatial) restrictions (e.g., "meeting friends"). It can also be easily seen that there was a lot of joint inner-household activity performance (see top figure: joint activity "active sports", grey shading). Inner-household activity-demand analysis and modelling are of great interest in activity-based research, which has been stressed in many recent publications (see, for example, Simma 2000; Gliebe and Koppelman 2002, 2005; Srinavasan and Bhat 2005, 2006; Kang and Scott 2008). For an analysis of joint inner-household trips in the Mobidrive survey, see Singhi 2001.

Clearly, this striking visual regularity is by nature a result of the level of detail applied to the data representation and reduction. The result would be relativized to some extent if trips were classified by several attributes instead of only one (here: trip purpose). The similarity of trips or activity patterns could then vary considerably subject to the researcher's actual characterization of similarity – which is, in fact, a triviality, however important when interpreting results on regularity and variability. The combination of various attributes might greatly increase the number of different categories of similar trips. This methodological discussion has been pursued intensively, leading to the development of similarity indices for repetitious travel (Huff and Hanson 1986; Hanson and Huff 1988a, 1988b; Pas 1983; Schlich 2004).

Model estimations results

The econometric analysis, which uses the semiparametric approach presented above, refers to a selection of activity purposes with a focus on service and leisure. The durations (*spells*) between two activities of the same type are defined to constitute the periodicity of activity demand. Intervals were generated from the Mobidrive and Thurgau travel-survey data sets due to their comprehensiveness and exactness.

Because survey respondents were explicitly asked to provide the exact activity purpose for all leisure as well as all non-precoded activities, a detailed categorization of the activity purposes was possible, exceeding the usual number of ten or even less. A simple differentiation between obligatory trips (school and work, etc.) and voluntary trips (shopping, maintenance and leisure, etc.), which is often the case in mobility research, might be an overly simplistic aggregation of the human activity system. Even the category *leisure* covers a wide spectrum of activity types with different regularities, priorities and interconnections with other activities, which result in different activity programmes. The categorization was made comparable to the coding applied in the earlier research project, City:mobil (Götz et al. 1997), which is given in Appendix A1.

The following activity purposes are covered in our analysis:

- Daily shopping;
- Long-term shopping;
- Private business;
- Club meetings;
- Active sports;
- Meeting family or friends;
- Going for a stroll;
- Going out (bar, restaurant, cinema).

Our analysis focuses on voluntary trip purposes and neglects obligatory activities (i.e., work and education), which by nature exhibit strong regularity. However, this should not imply that important and interesting investigation into the variability and stability of compulsory activities can not be undertaken. For example, Mahmassani, Bhat and others (Jou and Mahmassani 1996, 1997; Bhat 1996b, 1997, 1999, 2001) have done substantial work on the dynamics of departure-time choice and the trip chaining of commuting trips.

Censored spells, i.e., intervals which could only be partially observed and measured[4], were excluded.

Selected important characteristics of the activity performance are displayed in Table 9.1 and Table 9.2. As could be expected, there is great variance in the determinants given the wide range of purposes. This is especially true for activity durations. In addition, the tables present the differences in travel and activity characteristics between the Thurgau and the Mobidrive surveys. The differences between the suburban or rural lifestyle in the canton of Thurgau and the urban demand structures of Karlsruhe and Halle are evident. The urban areas featured:

- a lower share of car usage over most activity purposes,
- smaller travel distances due to higher land-use densities, and
- generally lower speeds, partly due to the different mode-choice structure, but mainly due to the urban traffic situation and congestion.

A first insight into the long-term structure of activity demand is provided by the shares of the interval lengths between two activities of the same type. Table 9.2 shows that many activity types were performed twice or even more often per day (interval length = 0). In addition, there is a strong indication that for some particular activities such as shopping, there was a one- or two-day rhythm, albeit with a flexible background pattern. A clear weekly rhythm can be identified for

4 Limited observation periods usually affect the completeness of the measurements, since the relevant processes may have started before the beginning of the investigation or continued beyond its end.

Table 9.1 Characteristics of selected activity types (unweighted; Mobidrive: main study, Thurgau: total sample)

Activity type		N	Share car * [%]	Mean distance (Std.) [km]		Mean trip duration (Std.) [min.]		Mean activity duration (Std.) [min]	
Daily shopping	MD	4,085	41	3	(15)	11	(10)	36	(97)
	TH	2,033	51	4	(9)	9	(13)	45	(148)
Long-term shopping	MD	1,638	54	6	(10)	17	(15)	62	(110)
	TH	993	70	10	(16)	16	(21)	53	(113)
Private business	MD	1,335	73	19	(48)	26	(37)	134	(210)
	TH	2,024	66	8	(16)	12	(22)	58	(161)
Club meeting	MD	649	37	7	(22)	15	(19)	140	(169)
	TH	845	62	7	(10)	11	(12)	137	(117)
Active sports	MD	1,146	58	6	(11)	18	(25)	150	(164)
	TH	1,144	50	7	(10)	21	(37)	178	(216)
Meeting family / friends	MD	2,361	53	16	(49)	24	(37)	265	(475)
	TH	1,733	66	16	(33)	17	(66)	202	(251)
Going for a stroll	MD	1,592	16	6	(11)	38	(35)	398	(532)
	TH	1,189	16	4	(6)	48	(36)	492	(568)
Going out (bar, etc.)	MD	1,183	46	6	(14)	18	(18)	136	(120)
	TH	1,584	44	7	(22)	6	(91)	114	(141)
For comparison:									
Work	MD	4,134	49	9	(15)	20	(15)	407	(208)
	TH	3,702	62	15	(21)	20	(28)	312	(215)
School / education	MD	2,324	13	5	(8)	18	(14)	296	(132)
	TH	4,476	34	7	(15)	15	(23)	161	(198)

* Car driver and passenger; MD = Mobidrive, TH = Thurgau.

leisure activities such as club meetings or active sports. Finally, for a range of other purposes no obvious temporal pattern of demand is visible.

Before the effects of travellers' socio-economic attributes are examined in detail, the empirical survival and hazard rates of the intervals for the different activity purposes are presented in Figure 9.6. It shows selected rates for Mobidrive (Karlsruhe subsample) based on the life-tables method (see, e.g., Berkson and Gage 1950). The method efficiently calculates survival and hazard rates, especially for large-event time-data sets. Life tables, in contrast to the commonly used Kaplan-Meier estimator (Kaplan and Meier 1958), group durations into user-defined intervals. Here, interval lengths of one day were chosen.

The depiction of the temporal structure of activity demand corresponds to Table 9.2. Interestingly, most of the hazard curves reach a local maximum after one and/or two weeks. This is especially apparent for the often-structured leisure activities "club meetings" and "active sports". However, this only partially shows

Table 9.2 Share of interval lengths between two activities of the same type in days (unweighted; Mobidrive: MD, Thurgau: TH) (%)

Activity type		N	0	1	2	3	4	5	6	7	8	9	10	11	12	13	14
Daily shopping	MD	4,085	**18**	**30**	16	10	6	3	3	**2**	1	1	1	1	0	0	**0**
	TH	2,033	**14**	**26**	16	10	6	4	3	**5**	1	1	0	0	0	0	**1**
Long-term shop.	MD	1,635	**15**	**14**	11	7	5	4	4	**5**	2	2	2	1	2	1	**1**
	TH	993	**18**	**10**	8	6	6	5	4	**5**	2	2	2	1	1	1	**1**
Private business	MD	3,524	**24**	**25**	11	8	5	4	3	**3**	1	1	1	1	0	1	**1**
	TH	2,024	**23**	**20**	11	7	4	3	3	**3**	1	1	1	0	0	1	**1**
Club meeting	MD	643	**6**	**17**	11	8	7	4	2	**15**	1	0	0	1	0	0	**3**
	TH	845	**7**	**15**	13	9	6	6	5	**11**	2	1	1	0	0	0	**2**
Active sports	MD	1,146	**6**	**26**	16	7	7	4	2	**9**	2	1	1	0	1	1	**2**
	TH	1,144	**9**	**22**	14	10	8	3	3	**9**	1	1	1	1	0	0	**2**
Meeting family / friends	MD	2,358	**15**	**26**	12	8	6	5	3	**2**	1	1	1	1	1	1	1
	TH	1,733	**15**	**20**	8	7	4	4	4	**3**	2	1	1	1	1	1	**2**
Going for a stroll	MD	1,592	**29**	**37**	5	3	2	1	2	**2**	1	0	0	0	1	1	**1**
	TH	1,189	**20**	**38**	8	4	4	2	2	**3**	1	1	1	0	1	0	**1**
Going out	MD	1,183	**9**	**21**	10	8	5	4	4	**5**	3	2	1	1	1	1	**1**
	TH	1,584	**16**	**30**	10	8	4	3	4	**4**	2	1	1	1	1	0	**0**

Note: Longer intervals (>14) and missing values excluded, i.e., the sum is not necessarily 100%; MD = Mobidrive, TH = Thurgau.

that there is a predominant seven-day periodicity for the whole sample, as the hazard rate does not consider the total number of observations for a point of time, but only the risk set. In principle, the survival rates indicate the real significance of the trend at the respective points of time. For example, the relatively high probabilities for the activities "daily" and "long-term shopping" at seven days are true only for a few respondents or observations (i.e., the survival rate is around or below 0.2).

Covariate effects

A set of personal and household-related characteristics which represent common determinants of life cycles and lifestyles were chosen as explanatory variables for the model estimation (Table 9.3). Per capita income and car availability were plausibly imputed using the modal value of the socio-economic group based on household size, number of adults as well as number of vehicles in the household.

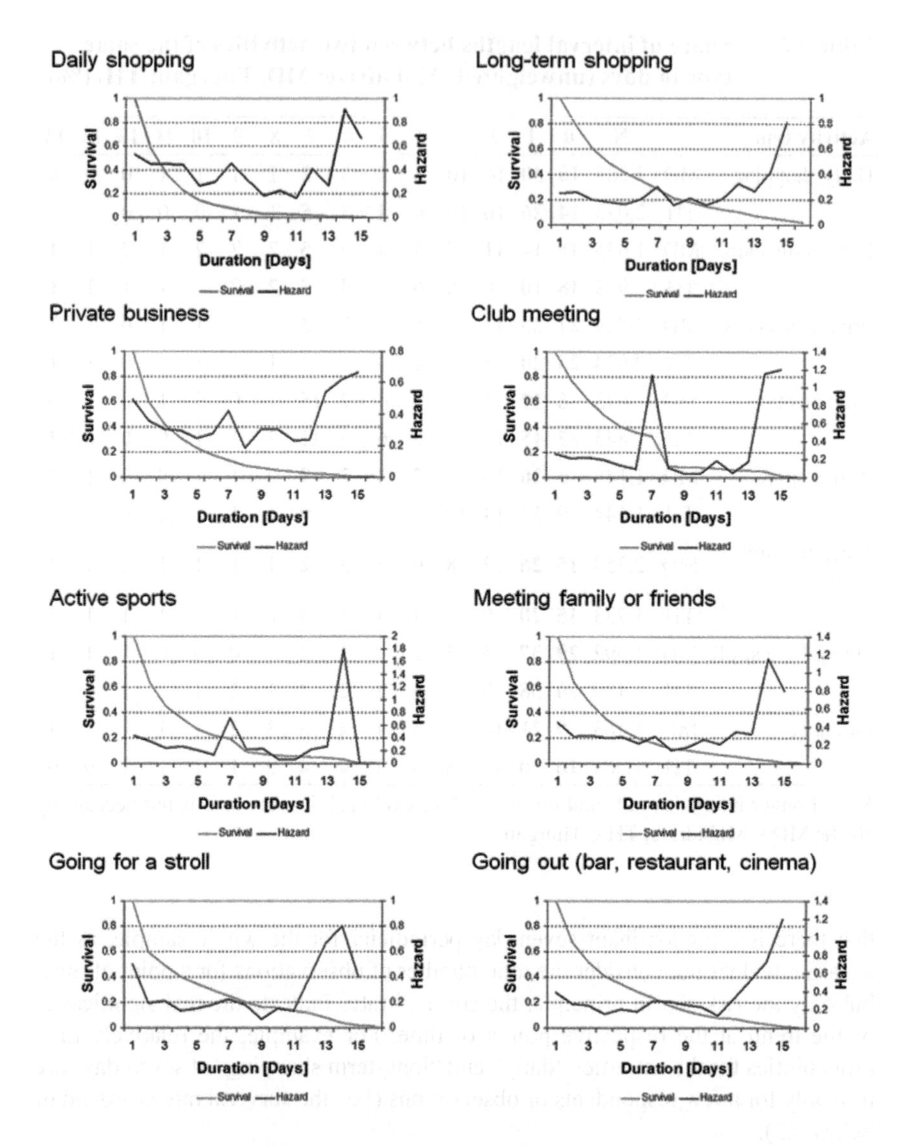

Figure 9.6 Empirical survival and hazard rates based on life tables (Mobidrive, Karlsruhe subsample)

The model estimation for the Mobidrive data distinguishes between the cities of Karlsruhe and Halle by incorporating a city dummy. This takes account of differences in travel behaviour between the two cities (see, e.g., Schlich et al. 2000). A similar differentiation was made for the Thurgau data with a dummy for

Table 9.3 Selected covariates: Means (Std.)

Covariate	Mobidrive	Thurgau
Personal information		
Male	0.5 (0.5)	0.5 (0.5)
Age	39 (18)	39 (18)
Age^2	1,880 (1,476)	1,916 (,1417)
Married or cohabiting	0.5 (0.5)	0.6 (0.5)
Parent	0.4 (0.5)	0.2 (0.4)
Club member	0.3 (0.4)	0.6 (0.5)
Works full time, i.e., working hours > 30 h / week	0.4 (0.5)	0.6 (0.5)
Dog owner (>10% of all trips with dog)	0.1 (0.3)	0.1 (0.3)
Household-related information		
Number of household members	2.9 (1.2)	3.1 (1.6)
Net income: > 1.000 Euro / 3.000 CHF per HH capita / per month	0.3 (0.4)	0.6 (0.5)
Car usage		
Number of cars in the household	1.2 (0.6)	2.0 (1.5)
Main car user: Holds a driving license and has permanent access to a car	0.4 (0.5)	0.8 (0.4)
Local differentiation		
Lives in Karlsruhe (Mobidrive) / Frauenfeld (Thurgau)	0.5 (0.5)	0.5 (0.5)

Note: Means based on total sample; for particular covariate means for single models by activity purpose, see estimation results in Appendix A2.

the (small) town of Frauenfeld (which is also the canton's capital) in contrast to the surrounding villages.

The (overall) covariate means show the socio-economic parallels and differences between the two samples considered for the following analysis. Differences are evident with regard to family structure (married/parents), club membership, occupational status (working full time), income structure and car availability/car usage. This again is partly due to differences in urban and more rural lifestyles, but it is also simply due to the socio-economic composition of the respective samples. A reweighting of the Thurgau sample to match the Mobidrive characteristics was not part of the Thurgau study.

The following tables present the Han and Hausman model estimation results using the statistical software package LIMDEP 7.0/NLOGIT 3.0 (Greene 1998). While Table 9.4 (Mobidrive subsample) and Table 9.5 (Thurgau) provide exemplary parameter estimates for the models "daily shopping" and "going for a stroll", Table 9.6 and Table 9.7 give summaries of the direction of effects for all activity categories considered (the detailed model estimates for the other activity purposes may be found in Appendix A2).

Table 9.4 Exemplary ordered logit model results (Mobidrive)

Model	Daily shopping			Going for a stroll		
Covariate	Coefficient	SE	P	Coefficient	SE	P
Personal information						
Male	-0.02	0.08	0.83	-0.21	0.19	0.26
Age	0.00	0.01	0.92	**0.05**	0.02	0.03
Age^2	0.00	0.00	0.81	0.00	0.00	0.17
Married / cohabiting	**-0.19**	0.09	0.03	-0.19	0.25	0.43
Parent	**-0.54**	0.09	0.00	**-1.10**	0.27	0.00
Club member	**0.19**	0.09	0.03	0.29	0.27	0.29
Dog owner	**-0.27**	0.10	0.01	**-2.25**	0.17	0.00
Works full time	**0.71**	0.09	0.00	**0.47**	0.21	0.03
Household						
N household members	**0.18**	0.04	0.00	0.10	0.09	0.27
High income	**-0.27**	0.09	0.00	**-1.16**	0.25	0.00
Car availability						
Number of vehicles	0.08	0.07	0.22	-0.03	0.19	0.87
Main car user	0.03	0.08	0.75	0.10	0.22	0.66
Type of area						
Karlsruhe	-0.02	0.07	0.78	**0.89**	0.20	0.00
Iterations completed		31			36	
N		3,019			883	
Log likelihood constant		-5,409			-1,260	
Log likelihood β		-5,352			-1,104	
-2 Log likelihood		115			311	
DF		12			12	
Prob. chi-squared		0.00			0.00	

Note: Dependent variable: Interval length in days; **Bold**: Covariate significant at 0.05 level.

The resulting effects of the covariates in the daily (grocery) shopping model for Mobidrive and Thurgau are plausible and intuitive. The parameter estimates for the variables gender (male), car availability, household size and full-time work are statistically significant and positive, which means that daily shopping was performed little or less frequently. The opposite is true for the covariates "parent" and "high income". Together this makes clear that the group of male, highly mobile full-time workers shop significantly less regularly than, for example, mothers whose domestic work commitments are traditionally greater.

The "going for a stroll" model illustrates the effect of dog ownership as a strong fixed commitment, with the covariate having high statistical significance and a large coefficient. Caring for the pet naturally forces respondents to go out

Table 9.5 Exemplary ordered logit model results (Thurgau)

Model	Daily shopping			Going for a stroll		
Covariate	**Coefficient**	**SE**	**P**	**Coefficient**	**SE**	**P**
Personal information						
Male	**0.43**	0.11	0.00	0.23	0.20	0.25
Age	-0.02	0.01	0.15	**0.07**	0.03	0.01
Age^2	0.00	0.00	0.25	**0.00**	0.00	0.00
Married / cohabiting	0.05	0.13	0.66	**-0.81**	0.26	0.00
Parent	**-0.81**	0.16	0.00	0.07	0.24	0.76
Club member	**-0.30**	0.10	0.00	**-0.44**	0.17	0.01
Dog owner	-0.01	0.14	0.92	**-2.46**	0.17	0.00
Works full time	**0.75**	0.12	0.00	0.13	0.20	0.52
Household						
N household members	**0.31**	0.06	0.00	**0.32**	0.08	0.00
High income	**-0.32**	0.11	0.00	-0.07	0.18	0.69
Car availability						
Number of vehicles	-0.01	0.04	0.88	-0.02	0.08	0.81
Main car user	**0.41**	0.16	0.01	-0.11	0.42	0.78
Type of area						
Frauenfeld (town)	-0.93	0.11	0.39	**0.42**	0.17	0.01
Iterations completed		31			36	
N		1,526			781	
Log likelihood constant		-2,987			-1,261	
Log likelihood β		-2,937			-1,119	
-2 Log likelihood		102			284	
DF		12			12	
Prob. chi-squared		0.00			0.00	

Note: Dependent variable: Interval length in days; **Bold**: Covariate significant at 0.05 level.

for walks with great frequency and regularity. This underscores the necessity to include dominating precommitments of travellers in travel surveys to enable better explanations of routines and regularities. This was done in both the Mobidrive and the Thurgau studies.

Synopsis

To start with a methodological subsumption of the model results, the following may be noted: The models are almost entirely significant, but have only moderate explanatory power given the selected covariates (McFadden's rho, i.e., pseudo-R2). This in fact raises the question of the strength of the random variation in the regularity of the demand structure (see the discussion at the end of this book). However, covariate effects are often similar among studies using the same data and applying related methodologies (Bhat, Sivakumar, and Axhausen 2003; Bhat et al. 2004a; Bhat, Srinivasan, and Axhausen 2005).

The effects of the chosen covariates are not uniform enough to compare them with other surveys and studies. The particular characteristics of the activity types clearly led to great differences in the activity-demand structure. In addition, it is likely that the chosen covariates only cover part of all possible determinants for the temporal structures of demand.

However, some general trends could be identified, which are as follows:

- Full-time workers and persons with car availability show a less regular and less frequent pattern of activity demand for shopping (both surveys) and private business activities (Thurgau).
- A converse trend for daily shopping is visible for respondents from high-income households (both surveys).
- Intervals between some leisure activities were longer for members of larger households.
- As could be expected, parents (with children in the household) needed to go shopping on a (more) regular basis.
- Dog ownership significantly increased the frequency and regularity of strolls.
- The city/survey area dummy had only a few significant effects: for Mobidrive, the Karlsruhe sample tended to be less engaged in going for strolls; for Thurgau, the respondents who lived in the canton's main town of Frauenfeld went out less frequently (to bars, restaurants, etc.).

To summarize the results, these issues need to be stressed:

- The activities may be categorized into groups with daily or two-day rhythms and groups with no fixed temporal activity-demand structures. (This has also been demonstrated in studies with a stronger focus on classifying demand structures: Bhat, Sivakumar, and Axhausen 2003; Bhat et al. 2004a.)
- The socio-economic impact on temporal characteristics is visible, but does not seem to be a domination determinant within the activity-demand structure.
- The activity-demand structure is heterogeneous, i.e., there is no entirely clear picture of the chosen covariate effects. However, the results indicate that factors which are generally strong determinants of travel demand (occupational status and car availability) play an important role in predicting periodicity, too.

Table 9.6 Overview of covariate effects of the Han and Hausman model (Mobidrive)

Activity type / Covariate	Daily shopping	Long-term shopping	Private business	Meet family/ friends	Club meeting	Active sports	Excursion into nature	Going for a stroll	Going out (bar, restaurant, etc.)
Personal information									
Male					+		+		
Age							-	+	+
Age^2				+			+		-
Married / cohabiting	-								-
Parent	-	-	-	+	+			-	
Club member	+					-			
Dog owner	-		+					-	
Works full time	+	+			-		-	+	
Household									
N household members		+	+			+	+		+
High income	-		-			+	+	-	
Car availability									
Number of vehicles		+				+			
Main car user				-	-	-			-
Type of area									
Karlsruhe								+	
McFadden's rho[1]	0.01	0.00	0.01	0.02	0.02	0.03	0.08	0.12	0.02

+ increases interval length and decreases regularity.
– decreases interval length and increases regularity.
[1] McFadden's rho is used to evaluate the model fit. The value is a transformation of the likelihood ratio statistic intended to mimic R^2 values in logistic regression. Rho-squared values are normally lower than R^2 values (see, e.g., Hensher and Johnson 1981).
Note: Effects shown for all covariates statistically significant at the 0.05 significance level.

Table 9.7 Overview of covariate effects of the Han and Hausman model (Thurgau)

Activity type Covariate	Daily shopping	Long-term shopping	Private business	Meet family/ friends	Club meeting*	Active sports	Excursion into nature	Stroll	Going out (bar, restaurant, etc.)
Personal information									
Male	+								-
Age		+						+	
Age^2								-	
Married / cohabiting		-			-	+	-	-	
Parent	-	-				-			
Club member	-		-		-	+		-	
Dog owner					+	+		-	+
Works full time	+								
Household									
N household members	+	+		+	+			+	+
High income	-		-						+
Car availability									
Number of vehicles				-					
Main car user	+		+	-					-
Type of area									
Frauenfeld (town)				+				+	+
McFadden's rho	0.02	0.01	0.01	0.02	0.01	0.02	0.02	0.11	0.03

+ increases interval length and decreases regularity.
– decreases interval length and increases regularity.
* Model in total not statistically significant.
Note: Effects shown for all covariates statistically significant at the 0.05 significance level.

PART III
Human Spatial Behaviour and the Analysis of Activity Spaces

Chapter 10
Destination Choice and Activity Spaces: A Review of Concepts and a Framework for Analysis

Travel behaviour research is about human movement patterns. Where people head and how people decide on where to go has been the subject of countless conceptual and empirical studies. At least two different categories of destination choice may be discussed within the context of travel: long-term location choices (residential or workplace locations, etc.) and short-term choices in day-to-day travel for services, business or leisure. We will elaborate on the latter aspect in the chapter.

Transport modelling has operationalized short-term destination choice by applying both aggregate and demographically disaggregate approaches. Aggregate trip-distribution models widely rely on the well-known *gravity model* and refinements of this approach, which goes back to *Newton's law of gravitation.* The law states that "any particle of matter in the universe attracts any other with a force varying directly as the product of the masses and inversely as the square of the distance between them[1]." Transferred to travel analysis, the gravity model represents the aggregate relationship between (two) places or zones and their interaction. The level of interaction basically declines with increasing distance and increases with the "amount of activity at each location" (Isard 1956). In order to obtain a more realistic representation of trip distribution in space, the gravity model in its simple, original form has been augmented in many ways over the past eighty years (for early examples of refinements, see Reilly 1929; Stewart 1948; Ruiter 1967; Wilson 1967). The major drawback of early applications of the gravity model to destination choice is that they inherently produced great streams for nearby places and therefore prioritized short-distance origin-destination (OD) relations. Consequently, the original model neglects the advantages of walking over mechanical modes for short trips. Moreover, in the basic model, costs (travel times) are only given as ratios, irrespective of the absolute values (i.e., 5 min./10 min. = 50 min./100 min.). This is unlikely in realistic choice situations. Modern transport-modelling software makes use of more sophisticated impedance functions which consider destination choice not only as a function of distance, but also as an interrelationship of distance (trip distribution) and mode choice (e.g., Schnabel and Lohse 1997). The drawback of aggregate models in

1 Newton's law of gravitation (2008). Encyclopædia Britannica. *Encyclopædia Britannica 2007 Ultimate Reference Suite.* Chicago: Encyclopædia Britannica.

general (including the similar *intervening opportunity model* first presented by Stouffer 1940) is their failure to represent human behaviour and decision making appropriately ("Zones don't travel; people travel!", see Domencich and McFadden 1972). With the emergence of discrete-choice techniques, demographically disaggregated approaches, which considered variables other than pure travel time (based on interzonal distances) or at best generalized travel costs, were introduced (see Ben-Akiva and Lerman 1985 for an overview and Cascetta, Pagliara, and Papola 2007 as well as Bekhor and Prashker 2007 for state-of-the-art modelling approaches)[2]. However, for travel analysis and transport planning, destination choice remains one of the key challenges for analysis and strategy development as compared to other choice situations such as modal choice, route choice or departure-time choice. (Discrete) choice models have long failed to capture the complex decision-making processes underlying individual spatial choices (Hunt, Boots, and Kanaroglou 2004). Some researchers have even argued that choice models are not appropriate for the analysis of spatial choice (Fotheringham and O'Kelly 1989). This was probably true for the first attempts to apply choice models to destination choice, but the methodological development in this field over the last twenty years has shown substantial progress (see Fotheringham 1983 for an early example; see also Bhat 2000a; Bhat and Zhao 2002 for more recent examples). The most important advancement in the understanding of destination choice and its modelling was certainly the discovery that the rigid substitution pattern based on the *independence of irrelevant alternatives* (IIA) property in Multi-Nominal Logit (MNL) models does not correspond to choices for destinations. Some places might better substitute others than competing alternatives within the given choice set due to their particular characteristics of size, dimensionality, spatial continuity, proximity to other sites, etc. (Haynes and Fotheringham 1990).

Choice-set formation is another critical aspect of destination choice by discrete-choice approaches. As the number of possible alternatives in a destination-choice problem can be and often is considerably larger than in other travel choices such as mode choice, there is a great danger of an incorrect estimation of the model parameters and therefore an incorrect prediction of choices by a misspecification of the choice set (Manski 1977). Thill (1992) described several strategies to formulate choice sets by (conceptual) assignment:

- Defining the universal choice set: all possible destinations are considered. (The problem with this strategy is that it goes far beyond the actual considerations of an individual; see Ben-Akiva and Lerman 1985).
- Assigning all individuals the same choice set which captures all destinations in the area of interest (most often applied).

2 It should be mentioned that discrete-choice models for destination choice (in a logit form) and the gravity model do not necessarily contradict each other as they do have broad similarities (see the "entropy-maximization model", Wilson 1967).

- Defining a destination-specific choice set: a perimeter is set around each location in the universal choice set; the distance threshold is due to relative gains and losses in predictive power that result from excluding destinations in specific distance classes from the choice set. (The problem with this strategy is that the choice set is a function of the choices modelled, which results in a simultaneous equations bias; see Black 1984; Parsons and Hauber 1998.)
- Defining a choice set consisting of all destinations that were actually chosen by individuals living in the same area (the argument being that people living in the same area are constrained in similar ways, are affected by the same spatial structure of the urban environment and are familiar with the same shopping or recreational opportunities).
- Generating choice sets modelled by algorithms which simulate human learning (Meyer 1980).
- Preference-ranking destinations by asking the respondents (stated-preference method). (This strategy does not allow for any substitution among attributes, which would produce an overall favourable ranking even if one attribute is ranked poorly; see Arnold, Oum, and Tigert 1983.)
- Obtaining information about individual choice sets directly from the decision makers by naming potential alternative destinations and their actual choices. (The problem with this strategy is that people appear not to be able to report their choice sets accurately; see Lerman 1983.)
- Two-stage choice-set generation: Joint modelling choice sets and choice (Manski 1977) and choice sets as an outcome of an additional discrete-choice model which endogenously generates alternatives (Zhang, Fujiwara, and Kusakabe 2004).

As this list shows, the generation of choice sets is widely driven by researchers' presumptions about likely choices, search-area boundaries or potentially homogeneous search behaviour. As will be shown, the analysis of longitudinal data will add to the methodology to shape the size and structure of choice sets in spatial choice.

Spatial behaviour and activity spaces

Spatial behaviour analysis is a broader concept than destination choice; it stresses the interaction between individuals and their surrounding environment and goes beyond the question of actual choice.

Human geography, sociology and other related disciplines have developed concepts to represent, analyse and model location and destination choice as well as people's use of urban space. The approaches are both aggregate and disaggregate, i.e., focusing on the average distribution of places frequented and giving an individual perspective of a person's or household's mobility.

Conceptual approaches

One of the first aggregate approaches to estimating people's range of movement and contact is Hägerstrand's *Mean Information Field* (MIF) (Hägerstrand 1953). In brief, the MIF gives the average spatial extent of a person's short-term contacts. The conceptual idea of the calculation is simple: From a given centre of a coordinate system, a series of rings is drawn and the number of points of destination in each ring is tabulated. Based on this distribution, a Pareto curve of the form $Y=aD^{-b}$ is calculated, with Y as the expected number of persons per square kilometre and D as the distance from the point of origin in kilometres. A cell grid is then constructed and an estimating equation is taken to give point estimates of the expected amount of people in each of the exterior cells. Dividing each cell entry by the sum of all cell values gives the respective probabilities. As Hägerstrand and his colleagues could not use longitudinal movement information, which would have fulfilled the research requirements, they used local migration data to test the model. It was later applied to other data sources and in different contexts, interestingly also to one of the first longitudinal travel-data sets ever, the Cedar Rapids movement study data (Garrison et al. 1959; Marble and Nystuen 1963).

Lynch's work (1960) on *cognitive* or *mental maps* focuses on the assumption that perception of space is a highly subjective process in contrast to the generalized representation of space in cartography. Based on his interest in the relationship between the structures as well as the quality of architecture and human perception, Lynch found out that the mental maps of individuals, i.e., the image which human beings develop about their (travel) environment, are:

- more or less biased;
- are simplifications of the real world;
- are group-specific; and
- are composed of about five basic elements which have different meanings for the structure of urban space in different cities (paths, border lines, areas, foci and landmarks).

Mental maps mainly act as an individualized cognitive support for spatial ordering and orientation. Mental maps and their formation can only be methodologically captured indirectly. Lynch used memory protocols and, as a main approach, map sketches of test persons. As mental maps have great potential for "testing" the acceptance, efficiency and clarity of urban design for users and citizens, the methodology has been widely applied in space-related scientific disciplines. In addition, Lynch's idea was the starting point of a conceptual dispute in human geography because the mental-map approach raises questions about the common behavioural perspective (*stimulus-response relationship*) in perceptive geography (Anderson 2000).

In a broad sense, the action-space concept by Horton and Reynolds (1970) and others comprises both those locations of which a traveller has had personal experience as well as the traveller's knowledge space of locations of which he or she has had second-hand experience through family, friends, books, films or other media. Jakle, Brunn, and Roseman (1976) summarized the action-space concept as the total interaction of an individual with his or her surrounding social and physical environment, comprising all those places in which people potentially operate. Another approach to action space is the individual evaluation of spatial alternatives: Each possible destination is assigned a place utility, which yields a degree of satisfaction or dissatisfaction when considered or chosen. The action space as a whole may be seen as the sum of those utilities (see also Wolpert 1965). When the above perceptual space approach is linked with the idea of action space, action space may be defined as a part of perceptual (cognitive) space, wherein the traveller not only knows particular locations but can potentially choose destination alternatives (Dürr 1979). This definition is closely connected to the principles of space-time geography in which travel behaviour is considered to be an outcome of a complex system of individual and external constraints (Hägerstrand 1970).

Dürr (1979) also added the phenomenon of selective perception of spatial structures and the idea of *perceptual space*. In contrast to a universal representation of an action space, perceptual space captures an incomplete section of the objective environment. Individuals select the information from their surroundings which appears important for satisfying their needs and achieving their objectives. The resulting perceptual space may be seen as a biased mental map, in line with work by Lynch as well as by Gould and White (1986).

Inspired by Hägerstrand's space-time paths, Lenntorp (1976), a member of the Lund School, developed the concept of space-time prisms (see also Chapter 4). He operationalized Hägerstrand's ideas to create a measure of individual accessibility based on the notion of a person's reach. Space-time prisms define the possible locations for a space-time path with obligatory activities such as work fixing the shape of the prism by predefining a person's location. Figure 10.1 gives an example of a fictive prism (Miller 2004). The two anchor points represented in Figure 10.1 are home and workplace, with a given minimum (fixed) departure time t_i and a maximum arrival time at work t_j. The gap between those times is planned to be used for another activity at some location which requires at least a time units. In addition, the fictive traveller is able to move with an average maximum speed v. The interior of the prism is called the *potential path space* and contains all points in space and time that the traveller is able to reach within his or her travel episode. A traveller will not have the chance to execute an activity unless the space-time path (reflecting his or her location and available times) intersects the potential path space sufficiently. The projection of the potential path space to geospace gives the *potential path area*, which consists of all locations that the person could potentially occupy. A traveller can not participate in an activity unless its location is within the potential path area (ignoring the temporal duration of activities).

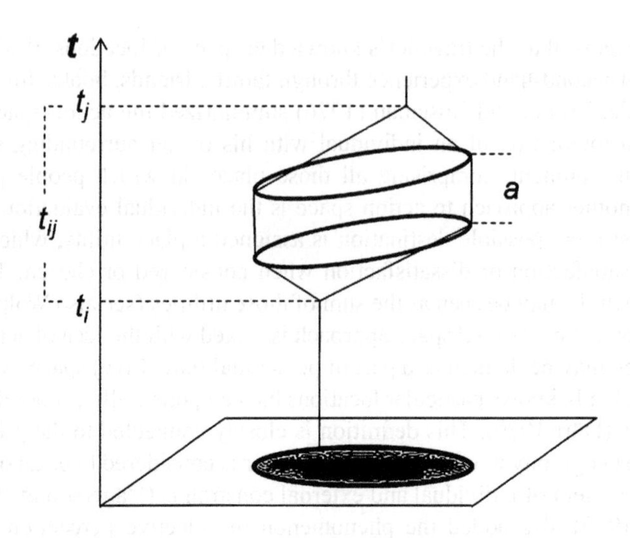

Figure 10.1 Example of a space-time prism
Source: Adapted from Miller 2004.

The activity-space approach and the daily level

Finally, the *activity-space* concept, which was developed in the 1960s and 1970s in parallel with several of the approaches presented above to describe individual perception, knowledge and actual use of space (see Golledge and Stimson 1997 for a discussion), is meant to represent the space which contains the places frequented by an individual over a period of time. Activity spaces are (geometric) indicators of *observed* or *realized* daily travel patterns (see also Axhausen 2005). This is stressed here because related concepts such as *action space*, *perceptual space*, *mental maps* or *space-time prisms* mainly describe individual travel *potentials*.

Early empirical studies on location choice and activity space

Empirical work on activity space, especially work using longitudinal travel data, is rare. The few studies that focused primarily on travel potentials or opportunities related to action-space analysis.

Early literature on the actual estimation and measurement of activity spaces was mainly based on cross-sectional data for groups of respondents. Treating many cross-sections as a quasi-panel of an average person (type) is problematic, as this ignores biographical elements in the mental map of an individual and is likely to bias the conclusions.

Marble and Bowlby (1968) undertook one of the rare studies on location choice using multiday data. By applying an enumerative and listing approach to the Cedar

Rapids travel-diary data (30-day period), the researchers found great stability in destination choice on the daily level. About three quarters of all trips were made to "repetitiously visited locations", with about 25 per cent to 50 per cent of these trips for shopping purposes. Interestingly, sensitivity to distance decay was lower for trips to regular destinations, which opens up the discussion on the particular characteristics of habitual spatial behaviour and variety seeking (see Chapter 12).

In another early study, Kutter (1973) linked his hypotheses about the stratification of the population according to groups with homogenous travel behaviour to the question of where those groups execute their activities and how spatial-usage intensities vary according to personal attributes. Based on a small (cross-sectional) sample from the city of Braunschweig, Germany, he investigated the spatial distribution of activities by area type, life-cycle group and distance from home. The study–which took into account the comparatively low car availability and usage rate for Germany in the early 1970s – confirmed Kutter's assumptions of a strong correlation between distance decay and activity intensity. There were, however, different sensitivities for different activity types. Home was an important anchor point of daily life, and there were different activity space sizes for different socio-economic groups.

An aggregated perspective of urban and regional space usage and travel densities was provided by the 1970s UMOT project (*Unified Mechanism of Travel*) and subsequent studies (Zahavi 1979; Beckmann, Golob, and Zahavi 1983a, 1983b). One focus of the UMOT project was to analyse densities of activity locations (or trips) and test hypotheses about the character of trip distributions at the regional level given a certain mode choice and the spatial structures of the regions studied. This work was based on one-day travel diaries. UMOT led to the calculation of ellipse-shaped *travel probability fields*, which are the geometric result of travel demand, network structure (system supply) and the number of activity opportunities (as an indicator for the urban form) (Figure 10.2). The major findings were that:

- the fields' directions tend to be towards the urban cores,
- the length of the fields is proportional to the distance of the zone's centroid to the main agglomeration centre,
- there are differences of shape between the different modes of transport, and
- there are strong relationships between the infrastructural supply of the region and the direction of the probability fields.

Schwesig (1988) analysed the importance of the home/work axis based on activity- and destination-choice frequency data collected for the Hamburg region in the early 1980s (see also Dangschat et al. 1982). This study is one of the few early investigations in which quasi-longitudinal data covering a period of one month was used.

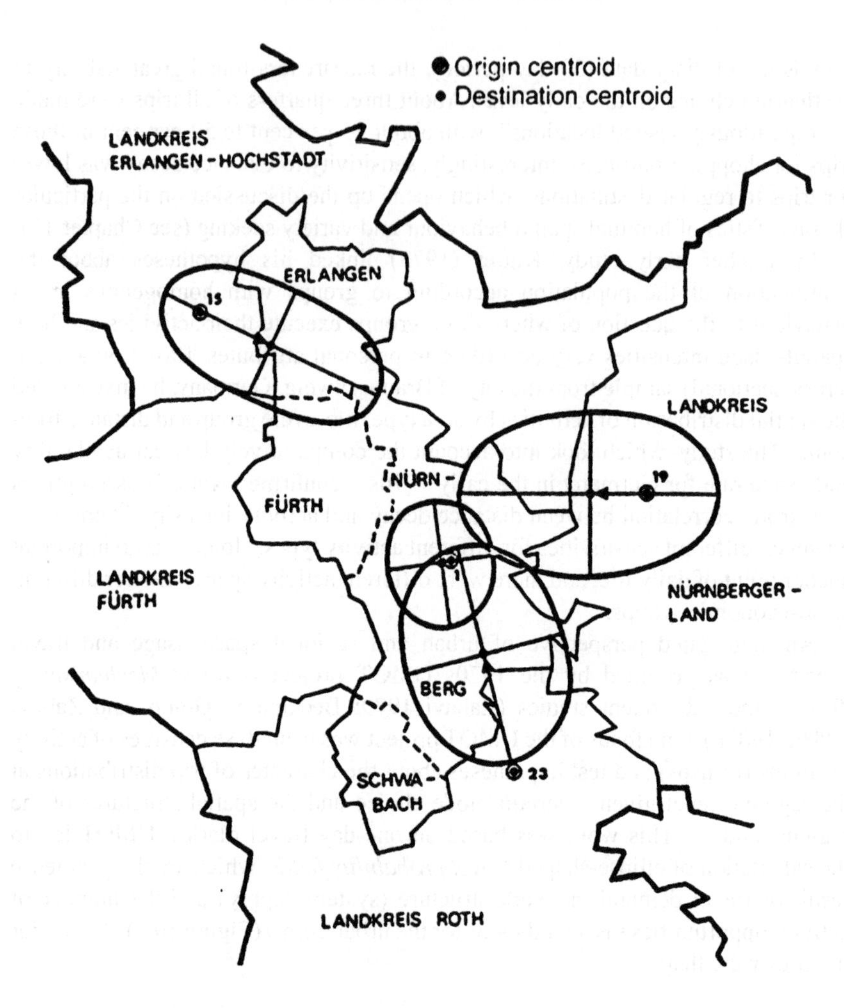

Figure 10.2 Travel probability fields in the Nuremberg region
Source: Zahavi (1979) 230.

While focusing on integrating complex travel patterns into concepts of accessibility, Miller (1991), Kwan (1999), Kim and Kwan (2001), Scott (2003) and several other researchers developed techniques (mainly GIS) to operationalize space-time prisms for daily travel. The basic aim behind operationalizing the heretofore theoretical Lund-School approach was to derive an individual *daily potential path area* (DPPA), which is the physically accessible part of space based on an individual's restrictions, commitments and opportunities (Hägerstrand). The DPPA, which is a three-dimensional diagram, may then be transformed into a (two-dimensional) map representation which gives the DPPA combined with the available road network and all spatial opportunities within the area of investigation. Compared to conventional accessibility measures, space-time measures of individual accessibility have the following advantages:

- Space-time measures evaluate individual accessibility from any place in continuous space rather than considering a single reference point (such as home or the workplace) as the focus of daily life. This is based on the notion that a substantial portion of travel consists of multistop journeys, which implies that various locations become more accessible from places which are visited or passed on the traveller's trip chain or activity programme.
- Space-time approaches include personal time-budget and space-time constraints as important determinants of accessibility. These have been neglected entirely in conventional approaches (Kwan 1999).

The approach was successfully used by Kwan and others to reveal ethnic and above all gender differences in individual access, and it challenged the traditional understanding of accessibility and its calculation. Many researchers (including Wu and Miller 2000, 2001; Wu, Miller, and Hung 2001; Pendyala, Yamamoto, and Kitamura 2002) enhanced the calculation and modelling of space-time prisms by integrating dynamic flow as well as access-utility concepts or by applying stochastic frontier models.

Without a doubt, space-time measures of accessibility may be seen as an activity-space representation, because revealed (often only one- or two-day) travel data is used to define individual DPPA. However, only a cross-section of

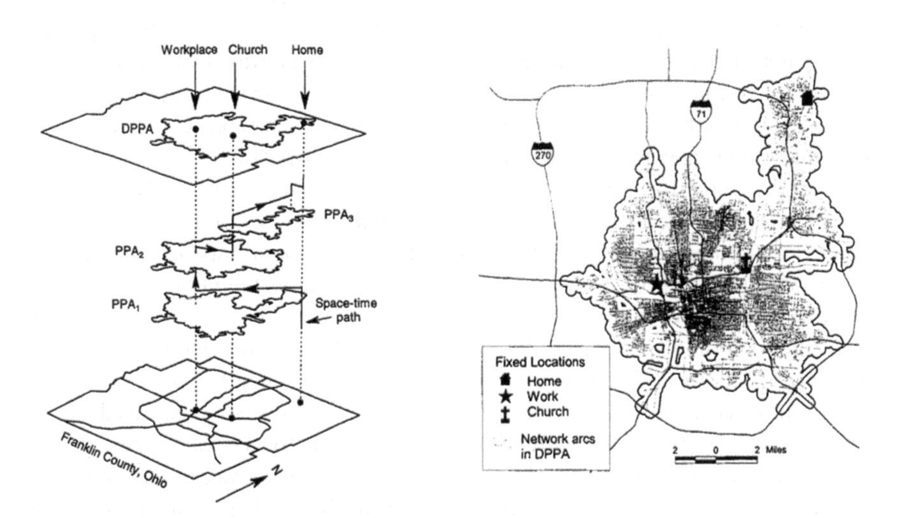

Figure 10.3 Daily potential path area (DPPA): Three-dimensional representation and map

Source: Kwan (1999), 214–15, with kind permission of Wiley-Blackwell Publishers.

the activity space could be visualized and calculated, as longitudinal data was not yet available.

From a more sociological perspective, Scheiner (2001) investigated the distribution of activity locations for a sample of 278 respondents living in eastern and western districts of Berlin. The purpose of the 1998 study, which was part of a comprehensive research programme focusing on transformation processes in Berlin after the reunification of Germany in 1990, was to reveal major differences between daily travel behaviour routines on both sides of the former Berlin Wall. The respondents were asked to state their main activity locations for shopping, services and leisure activities as well as the frequency of their visits. The study yielded interesting results on the integration of East and West Berlin with regard to travellers' everyday use of space: There were still significant differences between activity spaces in adjacent areas. East Berlin residents oriented themselves towards East Berlin opportunities; likewise, West Berlin residents oriented themselves towards West Berlin opportunities. However, the study also demonstrated that people tended to choose destinations selectively (e.g., for visits to the doctor), which indicates that habitual behaviour still dominated, but was being challenged by further considerations of spatial choice.

Newsome and her colleagues (Newsome, Walcott, and Smith 1998) used cross-sectional travel-diary data from Charlotte, North Carolina to test a method which gives a representation of the maximal area within which travellers could engage in activities. Based on Hägerstrand's space-time theory, they developed an ellipse to show the observed extent of an activity space. The home and work locations of a traveller were chosen as the foci of the ellipse, whereby the location of any combined discretionary activity was estimated as the greatest combined distance from those two points. Similar approaches were used to test the impact of policy measures and telecommunication developments on travel and accessibility (see, e.g., Saxena and Mokhtarian 1997). Even though these studies used revealed travel data, they belong to the group of approaches which represent space-usage potential rather than actually observed activity spaces over time.

Based on three-day travel and in-home diary data from Utrecht, the Netherlands and surrounding areas, Dijst (1999) investigated individual activity spaces and applied a typology of shapes based on different temporal, spatial and spatio-temporal characteristics. These included attributes such as the number of activity places visited between departure from a base and arrival at the same or another base; the total time spent on activities in the visited places (excluding time spent at a base); the area of actual action space; and the distance between bases and the farthest visited activity place. The classification system comprised about twenty such attributes. It finally yielded seventeen activity-space types, which may be described as circular, elliptical or linear activity spaces, depending on the identified shape. In addition, activity spaces of different sizes mainly covered neighbourhoods, the local area, the region or the whole country. This twofold categorization was finally linked to socio-economic attributes of the travellers, with a strong focus on the implications of part-time and full-time work on the quality of the activity spaces. It was generally found that full-time workers tend to have larger activity spaces than those with part-time jobs.

A framework for the analysis of activity spaces

To summarize our own concept of activity-space analysis, an activity space is defined as a two-dimensional form that is constituted by the spatial distribution of those locations a traveller has personal experience of (*contact with*). Important geographical reference points within the activity space are usually the traveller's home and other primary, regularly frequented locations. Consequently, activity spaces are mainly the result of:

- the traveller's home location;
- the traveller's duration of residence;
- the number of activity locations in the vicinity of home;
- the resulting trips within the neighbourhood;
- mobility to and from frequently-visited activity locations such as work or school; and
- travel between and around the centres (pegs) of daily life.

The *home location* in particular is often emphasized as a "pocket of local order", i.e., as a principal anchor point of time use in daily travel (see, e.g., Ellegård and Vilhelmson 2004). Further subsuming the more sociological characteristics of activity spaces, Jakle, Brunn, and Roseman (1976) gave the following definition:

- Activity spaces are manifestations of our everyday lives.
- They may be defined as an important process through which travellers gain information and attach meaning to their environment.
- Activity spaces are linked to the concept of territoriality, i.e., direct contact with locations has an influence on how we define territories or habitats.
- Movement between places is related to perceived territories.
- Activity spaces refer to an individual's role within society and are therefore linked to personal (socio-economic) attributes and group affiliation.
- A single activity space is the product of an individual's definition of a set of activities he or she wants to participate in.

Finally, activity spaces are subject to underlying fundamental geographical principles such as *distance decay* and *directional bias*, which implies that the probability of (regular) contact with a location usually decreases with its distance from the peg(s) of daily life (especially home) and the deviation from the main orientation or direction of daily travel. *Directional bias* refers to preferences for a particular place over other places of equal or similar distance due to some perceived quality of the preferred place (Golledge and Stimson 1997).

Chapter 11
Analysing Activity Space Using Longitudinal Data: Methods and Results

Having described selected principles of destination choice and a variety of earlier analysis approaches in Chapter 10, this section focuses on revealing the long-term structures of human activity spaces in the longitudinal travel-data sets introduced in Chapter 6. It comprises a description of the development of indicators to visualize and measure human activity space as well as a broad (comparative) analysis of the data.

Developing measures of human activity space: Two techniques

The lack of earlier empirical analyses of activity spaces as geometric indicators of *observed* travel patterns over prolonged periods requires the development of suitable measures to operationalize the microgeographical concept. Our investigation of the temporal structures of destination choice and revealed activity spaces is based on two techniques: the *enumeration of trips and unique destinations* and a *continuous representation of the use of space.*

Enumeration and listing of trips and unique destinations

The enumeration approach focuses on how many places we actually know, visit and discover over time. Our current understanding of the structure of mental maps and the spatial distribution of social networks suggests that a set of destinations should have a structure, i.e., certain locations and directions of travel should be systematically preferred beyond what the availability of competing opportunities or their associated generalized costs would indicate (Giddens 1984). It also suggests turnover in the set: new locations are added while other locations are dropped. The enumeration approach to revealing individuals' destination choice structures nicely shows the ambiguity between stability and variety seeking in travel behaviour.

Figure 11.1 shows how destination choice might be represented over prolonged periods. The combination of a unique geocode (coordinate) and purpose (if available) may be represented in a list which corresponds to the geographical visualization of travel and activity space. The destinations list, the like of which has never before been available in such detail (for a limited exception, see Marble and Bowlby 1968), allows us to develop indicators which reveal the inherent spatial structure and to characterize the temporal phenomena of destination choice.

Seq. No	X coordinate	Y coordinate	Trip purpose	Frequency
1	690398	260603	Home	84
2	690196	260468	Work	61
3	690034	260570	Leisure	5
4	690193	260703	Leisure	5
5	690905	260538	Shop	4
6	690046	260816	Shop	4
7	690026	260241	Work	3
8	690216	260982	Private business	3
9	690106	260252	Leisure	3
10	690926	260497	Business	2
11	690044	260855	Leisure	2
12	690379	260731	Shop	2
13	690030	260494	Leisure	2
14	690110	260740	Leisure	2
15	690125	260247	Leisure	1
16	690879	260034	Leisure	1
17	690308	260263	Shop	1
18	690119	260118	Private business	1
19	690328	260272	Leisure	1
20	690132	260530	Leisure	1
21	690575	260103	Leisure	1
22	690004	260760	Shop	1
23	690032	260860	Leisure	1
24	690795	260747	Leisure	1
cont.				

Figure 11.1 Exemplary list and graphical representation of destination choice over six weeks of reporting (Thurgau survey): Destinations according to coordinates, purpose and frequency of visits

The particular methods of measuring human activity space described here were developed in a series of papers (Schönfelder 2003; Schönfelder and Axhausen 2001b, 2002, 2003, 2004a, 2004b). They are summarized in Table 11.1. The indicators will be described in further detail in the respective analysis sections.

Table 11.1 Enumeration approach: Indicators of destination choice over time

Phenomenon	Brief description of the indicator
Volumes	Number of trips and unique locations visited
Stability/variability	Basic descriptives: Stability of departure time and mode choice Ratio between trips and unique locations Concentration of trips in a number of unique locations
Innovation rate and variety seeking	Number and share of locations previously not observed/actually visited Innovation rate: Share of unique places of the cumulative number of places visited
Dispersion and development of activity-space size	Mean distance of observed locations from home
Clustering	Clustering of activities in nearby locations

Measuring the continuous use of space

The second range of approaches to analysing human activity space focuses on the continuous representation and measurement of space. These methods of measuring activity space essentially capture the transformation of point patterns such as the spatial distribution of activity locations into geometrical shapes (Figure 11.2). The transformation process will provide answers to the following questions:

- Given observed location choices, which other locations are likely to be chosen (what is the probability of visits)?
- Which part of the region is used according to the traveller's needs and preferences (density/intensity of use)?
- When moving through nets, what adjacent area is perceived and possibly memorized (perception/memorization of infrastructure)?

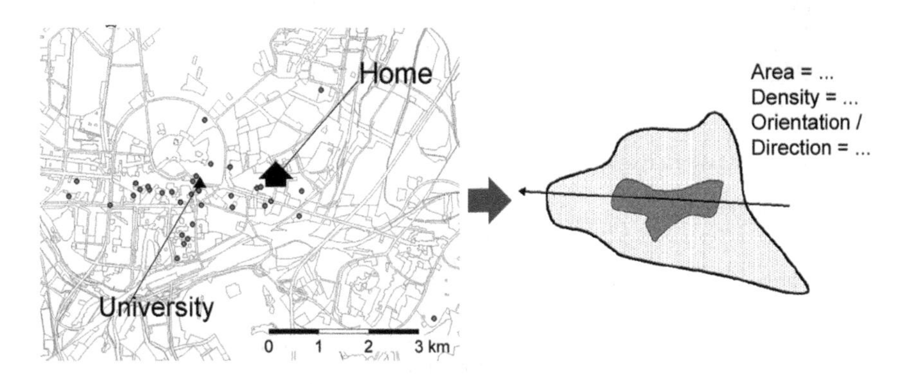

Figure 11.2 Transforming an activity-point pattern into a continuous representation of space usage

Three particular methods have been developed which model human behaviour while simplifying environmental perception and actual decision processes (Schönfelder 2003; Schönfelder and Axhausen 2002, 2004b). These are:

- a two-dimensional confidence ellipse or standard deviational ellipse similar to the Jennrich-Turner home range;
- measuring activity space based on kernel densities; and
- measuring activity space by shortest-path networks linking all destinations visited. This is conceptually similar to minimum spanning trees.

Figure 11.3 gives an introductory overview of the methods, which will then be described in more detail.

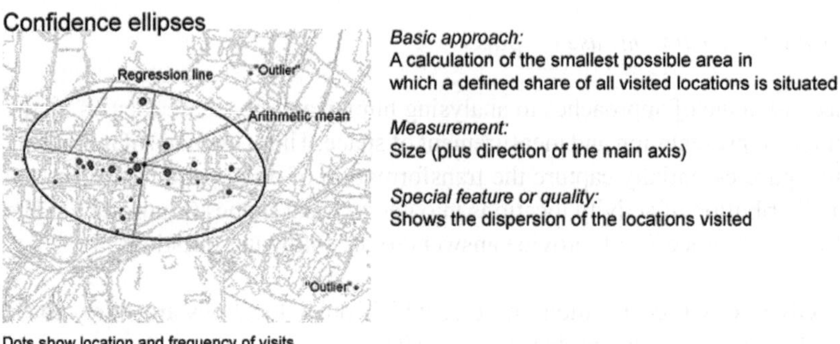

Confidence ellipses
Regression line
"Outlier"
Arithmetic mean
"Outlier"
Basic approach:
A calculation of the smallest possible area in which a defined share of all visited locations is situated
Measurement:
Size (plus direction of the main axis)
Special feature or quality:
Shows the dispersion of the locations visited
Dots show location and frequency of visits

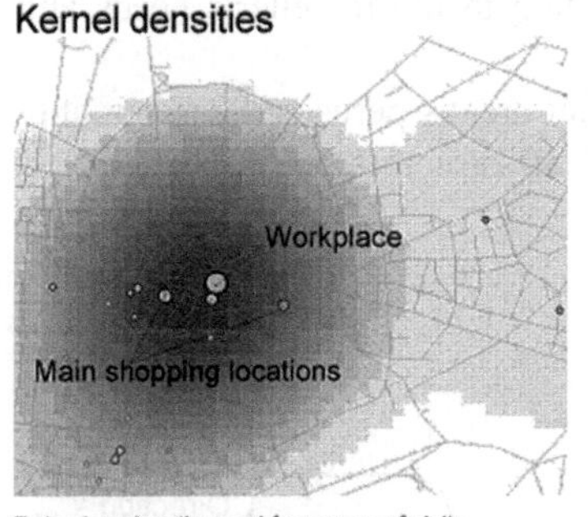

Kernel densities
Workplace
Main shopping locations
Basic approach:
Density surface; based on the proximity of activity locations
Measurement:
a) Area covered exceeding a certain threshold value
b) "Volume" (the sum of all kernel densities calculated)
Special feature or quality:
Represents local clusters or subcentres within individual activity spaces
Dots show location and frequency of visits

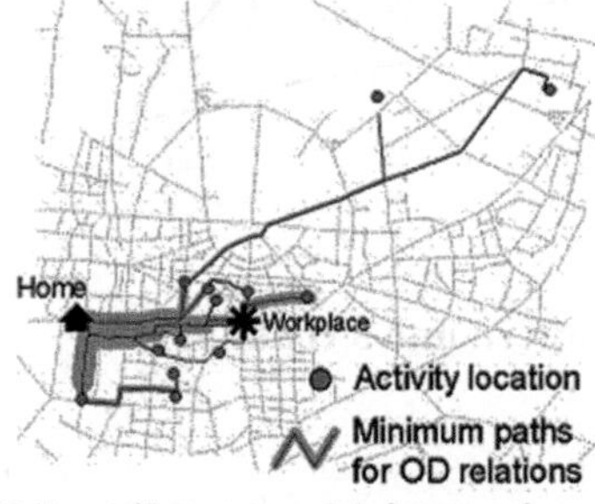

Shortest-path network
Home
Workplace
Activity location
Minimum paths for OD relations
Basic approach:
Set of shortest paths between all origin-destination relations observed
Measurement:
a) Length of the tree (unweighted / weighted by the frequency of single-link use)
b) Size of the buffered area around the tree, indicating potential knowledge spaces
Special feature or quality:
Indicator of perception of urban space and networks
Boldness of links corresponds to frequency of use

Figure 11.3 Measuring human activity space: Overview of methods

Confidence ellipses

Confidence ellipses, also called prediction-interval ellipses, are an explorative method of investigating the relationship between two variables (bivariate analysis). They are often used for testing hypotheses and detecting outliers. Confidence ellipses are analogous to the confidence interval of univariate distributions, defined as the smallest possible (sub-)area in which the true value of the population should be found with a certain probability (e.g., 95 per cent). Similar methodological techniques were already employed in the activity-space-oriented work of the late 1970s UMOT project (Zahavi 1979; Beckmann, Golob, and Zahavi 1983a, 1983b).

Confidence ellipses, like the kernel density approach below, belong to the descriptive and analytical concepts used in *habitat research* in zoology (Worton 1987). Zoologists have analysed longitudinal and spatially referenced data to define territories or so-called *home ranges* of individual creatures since the 1940s. Confidence ellipses were introduced later as the Jennrich-Turner home range concept (Jennrich and Turner 1969). This concept relates to the so-called *centre-of-activity approaches,* which define an arithmetic mean as a (biologically virtually meaningless) centre of an animal's home range and focus on the analysis of territory around that point. The extent of the use of space is often limited by a given geometrical shape, e.g., concentric rings, which define a fixed-percentage confidence region based on the animal's utility distribution. Centre-of-activity approaches are therefore *parametric, predetermined* or *probabilistic,* as it is necessary to define a distribution of the intensity of use about the centre. In our case, we assume bivariate normal distribution for human activity locations, which was shown earlier by Moore (1970).

In human geography, the concept of the confidence ellipse has never been applied to travel-diary data as such; however, the approach has been used to analyse social interaction based on activity-frequency or density data (Hyland 1970; Buttimer 1972; Herbert and Raine 1976). Raine (1978), for example, applied the standard deviational-ellipse approach to the activity-frequency data of a small sample of Cardiff residents. His study focused on different spheres of activities (e.g., visiting friends or conducting private business) and the main spatial opportunities within a limited residential area[1]. Raine found that individual ellipses intersected considerably, which shows that movement to particular places reflected and even initiated other patterns of interaction.

The size of the ellipse area shall represent the actual size of the activity space. It may be used to compare the dispersion of activity space between travellers or between subperiods of observation for single travellers. As an example for the latter, Figure 11.4 shows the daily activity space represented by the 95 per cent-confidence ellipses of one Mobidrive respondent over the course of one week. Whereas differences in the extent of the activity spaces can easily be identified, their orientation within the urban context of Karlsruhe remained similar for most of the weekdays.

In order to obtain a more realistic representation of human behaviour for the travel data we analysed, we made modifications to the basic mathematical concept. The traveller's home location was taken as a substitute for the mathematical centre (i.e., the arithmetic mean point) in the calculation of the covariance matrix. This

1 The places were prespecified by Raine's research team, which is a fundamentally different approach compared to longitudinal travel-diary surveys or GPS observations, which capture locations actually visited.

stresses the importance of home for daily travel, using a real-world location instead of the artificial mean point of the chosen locations.

Ellipses were computed with the covariance matrix of all points (activity locations) of a person:

$$S = \begin{pmatrix} s_{xx} & s_{xy} \\ s_{yx} & s_{yy} \end{pmatrix},$$

where each covariance is defined as

$$s_{xx} = \frac{1}{n-2}\sum_{i=1}^{n}(x_i - \overline{x}/HomeX)^2$$

$$s_{yy} = \frac{1}{n-2}\sum_{i=1}^{n}(y_i - \overline{y}\,/\,HomeY)^2$$

$$s_{xy} = s_{yx} = \frac{1}{n-2}\sum_{i=1}^{n}(x_i - \overline{x}\,/\,HomeX)(y_i - \overline{y}\,/\,HomeY)\,.$$

The determinant of the covariance matrix (generalized variance) is

$$|S| = s_{xx}s_{yy} - s_{xy}^2,$$

with the ellipse size A

$$A = 6\pi\,|S|^{\frac{1}{2}}\,.$$

The orientation of the ellipse is determined by the sign of the linear correlation coefficient between the coordinates X and Y of the activity locations. The longer axis of the ellipse (if shown) is the regression line.

Kernel densities

The Kernel density measurement approach also originates from habitat analysis in biology (see Silverman 1986 for basic information or Kirkby 2001 for an example of investigation). The technique is a non-parametric method which does not require any assumptions about the distributional form of underlying point patterns when building the geometry. Non-parametric approaches mainly involve interpolating or smoothing the two-dimensional locations observed. To interpolate the locations, data is often represented in the form of a grid cell. Every cell containing an observation influences its neighbouring cells by contiguity rules, which leads to an illustrative representation of movement directions and eventual biases (Voigt and Tinline 1980). In many cases, the point data may be smoothed by a kernel-density estimation. Other approaches involve Fourier transformation (Anderson 1982) or harmonic-mean methods (Dixon and Chapman 1980). The application and visualization of non-

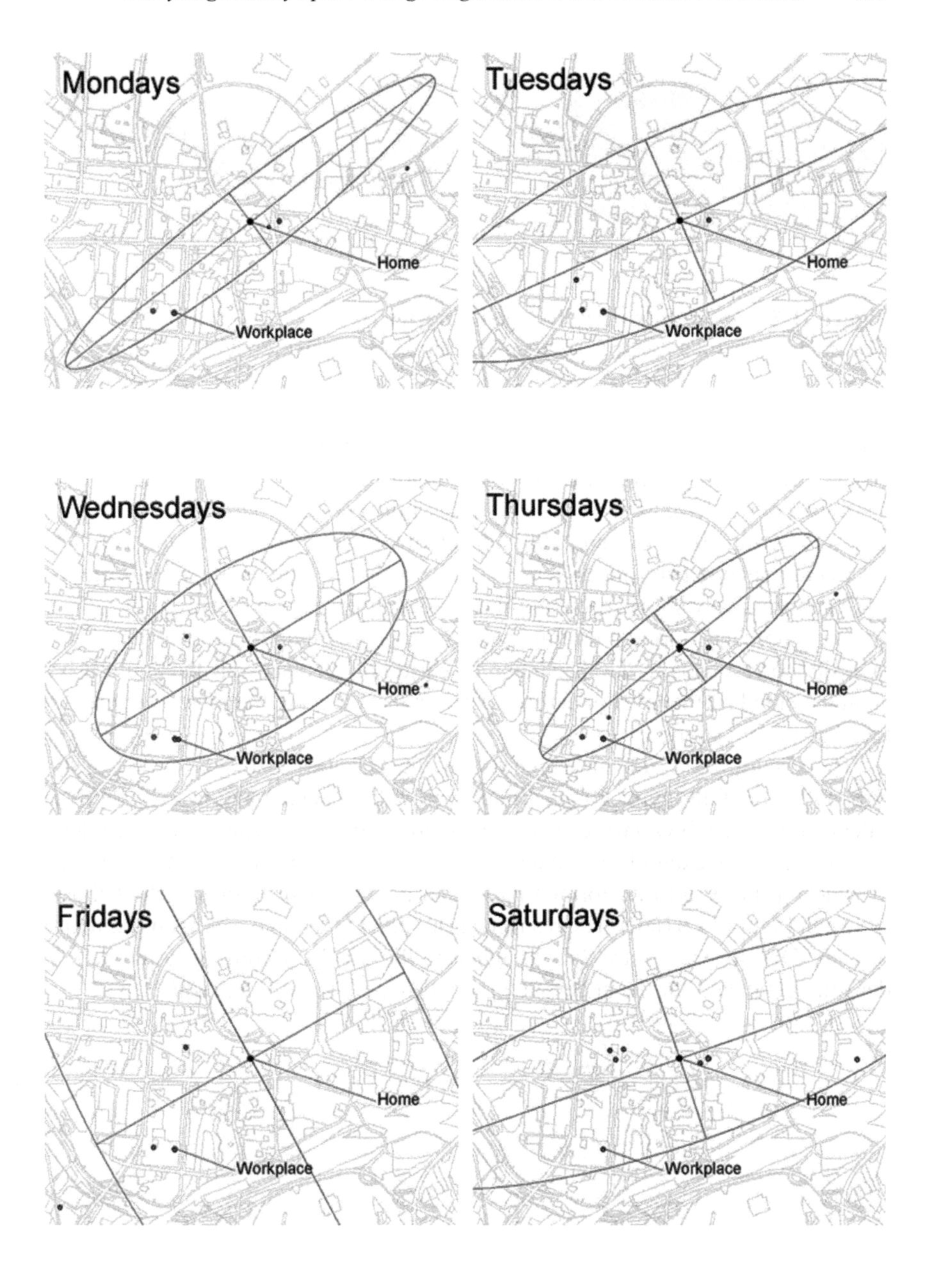

Figure 11.4 Human activity space over time by 95% confidence ellipses

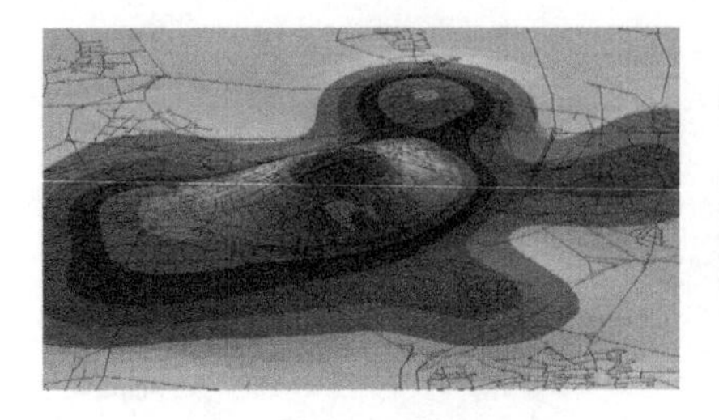

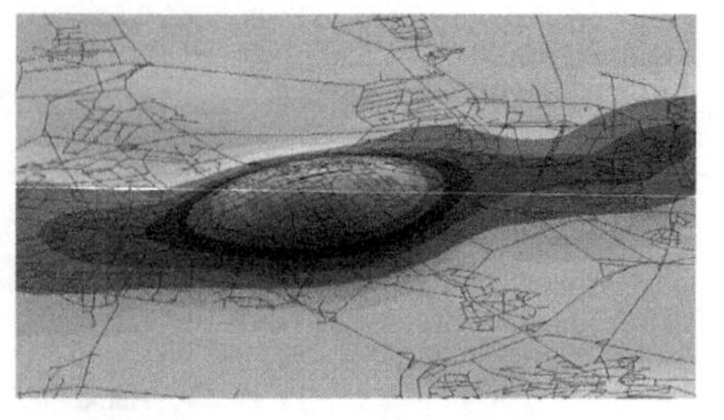

Figure 11.5 Aggregate activity density patterns
Note: Mobidrive: Total Karlsruhe subsample. Left: Leisure activities; Right: Work.

parametric methods have particularly benefited from the development of advanced geographical-information-system (GIS) technology since the 1980s.

Kernel densities have already been successfully applied to large cross-sectional data sets (Kwan 2000; Buliung 2001). Modern GIS applications include tools for calculating such density measurements effectively, including 3-D visualizations which impressively show space-and-time interactions (Figure 11.5).

The approach applied in this book focuses on individual densities. The intensity corresponds to the dispersion or clustering of places visited and can be complemented by the level of activity performance, i.e., the frequency of visits to the observed locations.

The visualization and measurement of the densities were performed using GIS software. GIS applications usually provide special modules for density calculation. ARCINFO® (which was used in this study along with its sister product ARCVIEW®), for example, estimates densities within its integrated GRID module, in which surfaces are transformed into raster grids or wire frames such as those shown in Figure 11.6 (left). The resulting grids are divided into a definable amount of cells. Density values are then assigned to those cells according to the kernel densities estimated for the underlying point pattern (Figure 11.6, right).

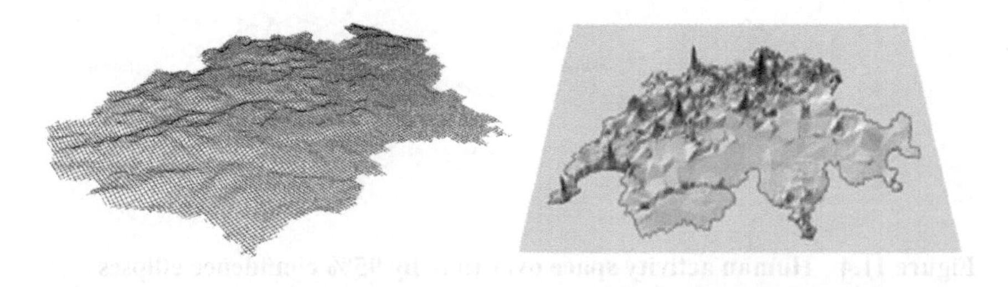

Figure 11.6 Transformation of surfaces into raster grids (left) and GIS-based density visualisation (here: rail accessibility in Switzerland, 1950)
Source: (left) Reproduced by permission of SAGE publications, from Fotheringham et al. (2000) and (right) Tschopp, Fröhlich, and Axhausen 2006, with permission.

The basic process behind estimating kernel densities is the transformation of a point pattern (such as the set of activity locations visited) into a continuous representation of density in a wider area (see Silverman 1986 or Fotheringham, Brunsdon, and Charlton 2000). Generally speaking, the estimation is an interpolation or smoothing technique which generalizes events or points to the area where they occur. Interpolation then leads to the calculation of a value for any point, cell or subregion of the entire area, which characterizes the density.

Probably the most common approach, implemented in several GIS packages, is the *fixed-kernel method* (also applied in this book). Similar to histogram techniques, a symmetrical or variably distributed *kernel function* is placed over each data point. The overlapping values are summed for all locations – not only for the data points – in the entire area ($\mathfrak{R}$), which yields the density or intensity estimate (Figure 11.7). This then leads to a smoothing of the surface, whereby the level of smoothness depends on the *bandwidth* of the kernel function, analogous to the width of ordinary histogram boxes. The bandwidths may be varied according to the necessary degree of smoothness, with greater smoothing at bigger bandwidths or values of the smoothing parameter. The GIS finally may represent the resulting estimates for all grid cells as a continuous surface.

Considering a grid structure in which single points are substituted by grid cells, the base kernel density is given by the formula

$$\lambda(s) = \sum_{d_i < \tau} K\left(\frac{d_i}{\tau}\right)$$

with

- λ density estimate at grid point s,
- T bandwidth or smoothing parameter,
- K kernel function (to be further specified), and
- d_i distance between grid point s and the observation of the ith event.

The kernel function K itself may take different forms, such as normal, triangular or quartic. The results do not differ significantly as long as the distribution is symmetrical. In our analysis, a quartic kernel function was used which was implemented by default through ARCINFO® (see Mitchell 1999 for details), leading to the kernel density

$$\lambda(s) = \sum_{d_i < \tau} K\left\{[\frac{3}{\tau^2 \pi}][1 - \frac{d_i^2}{\tau^2}]^2\right\}.$$

A particularity of the quartic function compared to a normal distribution is that outside the specified bandwidth τ, the function is set to zero per definition, which has implications for the behavioural model. This means that activity locations outside a specified radius do not contribute to the density estimation of the particular point (cell) in space. In other words, a quartic distribution of the kernel function adds

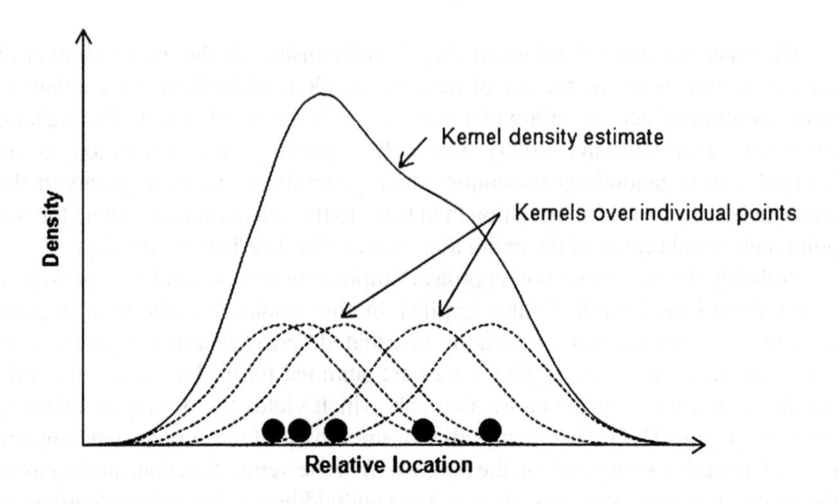

Figure 11.7 The principle of kernel density estimation
Source: Adapted from Levine (2004).

more weight to locations closer to the centre of the bandwidth than to those further away (see Levine 2004 for characteristics of the different kernel forms).

The actual measures of activity space are defined by (1) the number of cells which exceed a given density threshold and (2) the sum of all grid-cell density values (i.e., the *volume*).

Figure 11.8 shows a visualization of kernel densities for one Borlänge test driver. The observation period lasted approximately four months. The figure nicely shows the variation of the size and structure of the location-choice patterns over the course of a week: there was a large activity space on weekdays, similar densities for weekdays and Saturdays in the city-centre area and around the home location, and reduced local travel intensity on Sundays.

Shortest-path networks (SPN)

Transport network structures shape travellers' perceptions of potential activity locations as well as their knowledge of place and spatial orientation (Golledge 1999). Finally, the third measure of activity space which aims at the continuous representation of locational choice, the *shortest-path network* (SPN) measurement, considers the paths chosen by the travellers.

One way to consider network supply and travel interactions is to identify the portion of the network which was actually used by a traveller during the reporting period. This particular portion as well as the built environment adjacent to the roads can be assumed to be known to the traveller. *Shortest-path networks* (SPN) are constructed by merging the calculated shortest paths for all reported trips and their origin-destination pairs.

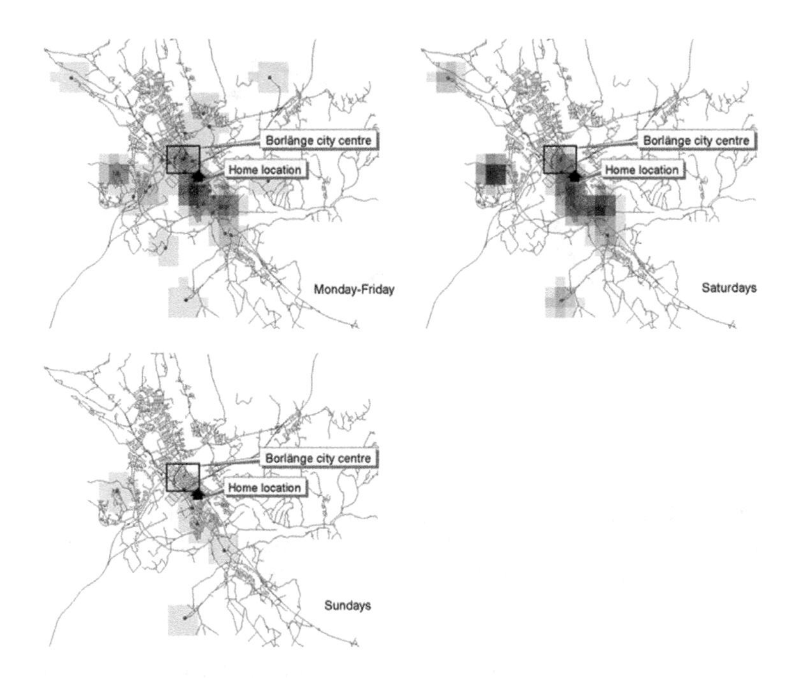

Figure 11.8 Kernel density visualization example (Borlänge GPS data): Human activity space by days of the week

Note: Maps show the activity space of a 71-year-old male retiree. Observation period: approximately four months; grid-cell size: 500 by 500 metres; activity locations weighted by frequency of visits; bandwidth: 1,000 m.

This concept was modelled on similar approaches such as minimum spanning trees. Within the framework of graph theory, Kruskal (1956), Prim (1957), Dijkstra (1959) and others developed algorithms that find minimum spanning trees for a connected and undirected graph weighted by edges (Figure 11.9). This means that they find a subset of the edges that form a tree which includes every vertex and in which the total weight of all the edges of the tree is minimized. If the graph is not entirely connected, a minimum spanning forest is generated (with a minimum spanning tree for each connected component).

The SPN measurement used in this book is an approximation of actual spatial decision making, except that observed route-choice information is not available

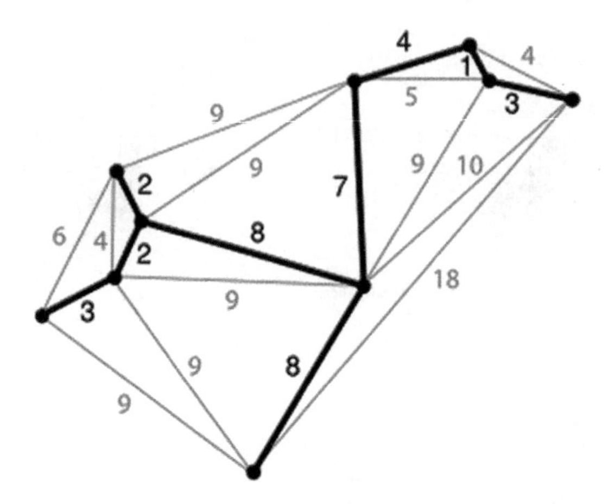

Figure 11.9 The minimum spanning tree of a planar graph
Note: Each edge is labelled with its weight, which here is roughly proportional to its length.
Source: http://en.wikipedia.org/wiki/Minimum_spanning_tree.

for the travel-diary data sets used[2]. The route-choice algorithm chosen is the default Dijkstra procedure implemented in the ARCINFO® NETWORK module[3].

The structure and size of the network may be also interpreted as quantitative indicators of travellers' perception, knowledge and especially use of urban space. Regarding their perception of the (built) environment, it can be assumed that there is a considerable correlation between the frequency of using a network link and a traveller's knowledge of the surrounding area. Psychologists and geographers widely agree that travelling through an environment is the most common way to acquire spatial learning and spatial expertise (Golledge 1999).

In the first of two examples in Figure 11.10, the home location is clearly the *major hub* for daily travel, acting as a central node in the given road network. This is not surprising, as the proportion of complex trip chains with diffuse travel relations is much smaller than the amount of simple home-based trips such as: home→work→home, home→shopping→home or home→leisure→ home. For example, more than 70 per cent of all Mobidrive home-based activity chains (i.e., *tours* or *journeys*) involved only one out-of-home activity.

2 A digitalized road network was only available for the City of Karlsruhe and the town of Borlänge at the time of analysis.

3 Enhancements of this procedure are conceivable, e.g., substituting the deterministic shortest-path algorithm by a probabilistic one (Sheffi 1985; Bovy 1996). Furthermore, the paths taken could be properly assigned to the different modal networks according to the modes actually chosen for the different trips.

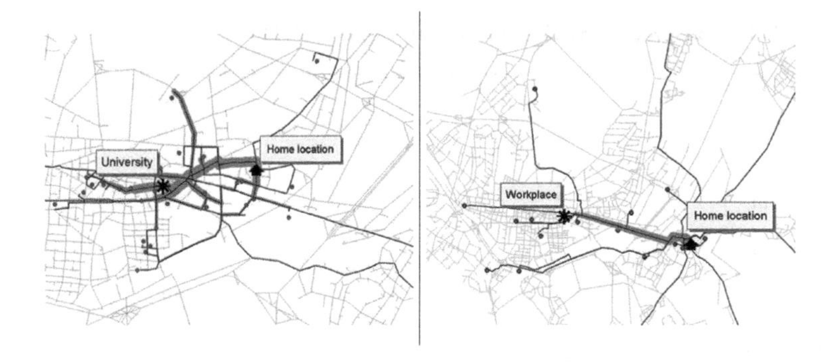

Figure 11.10 Visualization examples of shortest-path network measure (Mobidrive)

Note: The width of the network links indicates frequency of use.

Applying measures of activity space

The second part of this chapter turns to the application of the measurement approaches to the longitudinal travel-data sets. This final analysis starts with a description of trip and location rates. The number of trips and locations (*travel volume*) is not an indicator of regularity or variability per se. However, as travel volume differs substantially between individuals and data sets, the amount of travel is believed to have direct impact on most of the following indicators. In addition, it may be assumed that the number of trips over a given time period will also affect the number of unique locations and their spatial distribution. Finally, the number of trips which may be expected over a period of several weeks has not previously been investigated and is an interesting quantity in its own right.

Trip rates across all modes mainly follow a gamma distribution with zero as the lower limit of the underlying random variable (per definition, only positive trip rates exist)[4]. The median over all data sets comprises about 23 trips per week, which corresponds to cross-sectional results of three to four trips per day and per traveller. This is a number which is found often in travel surveys.

However, the distribution of numbers also shows differences in trip rates between the data sources. The Thurgau travel-diary data, which is based on a mainly rural but economically active survey area, show by far the highest trip rates for all modes. The Uppsala and Mobidrive data differ only slightly for both mode categories, which is interesting given the time gap of about 30 years between these surveys. The weekly and daily trip rates for vehicles in Atlanta and Copenhagen were about 15 per cent to 30 per cent higher in the (socio-economically unweighted)

4 Gamma distribution obtains the highest score in probability-distribution fitting using XPERTFIT (Law and Kelton 1999).

Table 11.2 Trips per week (details for Figure 11.11)

Survey	Mean	Std.
All trips		
Uppsala	24.2	11.3
Mobidrive	24.4	8.8
Thurgau	28.2	9.2
Car trips by regular car drivers		
Uppsala	19.2	9.8
Mobidrive	19.9	6.8
Thurgau	22.3	8.4
GPS car trips		
Borlänge	19.2	8.9
Copenhagen	25.9	11.0
Atlanta	22.5	9.9

GPS data compared to those of regular car drivers[5] in the travel-diary data. The difference in numbers was caused by the exact capturing of short car trips. In Borlänge, for example, the average distance travelled per trip was only 3.8 km, while the average trip duration was about six minutes. In Mobidrive – with an admittedly larger local survey area – the corresponding figures were 21 minutes and 13 kilometres. For Copenhagen the average trip duration was under 15 minutes, which is short considering the size of the greater Copenhagen area. In principle, one must assume the trip rates in the GPS observations to be even higher than shown, since the ad hoc cleaning procedure erases (probably too) many potentially correct short-duration trips (see Chapter 6 on data). The relatively low Borlänge GPS trip rates are an exception, as both the cleaning approach and the systematic underreporting of out-of-area trips bias the number of trips downwards.

5 For the travel-diary survey data, respondents who made more than 50% of their trips by car are considered "regular car drivers". This subsample acts as a comparison group for the GPS observations.

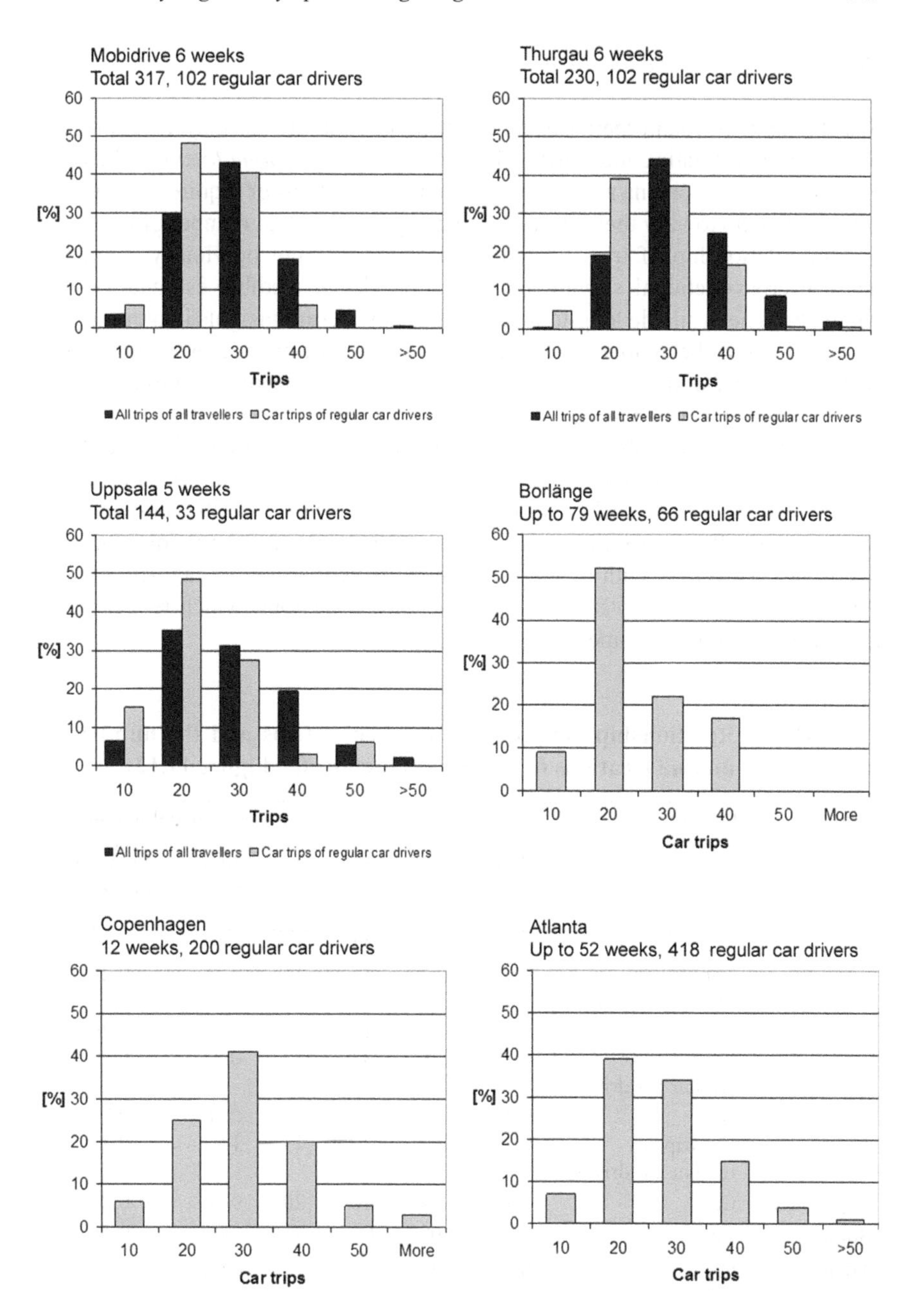

Figure 11.11 Mean number of trips per week (based on unweighted samples): Distributions by mode

Ratio of trips to unique locations

Stability and its counterpart *variability* in destination choice may be expressed by several interrelating indicators. The *ratio of trips to unique locations* helps to explain these phenomena as it shows individual aspirations or requirements which cause travellers to vary their location choices given a certain number of trips.

The relationship of trips to unique locations was not previously examined because cross-sectional surveys could not provide a credible estimate of this parameter. The available long-term travel data now permit insights into this aspect of spatial-choice behaviour. If the number of unique locations grows consistently with the number of trips, then variety seeking for its own sake becomes a credible explanation for those choices.

Figure 11.12 and Table 11.3 represent the ratios for the travel-diary data sets analysed here. Interestingly, the means are similar in spite of differences in the survey techniques and backgrounds. The average ratio for the travel-diary data varies marginally, approaching about three or four trips to one unique location over time[6]. Travellers with regular or even permanent access to cars and regular car use showed a more variable location-choice behaviour, which reflects their greater opportunities in time and space.

Table 11.3 Relationship between the number of trips and the number of unique locations in all surveys (details for Figure 11.12)

Scatter trend line (incept set to 0)				Unique locations: Distributions			
		Slope	R^2	Mean	Std.	Skewness	Mean ratio of locations to trips
Mobidrive	All	0.23	0.55	34	16	0.70	0.24
	Car trips by regular car drivers	0.27	0.63	31	15	0.78	0.27
Thurgau	All	0.26	0.46	41	19	0.88	0.26
	Car trips by regular car drivers	0.29	0.56	37	17	0.84	0.29
Uppsala	All	0.27	0.51	34	16	0.96	0.30
	Car trips by regular car drivers	0.29	0.62	29	15	1.93	0.32
Copenhagen	Car	0.19	0.34	46	20	0.76	0.24
Borlänge	Car	0.07	0.00	69	31	0.69	0.13
Atlanta	Car	0.14	0.47	148	77	0.95	0.17

6 This figure turns out to be the same for the travel-diary data if the trips are stratified by mode of transport.

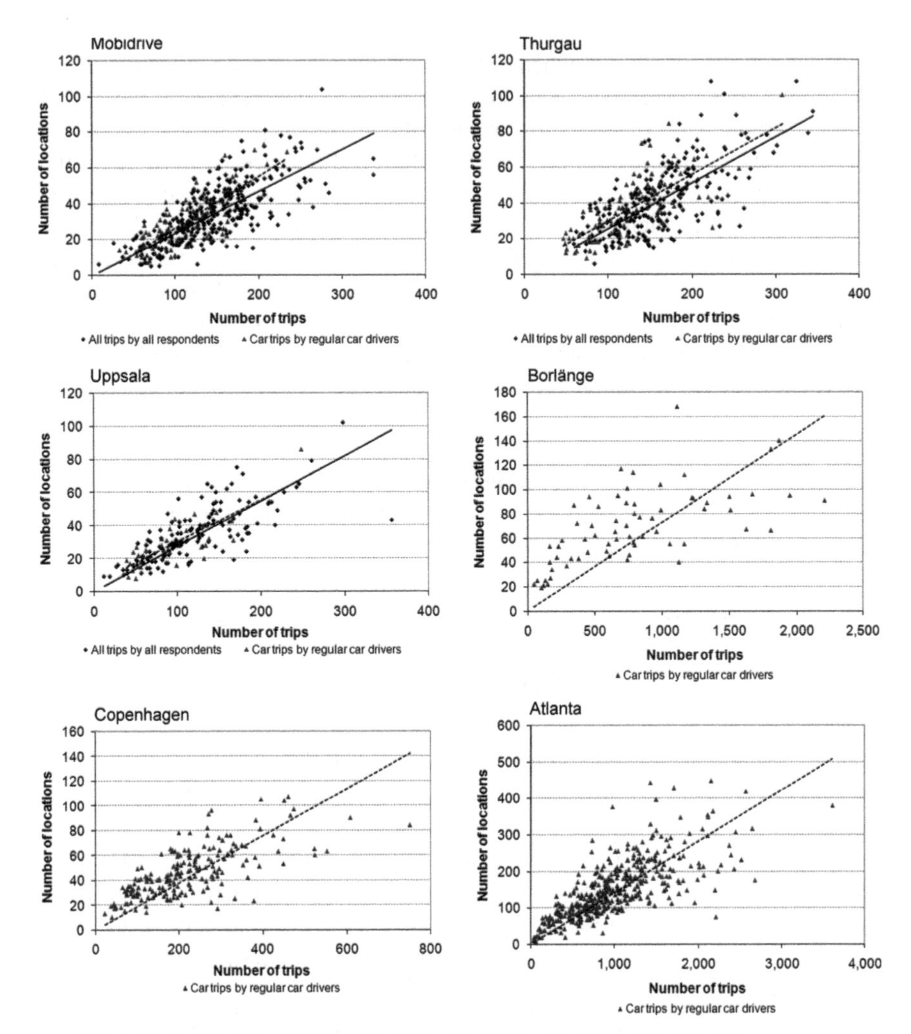

Note: Dark line = trend line for all trips and locations (for Mobidrive, Thurgau and Uppsala only); dotted trend line = trend line for car trips and locations of regular car drivers (all data sets).

Figure 11.12 Relationship between the number of trips and the number of unique locations

The GPS results deviate slightly from these results, indicating that the parameters of the cleaning and clustering processes used to identify unique locations need to be reconsidered for the observed trip ends. In all three cases, the parameters chosen for the clustering (i.e., radius = 200 m) seem to have been too large, as too few unique locations could be identified. Furthermore, the chosen cleaning thresholds clearly contributed to a misrepresentation of unique locations. Finally, the number of unique locations is smaller as trip purpose was not inputed.

An interesting question is whether these ratios can be explained by the survey background and/or the socio-economic attributes of the travellers. Table 11.4 shows a stratification of the ratio for out-of-home travel[7] per survey and a few selected socio-economic attributes. First of all, few differences are visible for the overall averages between the Mobidrive and the Thurgau results (0.40 unique locations per trip), which is in line with the values shown in Table 11.3. However, the socio-economic groups behaved differently in the two surveys: Whereas the ratios for the groups in the Mobidrive survey are generally homogenous, the Thurgau survey shows far more distinct differences. In the Mobidrive survey, the values for the elderly and the self-employed are above average, indicating a greater discretionary flexibility for the retired and an imposed flexibility on those who run

Table 11.4 Ratio between the number of unique places reported and the number of trips made over the six-week reporting period: Out-of-home travel only (Mobidrive [MD]/Thurgau [TH] surveys)

Attribute (N MD/TH)	Minimum				Mean (Std.)		Median	
Survey	MD	TH	MD	TH	MD	TH	MD	TH
All	0.12	0.12	1.00	0.78	0.41 (0.13)	0.41 (0.13)	0.40	0.40
Gender:								
Male (158/117)	0.13	0.13	0.68	0.12	0.41 (0.13)	0.41 (0.13)	0.39	0.39
Female (159/113)	0.10	0.13	1.00	0.18	0.41 (0.14)	0.42 (0.13)	0.40	0.40
Age group:								
<18 (60)	0.11	0.12	0.68	0.52	0.40 (0.12)	0.32 (0.09)	0.41	0.32
18-35 (61)	0.21	0.20	1.00	0.63	0.39 (0.12)	0.40 (0.09)	0.38	0.39
36-65 (171)	0.10	0.18	0.68	0.76	0.41 (0.14)	0.44 (0.13)	0.40	0.44
>65 (25)	0.17	0.34	1.00	0.78	0.46 (0.15)	0.54 (0.13)	0.45	0.52
Occupational status:								
Pupil (55/49)	0.13	0.12	0.74	0.52	0.41 (0.12)	0.32 (0.09)	0.41	0.33
Student (12/9)	0.16	0.36	0.54	0.63	0.34 (0.13)	0.45 (0.08)	0.33	0.45
Apprentice (11/11)	0.24	0.22	0.67	0.42	0.42 (0.13)	0.30 (0.07)	0.42	0.31
Homemaker (12/25)	0.20	0.20	0.55	0.69	0.39 (0.12)	0.47 (0.13)	0.40	0.49
Retired (53/20)	0.22	0.35	1.00	0.78	0.44 (0.14)	0.56 (0.12)	0.42	0.53
Unemployed (21/1)	0.20	0.36	0.63	0.36	0.41 (0.12)	0.36 (-)	0.42	0.35
Part-time work (29/-)	0.10		1.00		0.41 (0.16)		0.39	
Full-time work* (111/115)	0.11	0.18	0.79	0.76	0.39 (0.13)	0.43 (0.12)	0.39	0.42
Self-employed (13/-)	0.29		0.72		0.46 (0.12)		0.43	

* The Thurgau survey data does not differentiate between full- and part-time work.

7 Note that by nature the ratios for out-of-home travel are substantially higher than those capturing all trips (including home-directed ones).

their own businesses. The Thurgau data yield the same results for the elderly. Interestingly, the data sets show a greater discrepancy for younger respondents. In the Mobidrive survey, students were less spatially flexible than the average traveller, but in the Thurgau survey it was the other way around. As most of the students based in Thurgau were forced to travel long distances to universities in Zürich, St. Gallen or even farther away, their activity spaces were obviously more dispersed and variable than those of their counterparts from the big cities of Halle and Karlsruhe (Mobidrive survey). German students often live close to their universities in student accommodations or shared flats. Thurgau pupils by contrast were less flexible, which mirrors the concentration of their travel between home and school. Finally, homemakers in Thurgau tended to be more spatially flexible than the average traveller. This indicates that their travel behaviour was less tied to one main activity purpose (such as work or school), which would have attracted many trips to only one or a few unique locations.

Given the differences in the survey lengths, an exact comparison of these ratios (or any other indicators) between the surveys is non-trivial. While it is straightforward to compare averages such as the mean daily trip rate or the mean daily distance per person, one needs to be cautious with direct comparisons of the variability indicators in spatial choice if the lengths of the observation periods

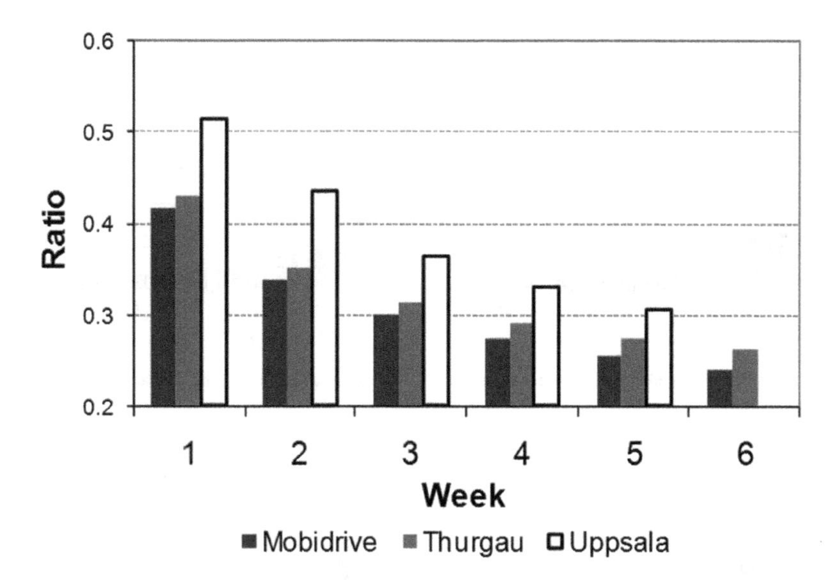

Figure 11.13 Mean ratio of the number of trips and number of unique locations over the course of the travel-diary survey periods

differ. In principle, stability might be less visible if a person is observed for only a few weeks (such as in Uppsala) compared to long-duration surveys such as Atlanta with a monitoring period of one year or longer. Figure 11.13 depicts the development of the ratio between unique locations and trips over time for the travel-diary data sets. As might be expected, the ratio decreased over time as regular visits to places of daily life became more important over the course of the survey period. Hence, after only a few weeks the ratio became dominated by frequently visited locations such as the workplace rather than by "novel" places that had not been observed before (see the discussion and analysis further in this chapter). However, the analysis in this book shows that after a sufficiently long

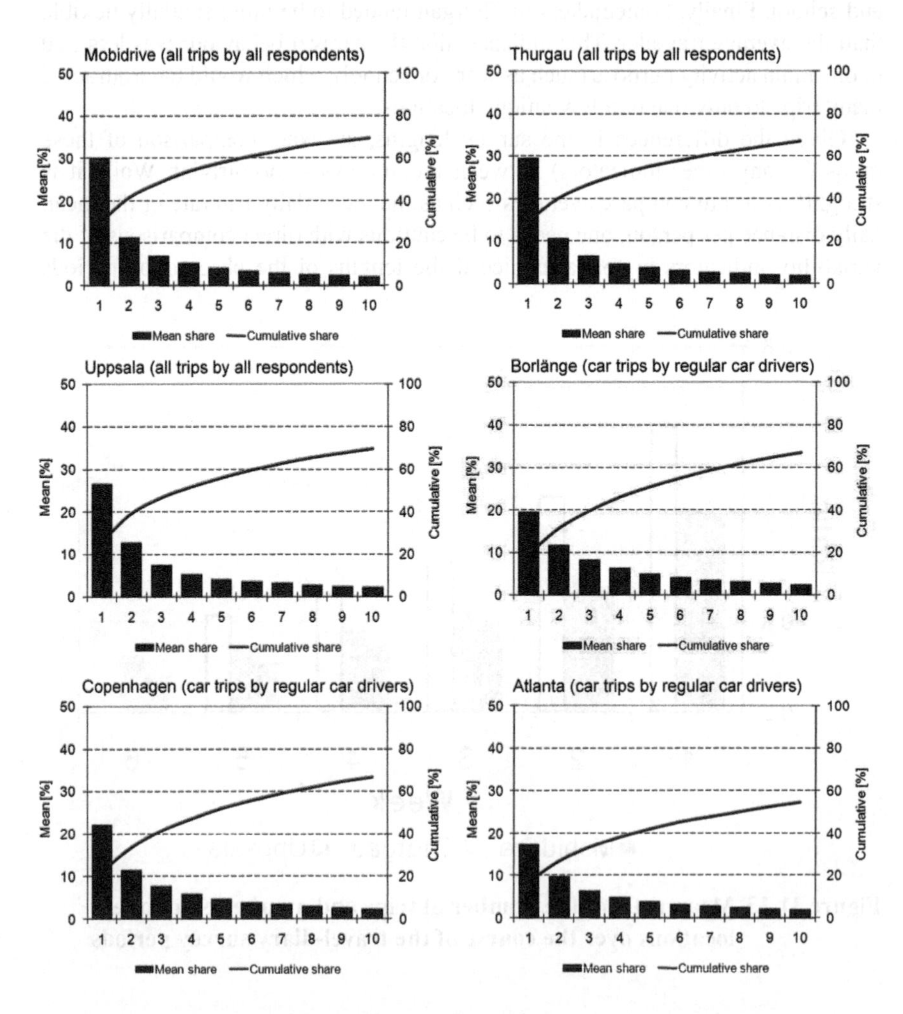

Figure 11.14 Mean shares of trips to the ten most-frequented locations (excluding home)

observation period (of about two to four weeks), the ratio approaches a fixed value of approximately one location to four trips, which seems to be typical of daily travel.

Concentration of trips in a few locations

Although most people seem to have many places to visit for different activities, this does not mean that each place is visited with the same frequency. People tend to *concentrate* their travel on a small number of locations for particular activities within a given observation period. For the purposes of methodology and planning, it would be interesting to know how many locations are necessary to describe a substantial part of a person's travel behaviour.

Figure 11.14 shows the average shares of trips to the ten most important unique locations identified (excluding home). The cumulative share of these first ten locations was about 80 per cent of all trips in the travel-diary surveys and from 40 per cent to 60 per cent of all trips in the GPS observations. This result confirms the notion that daily life notably concentrates on only a few places over longer periods–which is logical, considering that work or education obligations dominate daily activity and travel patterns for working people and students (Table 11.5).

Another interesting question is how the most important places may be categorized in terms of duration and distance. Figure 11.15 indicates that the most important destination (apart from home) naturally absorbs the greatest share of activity duration, whereas its trip-distance and trip-duration shares are generally less than its visiting-frequency average (compared to all trips made). Given that the

Table 11.5 Five most important trip purposes by occupational status and location (Thurgau)

	Pupil		**Student**		**Apprentice**		**Working**		**Home-maker**		**Retiree**		**Unemployed**	
	Purpose	**Share**	**Purpose**	**Share**	**Purpose**	**Share**	**Purpose**	**Share**	**Purpose**	**Share**	**Purpose**	**Share**	**Purpose**	**Share**
1	SE	98	SE	44	SE	45	WO	76	GR	44	LE	70	LE	100
2	LE	71	LE	44	SE	64	LE	48	LE	32	GR	45	LE	100
3	LE	96	LE	44	LE	55	LE	46	GR	40	GR	45	LE	100
4	LE	80	LE	56	LE	45	LE	35	LE	44	GR	40	GR	100
5	LE	80	LE	44	LE	55	LE	43	LE	40	LE	70	SP	100
N	49		9		11		115		25		20		1	

LE = Leisure, SE = School/education, WO = Work, GR = Grocery shopping, SP = Serving passengers.

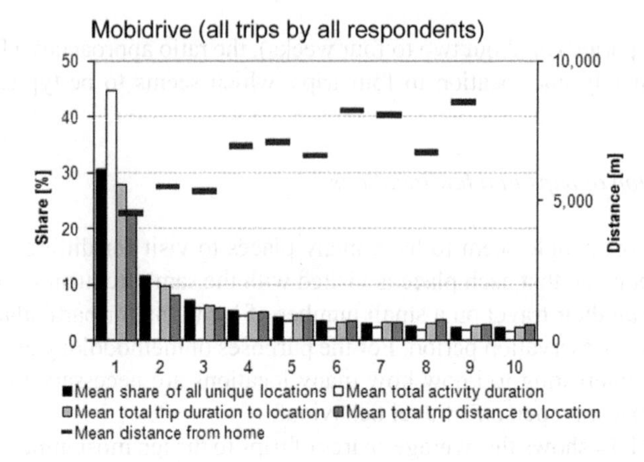

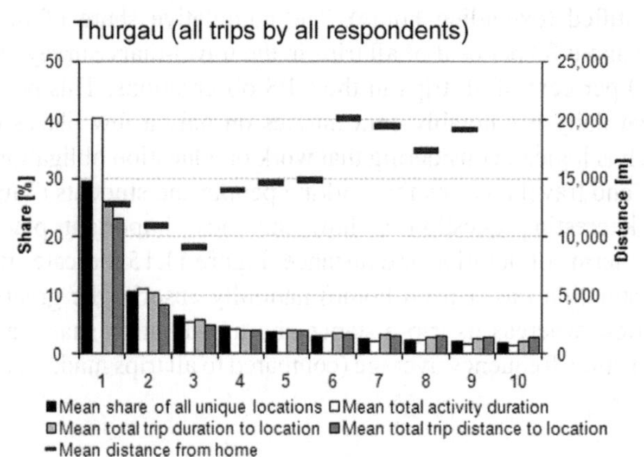

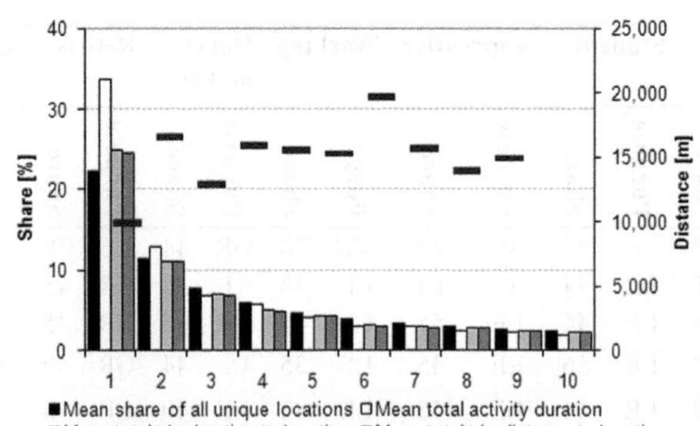

Figure 11.15 Mean shares of trips to the ten most frequented locations (excluding home): Distances and durations

most important location is related to an obligatory activity, this result is intuitive. Another general trend is that the average distance from travellers' home locations increases when the importance of the location decreases. This already provides insight into the structure of activity space: There are higher activity densities around home locations and lower densities at the edges of activity space. The finding suggests that distance decay remains a predominant motive in travellers' day-to-day destination choices in spite of advanced transport systems and a large degree of unlimited car availability.

Variety seeking and "innovation" in travel behaviour

Earlier analyses of the temporal aspects of travel using the Mobidrive data have shown that there is great regularity in individual travel behaviour, but also substantial variability (see, e.g., Schlich 2004 for a use of the Mobidrive data). The question remains whether this is also true for the locations visited. In other words, do people limit the number of places they know and visit? *Variety seeking* is a likely motive for travellers to "discover" novel or previously unvisited places over a certain time period. An initial means to reveal this trend is to identify every previously unobserved location over the course of the observation period.

The graph in Figure 11.16 shows the average number of additional "new" locations per day during the survey periods. It seems that people know or need to discover an almost unlimited number of places, because even after many weeks there were still places people travelled to for the first time.

The GPS observations show long-term averages of about 0.2 (Borlänge survey) to 1.5 (Atlanta survey) additional previously unobserved locations per week. The real value is probably closer to the higher range (1 to 1.5 new locations per week), as the Borlänge results refer only to the rather limited observation area of the Borlänge study.

Of course, the term "new" or "novel" location is a misnomer, as people visit some activity locations very infrequently, for example the dentist's office. Such locations are not genuinely new or previously unknown. In the two Swiss surveys

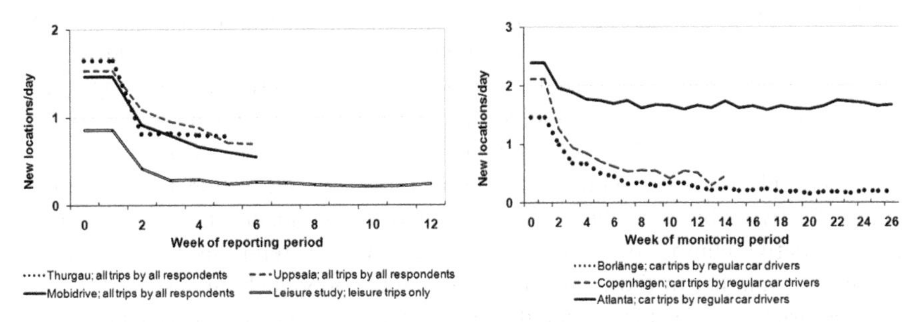

Figure 11.16 Comparison of studies: Mean number of new locations per day of survey (home excluded)

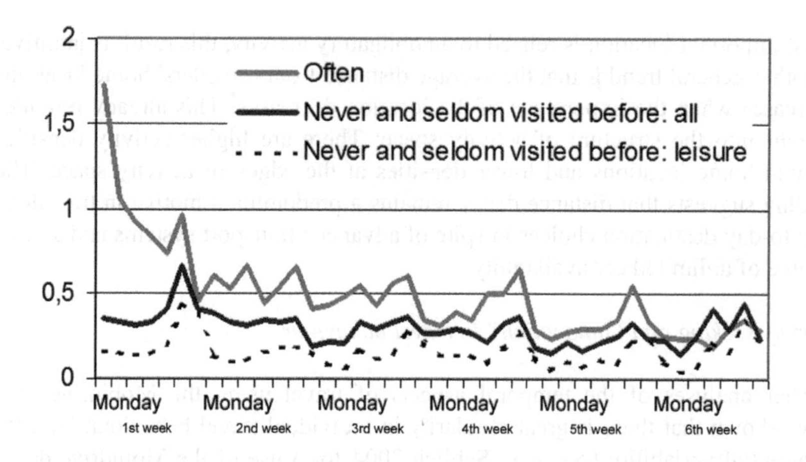

Figure 11.17 Mean number of previously unobserved locations per day and mobile person, and share of actual visiting frequency: Thurgau data

used in the analysis of this book (Thurgau and the Leisure Study), the respondents were asked if they had ever visited a place before, and if yes, how often. Compared to detecting previously unobserved places, this information yielded a more reliable indicator of innovation and variety seeking.

While most of the "added" locations shown in Figure 11.16 were not genuinely new, there were a steady number of truly new, never previously visited locations. In the Thurgau data (Figure 11.17), the mean of these is 0.3 locations per day (Std.: 0.1) for all days and purposes over the six-week reporting period. Saturdays show an even higher mean with 0.42 novel places visited (Std.: 0.13), while Sundays yielded a lower average than all weekdays with 0.26 new locations (Std.: 0.08).

Leisure travel especially contributed to the number of new locations discovered over time. On average, 53 per cent of all previously never- or seldom-visited locations were leisure destinations (dotted line in Figure 11.17). Our analysis of the Leisure Study produced similar results (Figure 11.18). The mean for genuinely new locations (defined by post code and purpose) per day and person added over the twelve-week reporting period was 0.37 (Std.: 0.18). From a more aggregate perspective, about 10 per cent of all leisure places visited during the survey period were previously unknown to the respondents (Figure 11.18, bottom).

Figure 11.19 shows another interesting aspect of innovation in destination choice for two arbitrarily chosen Thurgau survey respondents. The graphs depict the cumulative number of all locations visited over the reporting period and the cumulative number of those locations which were previously unobserved. It can now be assumed that the higher the share of previously unobserved locations, the greater the desire (or need) of the traveller to vary destination choice. The

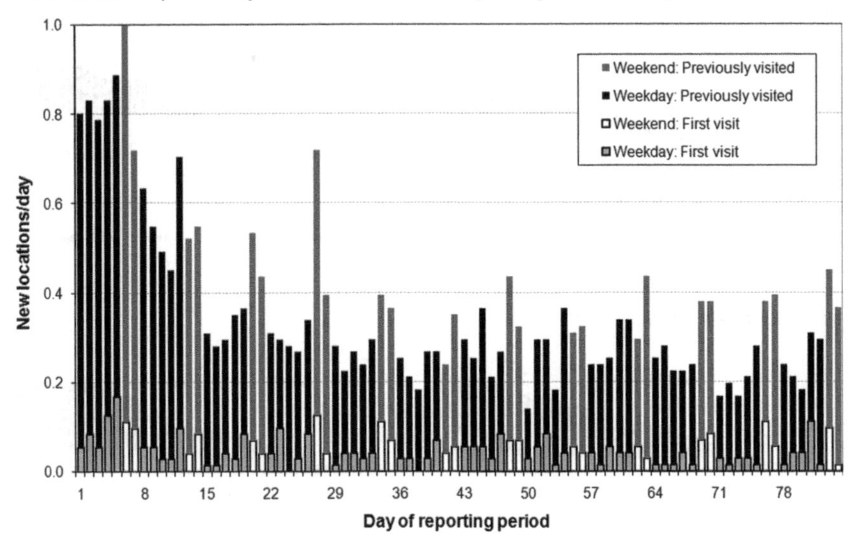

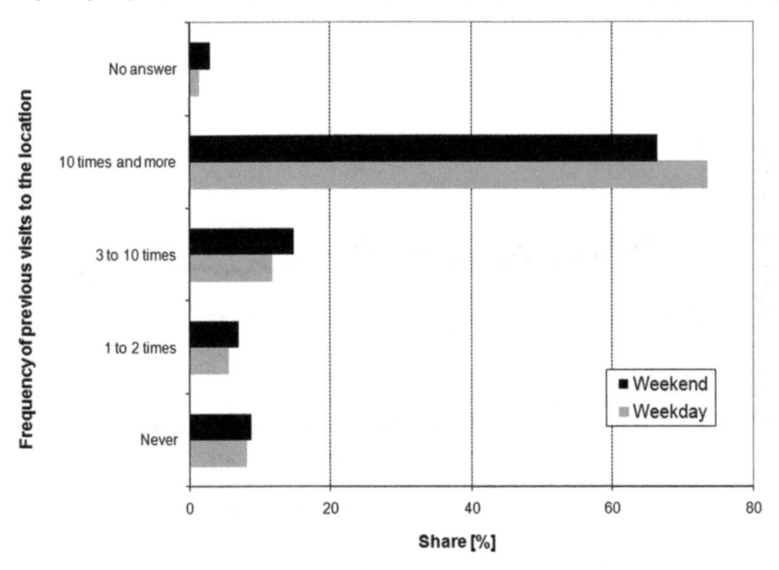

Figure 11.18 Innovation in location choice: Leisure study results

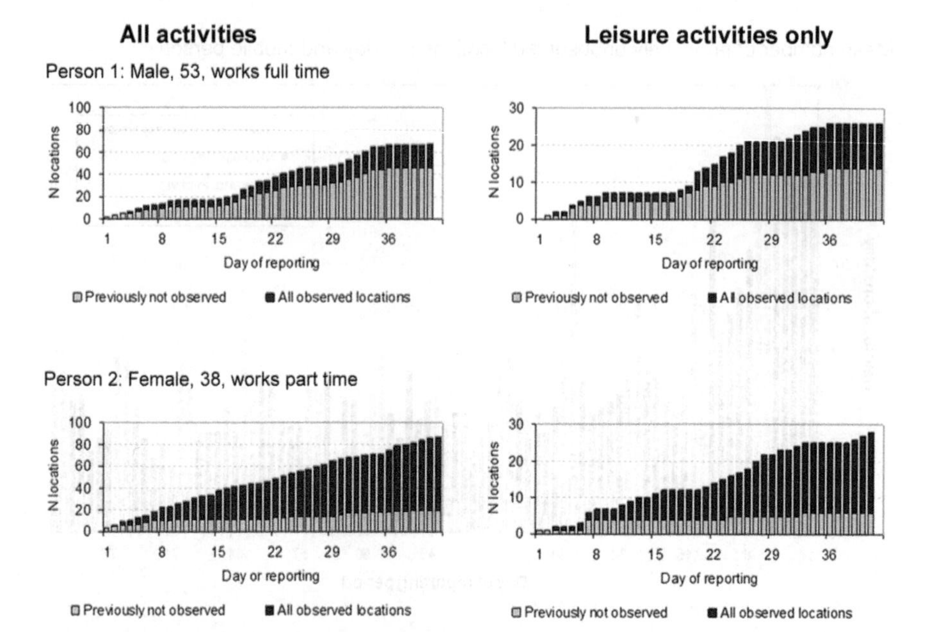

Figure 11.19 Individual characteristics of variety seeking in location choice: Two examples (Thurgau sample)

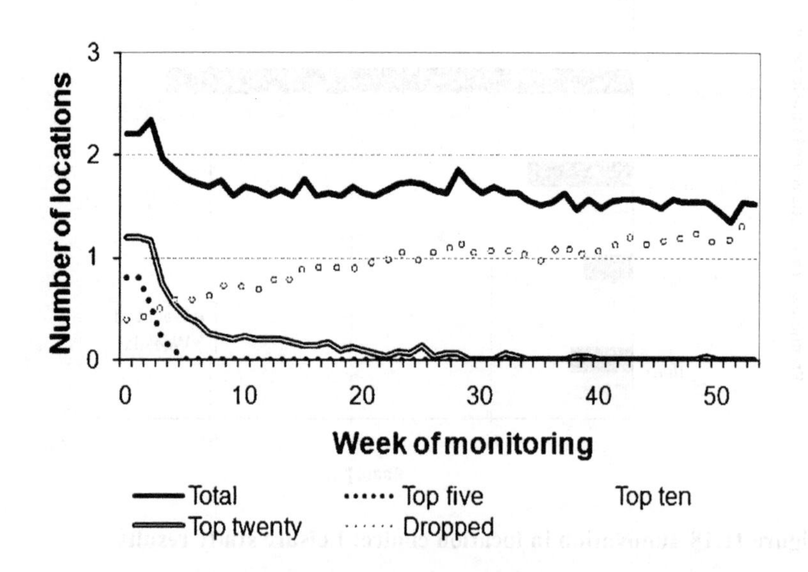

Figure 11.20 Number of "new", previously unobserved locations per monitoring day, by week of monitoring (Atlanta survey)

two respondents showed substantially different "innovative behaviour": the male traveller displayed much greater flexibility than the female traveller (bottom).

The results for previously never observed or visited locations raise the question of whether these "new" or at least unobserved places were then added to the travellers' personal standard destination repertoire. The desire to search for new places does not necessarily mean that those places will be built into a person's daily activity space. However, this issue can not be addressed explicitly, as the respondents were not asked to provide such information. Evidence of "*binding effects*" in destination choice may nevertheless be gained by listing:

- the total number of locations not previously observed;
- the number of locations which were added to a predefined standard locations repertoire; and
- those locations which were visited only once in the reporting period ("dropped places").

Figure 11.20 shows the resulting evidence gained from the Atlanta GPS observations. The standard sets represent the 5, 10 and 20 most-visited places over the total monitoring period. Unsurprisingly, the average share of places dropped increased steadily over time. Clearly, few new places became regularly visited destinations. However, the results also indicate that the standard destination repertoire of a traveller becomes apparent after just a few weeks, which is interesting in terms of future survey-design procedures. In other words, it takes about five to ten weeks of monitoring to gain relative certainty about individual destination-choice preferences. Given the complexity of daily life, this is a fairly short reporting period.

Dispersion of locations visited

The level of *dispersion* of locations visited and, in consequence, the *development of activity-space sizes* over time can be shown by the following enumeration exercise: As a straightforward indicator of dispersion, we choose the average distance (as the crow flies) of the locations from home. Home is by far the most important centre of daily life and acts for most travellers as the hub for obligatory as well as discretionary travel (see, e.g., Ellegård and Villhelmson 2004). By calculating the individual mean distance of places from home, one obtains a general impression of the extent of an individual's activity space.

Consider two hypotheses regarding the *development of activity-space sizes over the reporting period*: First, "new" locations tend to be chosen farther away from home. This is especially true for locations related to variety seeking and leisure activities. Second, despite this trend, the temporal development of day-to-day activity-space size is rather stable given the set of time, space, speed and social coordination restrictions travellers face (Hägerstrand 1974).

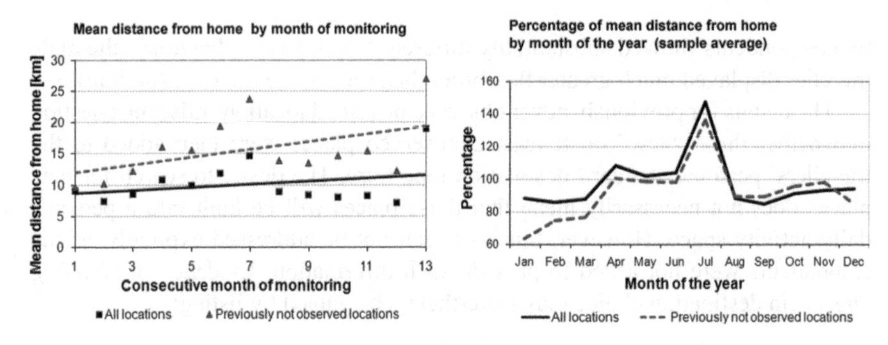

Figure 11.21 Development of activity-space size: Average distances of locations from home (Atlanta survey)

The Atlanta survey data show that these hypotheses can be confirmed at the aggregate level (Figure 11.21, left). The distance from home to previously unobserved places was substantially higher than to all locations visited. The average distance from home (whole sample) to previously unobserved locations even increased over the monitoring period (note the linear trend line with a slope of 0.61). However, the average distance to all locations from home remained more or less the same, with no visible increase in the spatial distribution of places.

A by-product of our analysis is an impression of how seasonality affects destination choice (Figure 11.21, right). If the monthly deviation of distance from home is calculated from the yearly mean, we find that the spring and summer months yield a significantly more dispersed choice of locations than the other months of the year – again, an indication of variety seeking in spatial behaviour. This is true for previously unobserved locations as well as for the total of all places visited. The spatial distribution of destinations will be analysed in more detail later in this chapter by examining the measurements of continuous space use.

Clustering activities at nearby locations

Another interesting location choice issue is whether travellers *cluster* their activities at subcentres of their activity space, and if so, to what extent. Destination choice is assumed to be determined by the needs, obligations and fixed commitments of travellers who therefore satisfy their activity demand at a few focal points of daily life. In order to minimize travel times and distances, people tend to group their activities at a few places of spatial proximity and density, which may be in the vicinity of home or other pegs of daily travel.

Table 11.6 shows that a large majority of the survey respondents behaved this way. Given a rather rough definition of a cluster (i.e., a common catchment radius of 1,000 m distance as the crow flies, a minimum of 10 per cent of all trips directed to the cluster and at least three unique associated locations), most

Table 11.6 Share of survey respondents with spatial clusters (%)

Number of clusters	0	1	2	3	4	Median	Mean	Std.
Mobidrive all (317)	13	42	38	6	0	1	1.4	0.8
Car trips by regular car drivers (102)	29	44	22	4	1	1	1.0	0.9
Thurgau all (230)	9	45	36	10	0	1	1.5	0.8
Car trips by regular car drivers (102)	29	39	25	6	0	1	1.1	0.9
Uppsala all (144)	3	31	50	14	2	2	1.8	0.8
Car trips by regular car drivers (33)	6	33	21	36	3	2	2.0	1.0
Copenhagen (200)	12	36	33	18	2	2	1.6	1.0
Atlanta (418)	11	34	40	13	2	2	1.6	0.9
Borlänge (66)	2	23	39	30	6	2	2.2	0.9

Note: Clusters were defined by a catchment radius of 1,000 m, a minimum of 10% of all trips to the cluster and a minimum of three unique associated locations.

Table 11.7 Internal structure of activity spaces: Activity-cluster cores

Purpose	Mobidrive survey all	Mobidrive survey full-time workers	Thurgau survey all	Thurgau survey full-time workers	Uppsala survey all	Uppsala survey full-time workers
Home	55	57	43	42	44	44
Leisure	12	11	14	10	12	12
Work	11	24	15	22	18	25
School	8	1	8	11	0	1
Daily shopping	6	4	9	5	19	12
Private business	5	0	3	1	2	1
Long-term shopping	1	1	0	1	1	0
Serving passengers	1	1	4	4	2	3
Work-related	1	0	4	4	0	0
Other	0	1	0	0	2	2

Note: Results only available for travel-diary data, as trip purposes have not yet been imputed for GPS observations.

of the travellers had at least one such distinct centre of daily life[8]. The statistics provide some indication that the number of clusters is larger for respondents from smaller places (Borlänge, Uppsala), which indicates the greater compactness and better accessibility of towns in contrast to bigger cities. In addition, the number clearly increased slightly over the course of the reporting period. However, this

8 The clusters were generated using a nearest-centroid sorting cluster method (Anderberg 1973) which is implemented in the SAS software package.

might have been biased by the GPS data-cleaning procedure, which did not return the real number of unique locations. Nevertheless, the total number of clusters never exceeded five, even after fifty or more weeks of monitoring such as in the Borlänge and Atlanta studies.

Using the same definition of clusters, it becomes clear that activity clusters evolve to a large extent around the home location. This again confirms the importance of home for travellers' activity patterns. In the Mobidrive study, more than half of all cluster centres (i.e., the cores defined by the most important locations in terms of visiting frequency), were home; other activity purposes were of lesser importance (Table 11.7). There is no indication that the workplace and its surrounding area played a significant role in combining work and the rest of the spectrum of activities to form distance-minimizing clusters.

If home is such a central anchor of daily life, it is interesting to explore which other activities were performed within walking distance from that point, and how intensely. Table 11.8 shows that for the Mobidrive (Karlsruhe) study, a large share of inner-urban daily travel took place within a radius of 1,000 m from home (as the crow flies): 70 per cent of all observed walking trips fell within this class of distance. Even considering the great diversity of the respondents (see large standard deviations) and differences between the infrastructural quality of their home vicinities, their recreational, private business and shopping activities were generally tied to home. There were differences between the various socio-economic groups regarding the degree of close-to-home activity performance (Rindsfüser, Perian, and Schönfelder 2001, 98 ff.). Whereas less mobile persons such as pupils and the unemployed made intensive use of the home's surrounding area for leisure activities, highly mobile persons such as the self-employed and students tended to have significantly more dispersed location choices for leisure activities. Table 11.8 also shows that the vicinity of the workplace apparently absorbed only a few daily trips, especially for leisure activities and daily shopping.

As mentioned, whereas the travellers' homes acted as an important anchor of daily life, there was significant variability between the Mobidrive respondents. This was clearly due in part to differences in the quality and supply of shopping and other opportunities around particular home locations. Exact information about the supply of opportunities and the infrastructural quality of travellers' home areas is still difficult to obtain in travel-survey settings. Fortunately, in the case of the Mobidrive study it was possible to obtain selected geocoded point-of-interest data for Karlsruhe using ordinary Yellow Pages business addresses and a geocode engine for digitalization. The data set covers about three thousand leisure, shopping and administrative locations in the Karlsruhe area. Using this data set and general information about the population density of the vicinity of the home locations as indicators for the level of supply, a significant relationship was determined between supply and demand for daily shopping (Table 11.9). The number of shopping trips within the home area (within a radius of 1,000 m) as well as shopping trips made by "slow modes" (walking and bicycling) increased with better shopping opportunities and higher population density. Even considering the

Table 11.8 Activity demand in the vicinity of home and workplace (maximum distance from the location: 1,000 m; Mobidrive, Karlsruhe sub-sample)

	Home							Workplace*						
	Respondents reporting the respective activity	Share (all activities of that type) [%]	Std.	Share duration [%]	Std.	Share expenditure [%]	Std.	Respondents reporting the respective activity	Share (all activities of that type) [%]	Std.	Share duration [%]	Std.	Share expenditure [%]	Std.
Private business: administrative	60	70	43	67	46	16	37	24	4	20	4	20	0	0
Group/club meeting	89	45	46	44	46	31	45	32	3	18	3	18	3	18
Daily shopping	149	47	32	40	34	43	37	59	13	22	13	23	12	23
Other	39	44	47	42	47	5	22	13	12	31	13	32	15	38
School	53	42	48	42	48	14	35	10	10	32	10	32	0	0
Private business: other	156	32	29	29	32	26	38	60	13	23	11	22	13	29
Walking or strolling	107	29	41	27	42	3	17	40	6	19	3	14	5	23
Meeting friends	146	26	32	22	30	4	19	57	3	9	2	7	0	0
Active sports	93	25	35	25	36	13	32	31	8	25	8	25	0	0
Serving passengers	110	24	35	21	36	6	22	42	11	26	9	24	3	17
Going out at night	137	18	28	17	28	15	31	54	13	25	11	22	10	22
Outing (cultural)	68	15	34	14	34	8	27	30	13	32	13	31	12	32
Long-term shopping	150	13	22	9	19	9	21	58	14	26	12	25	14	29
Work-related	68	13	30	13	31	4	16	36	24	36	21	37	12	32
Garden/cottage work	36	12	28	9	25	3	17	16		0	0	0	0	0
Meeting family	17	12	33	12	33	0	0	9	11	33	11	33	0	0
Window shopping	52	12	31	7	25	8	27	17	18	39	18	39	13	34
Work	82	11	30	11	30	4	20	61						
Further education	27	8	27	8	27	0	0	9	7	22	5	15	0	0
Nature excursion	68	4	21	4	21	0	0	25	1	7	0	0	0	0

* Only the group of respondents for whom the second most important location was the workplace.

Table 11.9 Pearson correlation coefficients between selected home-based shopping opportunities and shopping-trip demand (Mobidrive, Karlsruhe sub-sample)

	Number of shopping opportunities within a radius of 1,000 m from home	Share of shopping trips performed within a radius of 1,000 m from home	Share of shopping trips performed within a radius of 1,000 m from home by slow modes
Population density of home location vicinity (city block level)	0.64	0.26	0.26
Number of shopping opportunities within a radius of 1,000 m from home		0.26	0.27
Share of shopping trips performed within a radius of 1,000 m from home			0.83
N	149	149	149

All correlations shown are significant at the 0.05 level (two-tailed). Shopping opportunities included bakeries, butchers' shops, chemists' shops, local grocery stores and supermarkets.

initial character of this analysis, which should be deepened in more sophisticated destination-choice models, the trend seems clear and confirms the land-use policy approach of strengthening residential areas as centres of daily activity demand.

Continuous representation of activity spaces

The results of the continuous representation of space use will be presented in the order of concepts shown in this chapter: *confidence ellipses*, *kernel densities and shortest-path networks*. The results will be related to each other as well as to selected results of the enumeration exercise in order to reveal fundamental relationships.

Confidence ellipses

The pattern of activity-space sizes by the confidence ellipse measurement for all surveys follows a common trend[9] (Table 11.10 and Figure 11.22). In contrast to the

9 As the surveys originated from different spatial reference frames, the comparative analysis of the confidence ellipses will be limited to "local trips" where this appears necessary. Local trips are defined as trips not farther than 20 km from the home location (in the Mobidrive, Thurgau, Uppsala and Copenhagen studies); in the Borlänge study, all trips are considered

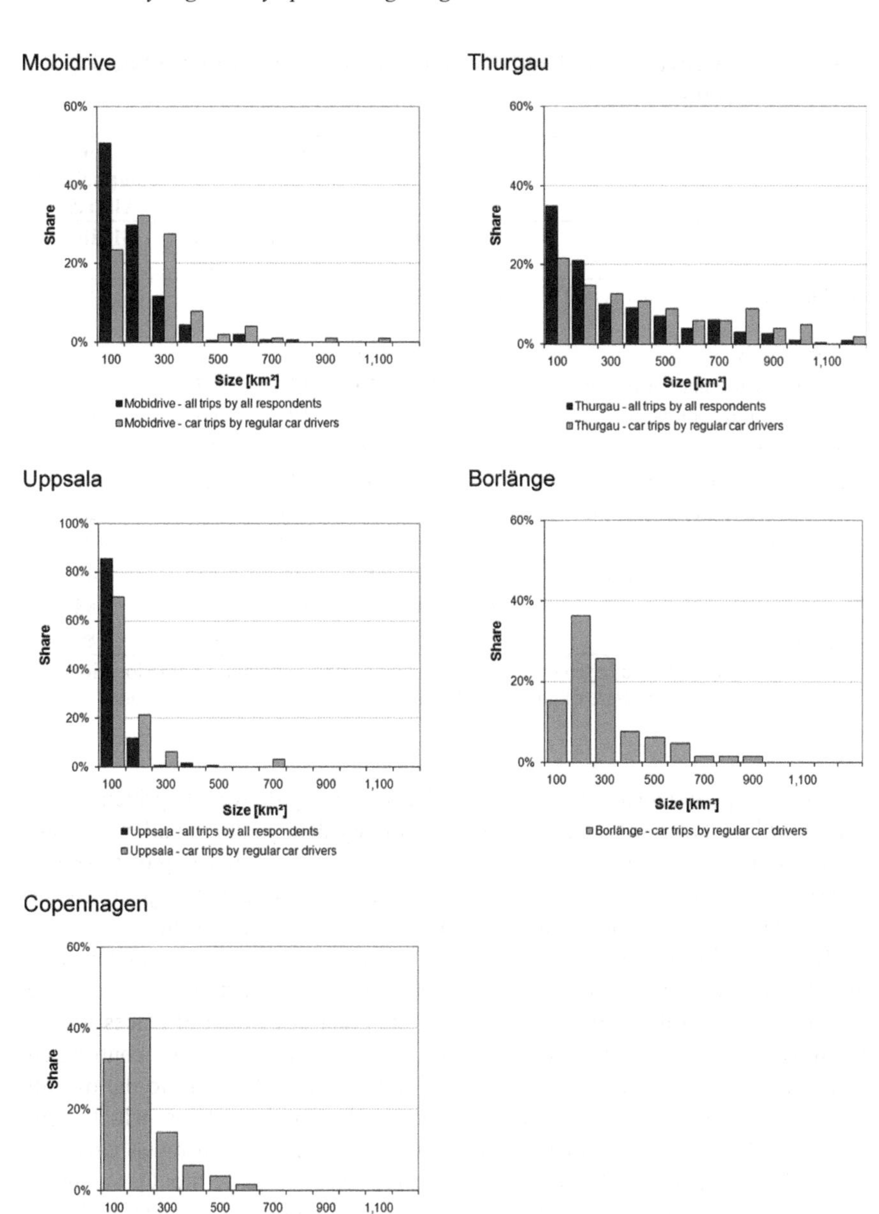

Note: 95% confidence ellipse based on local out-of-home trips; centroid = home location.

Figure 11.22 Distribution of activity-space sizes measured by confidence ellipses: Histograms

Table 11.10 Distribution of activity-space sizes measured by confidence ellipses

	Ellipse size* [km^2]					For comparison: All trips
Survey	**N**	**Mean**	**Std.**	**Median**	**Skewness**	**Median**
Mobidrive: All respondents / all trips	316	133	122	99	2.3	850
Car trips only	173	200	173	151	2.0	711
Car trips by regular car drivers**	99	212	169	177	2.3	1,009
Thurgau: All respondents / all trips	229	267	255	176	1.3	1,263
Car trips only	152	342	286	278	0.9	850
Car trips by regular car drivers**	102	382	297	311	0.7	987
Uppsala: All respondents / all trips	144	54	65	31	3.3	225
Car trips only	65	104	114	64	2.2	493
Car trips by regular car drivers**	32	94	112	69	3.5	643
Borlänge: Car trips	66	244	170	188	1.5	188
Copenhagen: Car trips	198	161	107	133	1.4	780

* 95% confidence ellipse based on local out-of-home trips; centroid = home location.
** Regular car drivers: Share of car trips (driving) exceeds 50% of all trips made.

number of trips and locations, the distribution is strongly skewed. In principle, this is true for both types of survey, i.e., the travel-diary data, including all modes and purposes, as well as the car-based GPS observations. A small group of travellers shows a very large dispersion of activity patterns, whereas the majority of the respondents' activity-space areas are below average (median < mean).

If the activity spaces are categorized or filtered by trip purpose, an interesting picture emerges: The medians for job-related and leisure-activity locations are far above the overall median, which shows the great dispersion of places visited for those purposes. Hence, leisure, with its large share of trips, contributed particularly heavily to the total dispersion of places and therefore to the overall size of the activity space. Shopping and private business locations, which were also visited with great regularity, were found to be distributed much closer to home, the centre of the ellipse and the assumed centre of daily life. Our analysis of activity clustering yielded similar results (see above in this chapter). It should be noted, however, that the informational value of Figure 11.23 has its limitations: The categories "work" and "school" were dropped as the ellipses could not be

"local trips" as monitoring was limited to the town of Borlänge and its surrounding area (20-km radius around the centre of town). Clearly, this ad hoc approach constrains the maximum size of the geometries, but it is acceptable for comparative purposes.

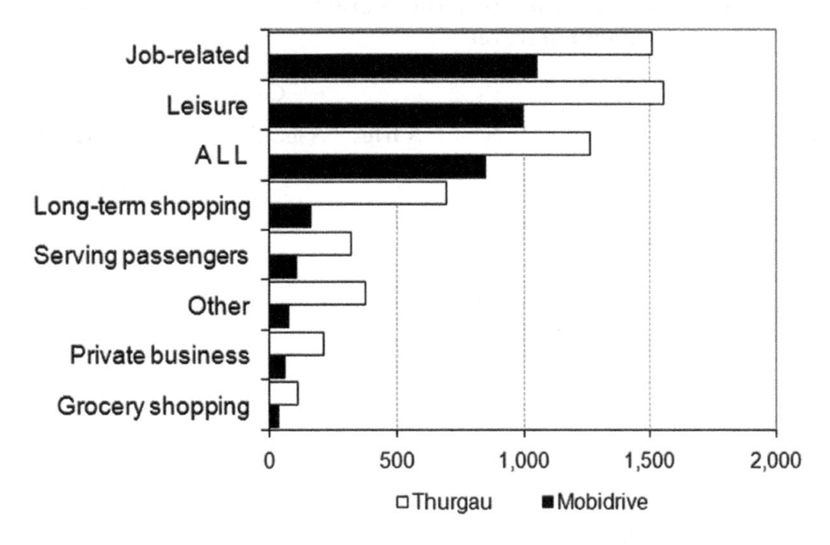

Note: All (!) out-of-home trips; 95% confidence ellipse; centroid = home location.

Figure 11.23 Median confidence-ellipse size by purpose: Mobidrive and Thurgau surveys

calculated if only one location was identified. This was especially necessary in the case of Thurgau, a rural region where many respondents had their workplace in the Zürich area, which might have been 50 km away from their home location.

The impact of a first set of determinants on the distributions remains inconclusive. Nevertheless, a few trends can be made out: First, activity space grew with the use (availability) of a car. The mean ellipse size of the activity space of regular drivers was higher than the overall sample average. This was to be expected and will be confirmed in the concluding analysis of variance (Table 11.10). Second, clustering activities in groups of nearby locations, as analysed in the enumeration section, had a slightly negative impact on the size of activity space (Table 11.11). This was also to be expected, as the confidence ellipse is by nature a measurement of dispersion. This finding is true for the all-mode analysis of the Mobidrive and Thurgau data with correlations of less than 0 between the ellipse size and the cumulative share of trips to the five most important locations. Finally, it is interesting that a significant negative correlation between the number of trips and the ellipse size could be found for GPS observations. (However, similar non-significant trends are observable for all other surveys and groups). The spatial concentration of activity patterns noticeably increases with the length of the observation period, which reflects the dominance of the few important poles of daily travel such as daily grocery shopping and travel to the workplace or school. This again is consistent

Table 11.11 Confidence ellipses: Basic characteristics and correlation with the amount of travel

		Correlations*		
Survey	**N**	**N trips**	**N locations**	**Concentration of trips in 5 locations****
Mobidrive: all respondents / all trips	316	-	-	-0.1
Car only	173	-	-	-
Car trips by regular car drivers	99	-	-	-
Thurgau: all respondents / all trips	229	-	-	-0.1
Car only	152	-	0.2	-
Car trips by regular car drivers	102	-	-	-
Uppsala: all respondents / all trips	144	-	-	-
Car only	65	-	-	-
Car trips by regular car drivers	32	-	-	-
Borlänge	66	-0.4	-	-0.4
Copenhagen	198	-0.2	-	-

Note: 95% confidence ellipse based on local out-of-home trips; centroid = home location.

* (Pearson) correlations shown are significant at the 0.05 level (two-tailed).

** Cumulative share of trips to the five most important locations.

with the findings of the enumeration exercise (see further above in this chapter). Nonetheless, the resulting correlations are relatively weak, which illustrates the ambiguity between concentration and the permanent (moderate) extension of a traveller's activity space, even though novel places never or only gradually gain the same importance as locations belonging to the standard activity-space repertoire.

One of advantages of the multimonth GPS observations is the possibility to compare the size of the activity spaces over extended periods. The stability of activity space has already been analysed for the Mobidrive study (Srivastava and Schönfelder 2003), but with no definite results for long-term stability. This was mainly due to the limited length of the reporting period, which did not allow sufficiently long continuous subperiods to be defined.

Such a comparison was possible for the Borlänge and the Copenhagen data sets. As a straightforward analysis approach, the monitoring period was divided into (non-overlapping) three-week intervals, and the sizes of the confidence ellipses were calculated. A period of two to three weeks was identified in earlier Mobidrive

Table 11.12 Correlation coefficients between selected activity-space characteristics of two consecutive (three-week) subperiods in the Borlänge and Copenhagen surveys

			"Last period"		
			Number of trips	**Number of unique locations**	**95% confidence ellipse, local trips**
"This period"	Number of trips	Borlänge	0.68		
		Copenhagen	0.60		
	Number of unique locations	Borlänge		0.62	
		Copenhagen		0.57	
	95% confidence ellipse, local trips	Borlänge			0.47
		Copenhagen			0.65
N (subperiods of monitoring)		Borlänge	862	862	862
		Copenhagen	451	451	451

Note: (Pearson) correlations shown are significant at the 0.05 level (two-tailed).

research as a relatively stable duration for studying the temporal phenomena of travel behaviour (Schlich and Axhausen 2003).

Investigation of the similarity of two consecutive subperiods shows that there was a remarkable degree of stability. On average, the indicators (number of trips, number of unique locations and activity-space size) correlated considerably for two consecutive periods: up to 0.68 (Table 11.12).

Kernel densities

Figure 11.24 illustrates the basic enumeration and calculation concept for measuring kernel density. For the first measurement (i.e., *number of cells* or *area covered*), the number of shaded cells which exceed a given density threshold (here: 0) are counted and, if necessary, multiplied by the chosen cell size. This yields the area which travellers presumably perceive, know or use.

The second measurement is the sum of all grid-cell values (here: 23), which may be interpreted as the *volume* of a three-dimensional surface representation, as in Figure 11.5.

To compare the density measure of activity space, we chose the following parameters for estimating and evaluating the kernel:

- Point-pattern base: Unique locations weighted by frequency of visits.
- Grid-cell size: 500 m by 500 m.
- Bandwidth of kernel function (search radius): 1,000 m.
- Threshold value for measuring the area covered: All cells with a kernel density greater than 0.

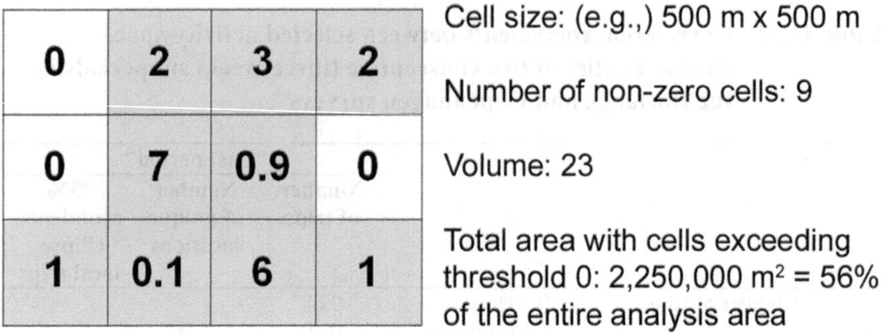

0	2	3	2
0	7	0.9	0
1	0.1	6	1

Cell size: (e.g.,) 500 m x 500 m

Number of non-zero cells: 9

Volume: 23

Total area with cells exceeding threshold 0: 2,250,000 m^2 = 56% of the entire analysis area

Figure 11.24 Enumeration and calculation of activity densities: Example

In order to obtain better comparability between the different surveys and different socio-economic groups, we determined the "search area", i.e., the area which contains the relevant places considered for analysis: The search area was defined as a square of 20 by 20 kilometres around the respective centre of the survey region (instead of a circle around the travellers' home locations, as for the ellipses). On average, this reduced the locations to be analysed by about 10 per cent to 20 per cent, which is within acceptable limits.

The distribution of the first measurement follows a gamma distribution similar to the distribution of the number of trips shown in Figure 11.25 and Table 11.13. Due to the different lengths of the observation periods, the mean differs considerably between the travel-diary data sets and the GPS observations, which is already an indication that the measurements depend on the amount of mobility observed. The Borlänge data show the highest cell-number and density means, which was to be expected due to the extremely long monitoring periods (for some vehicles up to fourteen months). This becomes especially obvious for the second sum of the kernel-densities measurement (Figure 11.26), in which the mean for Borlänge is seven to ten times higher than for the five- to six-week travel-diary data.

Again, one interesting question is whether the number of trips is a proxy for the size of the activity space represented by the kernel approach. Figure 11.27 relates the two different kernel density measurements to the number of trips, the number of unique locations, the number of days and finally, to each other. Clearly, there is a close link between the number of trips, the number of unique locations, the number of days and the size of the activity space. The underlying (significant) correlations are between 0.6 and 0.8, which is a stronger relationship than the link between the size of the confidence ellipse and the number of trips or locations (Table 11.11).

Finally, differentiation by day of the week accentuates this strong link between travel volumes and kernel density measurements. Figure 11.28 shows the analysis of this relationship for the two Mobidrive subsamples. Whereas the measure of activity space based on the number of non-zero cells peaked on Fridays and

Table 11.13 Distribution of activity-space sizes measured by kernel densities

Survey	N cells					Volume (in 10^3 units)				
	N	Mean	Std.	Median	Skewness	N	Mean	Std.	Median	Skewness
Mobidrive: all respondents / all trips	317	137	54	132	0.7	317	55	21	54	0.5
Car trips by regular car drivers	102	148	58	136	0.9	102	43	17	42	0.4
Thurgau: all respondents / all trips	230	147	73	134	1.1	230	57	23	54	0.6
Car trips by regular car drivers	102	162	74	145	0.9	102	46	20	45	0.6
Uppsala: all respondents / all trips	144	86	28	80	0.5	144	47	23	42	1.0
Car trips by regular car drivers	33	95	29	95	0.1	33	37	19	35	1.1
Borlänge	66	325	103	329	0.2	66	365	242	338	0.9
Copenhagen	199	256	92	248	0.4	199	89	54	82	1.0

Saturdays, there was a considerable decrease in the value of the volume measured from Friday through Sunday. This implies that the travel-intensity indicator (volumes) is somehow more frequency-sensitive than the measurement which represents the dispersion of places only. Hence, the dispersion aspect of activity space (i.e., the distribution of activity locations in space) was outweighed by the travellers' level of general mobility or level of activity performance at the particular destination per time unit.

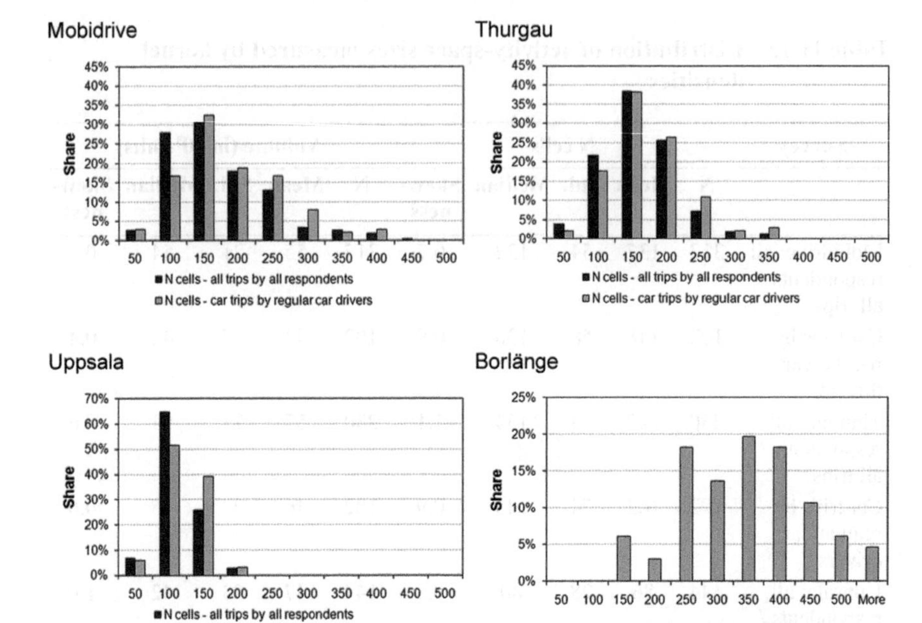

Copenhagen

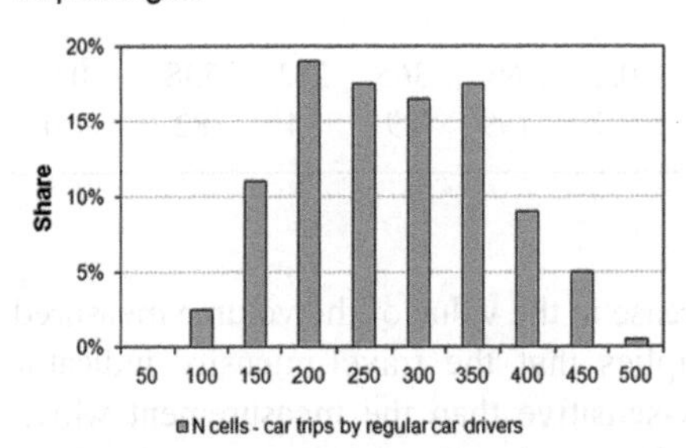

Figure 11.25 Distribution of activity-space sizes measured by kernel densities: Cells with positive kernel densities and their distribution

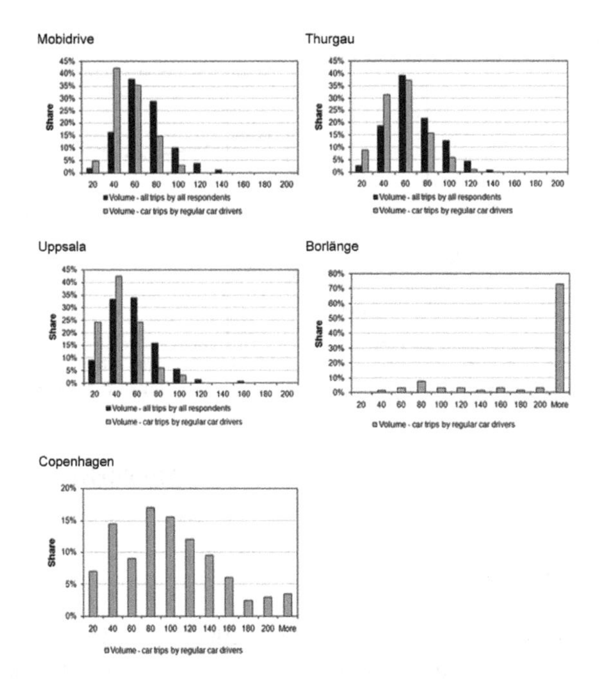

Figure 11.26 Distribution of activity-space sizes measured by kernel densities: Sum of kernel densities (volumes*10^3) and their distribution

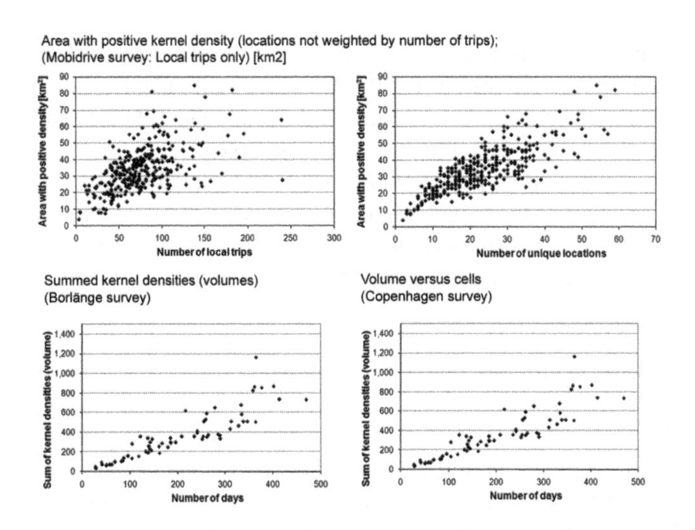

Figure 11.27 Activity space represented by kernel densities: Measures of activity space versus number of trips, number of unique locations visited, number of days and versus each other

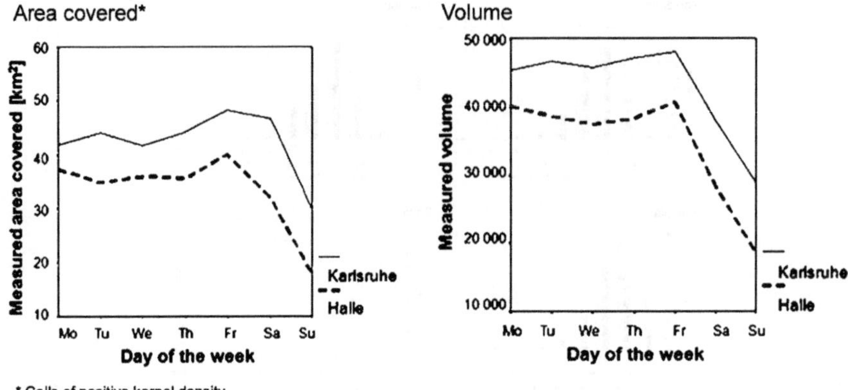

Figure 11.28 Kernel densities by day of the week (Mobidrive)

Shortest-path networks

In *shortest-path network* measurements, the length of the geometry is the focus of analysis. The measurement gives the sum of the lengths of all network links used. Due to missing network data for most of the surveys, measurements could only be generated for the Karlsruhe (Mobidrive) and Borlänge surveys. These encompass the link lengths of regional road networks. Note that the Karlsruhe results cover all purposes and modes, whereas the Borlänge survey yielded results for car trips only.

The Mobidrive sample again follows a gamma distribution. As the length of the monitoring period varied for the Borlänge respondents, the results were standardized by the number of monitored days in Figure 11.29. The Borlänge distribution is similar to that of the Mobidrive sample.

The size of the shortest-path networks is closely related to travel volumes and the spatial structure of the places visited. The measurement therefore reflects the dispersion of the activity pattern (Figure 11.30), which is in line with the outcome of the two other measurement approaches (confidence ellipses and kernel densities).

Activity-space size and personal characteristics

The distributions of the measures of activity-space shown in Figures 11.22, 11.26 or 11.29 indicate great variability in activity-space sizes among travellers and between the different surveys. However, many of the differences can simply be attributed to the amount of travel observed during the survey and monitoring period. Each of the measurements obviously correlates with the amount of travel, i.e., the number of trips made over the reporting period. This is especially true for the measure of travel volume (kernel densities), which resulted in an almost

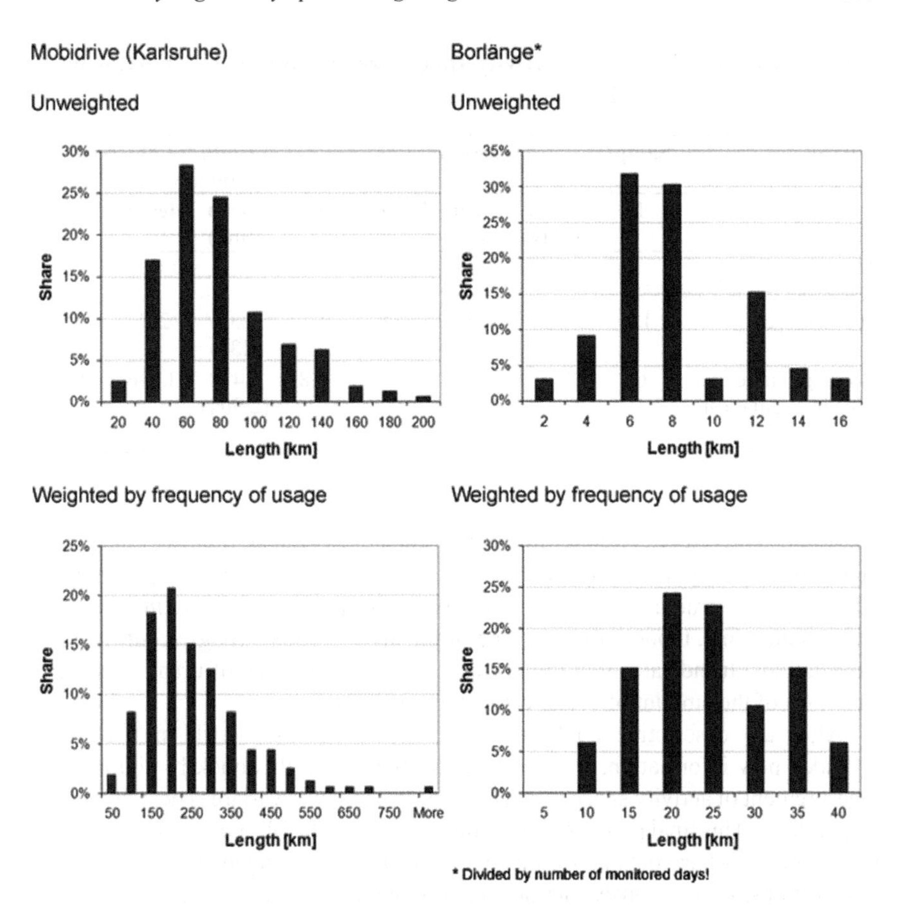

Figure 11.29 Distribution of activity-space sizes measured by shortest-path networks: Length of network used (km)

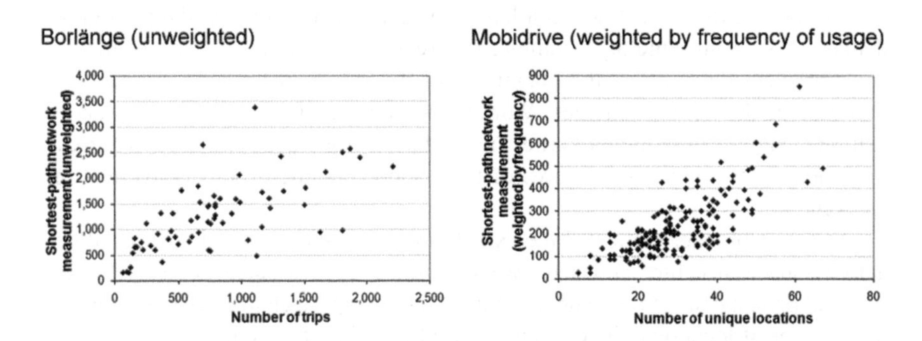

Figure 11.30 Shortest-path network measurement versus number of trips and number of unique locations

Table 11.14 Distribution of activity-space sizes measured by shortest-path networks (km)

Survey	Sample		Length			Length weighted by frequency		
	N	Mean N days	Mean (Std.)	Median	Skew.	Mean (Std.)	Median	Skew.
Mobidrive survey, Karlsruhe (all modes and purposes)	159	38	68 (34)	64	1.1	232 (131)	201	1.5
Borlänge survey (car trips by regular car drivers)	66	205	1,243 (669)	1.157	0.8	4,418 (2,904)	3.736	1.2

one-to-one correlation. At first, this finding appears to be insignificant. One could question the utility of an indicator for the size of individual activity space which tells us that the structures of spatial mobility are tied purely to the amount of travel. At the same time, though, the outcome of the investigation strongly confirms our expectations. It indicates that the use and current knowledge of urban space are functions of the amount of social contact a traveller has.

After the descriptive analysis of the measurements, which in itself has provided new information, we conclude the analysis in this book by linking the measurement of activity space to selected socio-economic variables describing the respondents. This final part of our investigation covers the Mobidrive, Thurgau and Uppsala travel-diary data as well as the Borlänge, Copenhagen and Atlanta GPS observations. As previously mentioned, continuous activity-space measurements were not calculated for the latter data set. Furthermore, data from the Leisure Study were not considered here due its focus on only one trip purpose and the different level of resolution for destination geocoding.

A general finding is that the influence of selected socio-economic factors on the measurements has distinct parallels to the general structures of daily mobility demand. As an introductory example, Figure 11.31 makes clear that occupation and life-cycle status affect the magnitude of the values of the measurements–in this case of the kernel densities. Working respondents in the Mobidrive survey exhibited significantly higher kernel values during workdays compared to retirees or pupils. Interestingly, the figures of the socio-economic groups converged on weekends.

To gain a broader picture of the extent to which socio-economic factors affect activity-space structure and size, we performed a covariance analysis to test selected personal attributes. The dependent activity space characteristics included the number of locations, the concentration of trips in a few unique locations, the clustering of activities and the size of the local activity space, as indicated by

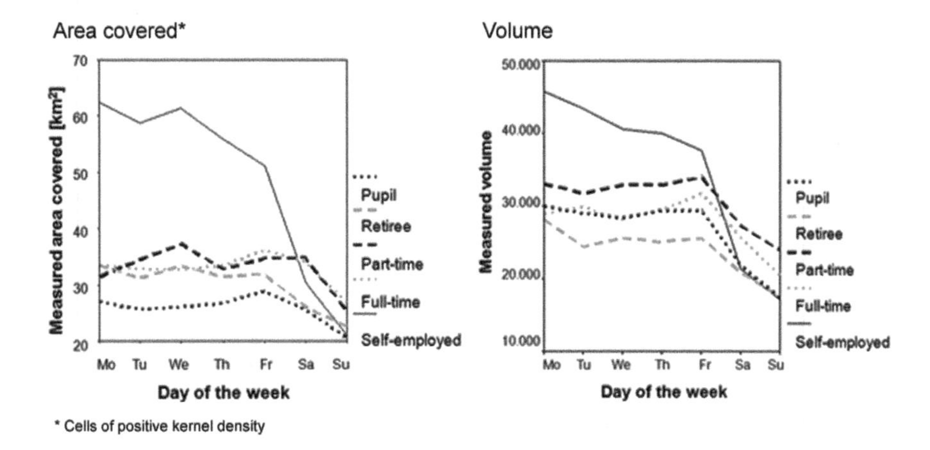

Figure 11.31 Mean values of measurements by selected socio-economic groups and day of the week (Mobidrive, Halle sub-sample)

the size of confidence ellipses, kernel densities and shortest-path networks (Table 11.15). Due to the limited number of socio-economic attributes recorded for the drivers in the GPS observations, our analysis focused on a few covariates: gender, age, occupational status, intensity of car use and home location. The combined effects of car use and agglomeration type(s) were also added. Further relationships have already been tested for the Mobidrive survey (Schönfelder and Axhausen 2002; Schönfelder and Axhausen 2004a).

Table 11.16 shows in a reduced form whether the chosen attributes had an impact on the activity-space indicator based on an analysis of variance (SAS General Linear Model [GLM] framework). A bold square for a classification variable or a combination of two variables indicates a significant main effect ($p<0.05$) on the dependent variable.

The GLM combines a variance-type analysis for the categorical variables with a regression-type analysis of continuous variables. The significance levels reported in the table imply that one or more of the categories of a variable differed significantly from those contained in the survey samples.

The models have only a poor statistical fit in most cases (low R^2). Some of the models are not even statistically significant as a whole. This somewhat contradicts our finding that there is a strong correlation between the measurements and the amount of travel. However, this shows that there is only an indirect link between the socio-economic attributes of travellers and indicators of activity-space size and structures. Furthermore, disaggregate models of trip generation based on small subsamples often suffer the same lack of explanatory power, which is an indication of random variance and the difficulty of predicting individual travel amounts.

Table 11.15 GLM by data source, activity-space indicator and model: Variables

Variables	Description	Survey particularities
Locations	Mean number of locations per week	
Ratio	Locations per trip	
Concentration	Cumulative share of trips directed to 5 most important reported locations	
Clustering	Number of real clusters over the entire reporting period	
Ellipse area	Size of 95% confidence ellipse of local trips analogous to description above (local trips)	Not for the Atlanta survey
Kernel: Cells	Number of cells exceeding a kernel density of zero	Not for the Atlanta survey
Kernel: Volume	Sum of kernel densities	Not for the Atlanta survey
Shortest-path network, unweighted	Length of shortest-path network	Mobidrive (Karlsruhe) and Borlänge surveys only
Shortest-path network, weighted	Length of shortest-path network weighted by frequency of use	Mobidrive (Karlsruhe) and Borlänge surveys only
Covariates		
Gender		
Age	Age classes: < 30, >= 30 < 40, >= 40 < 50, >= 50 < 60, > 60	
Household type	Types: single household, two persons, three and more persons	Copenhagen survey: no information available
Working status	Types: full-time work, part-time work, retired, pupil, other	
Income	Types: low (<25% percentile), medium 1 (25-50 percentile), medium 2 (50-75 percentile), high (>75 percentile) of the respective survey sample	Uppsala survey: no information available; Copenhagen survey: no high income class

Table 11.15 *continued*

Variables	Description	Survey particularities
Car use	Intensity of car use Respondent is a non-regular / regular car driver	Mobidrive, Thurgau, Uppsala surveys: More than 50% of all trips made by car Borlänge survey: >10,000 km yearly kilometrage, or more than 50% of trips stated to be made by car Copenhagen survey: >10,000 km or frequency of car use to work per week >= 5 Atlanta survey: driver does not share a car
Urban	Household location type 1: Agglomerational type urban / non-urban	Mobidrive, Copenhagen, Atlanta surveys: All households
Density	Household location type 2: Potential supply of facilities and shops in the vicinity of home	Mobidrive and Uppsala, surveys: All households; Thurgau survey: All households in the town of Frauenfeld; Borlänge survey: All households within Borlänge; Copenhagen survey: All households in Greater Copenhagen; Atlanta survey: All households located less than 50 km from downtown Atlanta
Combination of: Car use and urban; car use and density; urban and density		

Table 11.16 Summary of the GLM results by data source, activity-space indicator and model: Significance levels

Survey	Mobidrive survey: All trips by all respondents									Thurgau survey: All trips by all respondents							Uppsala survey: All trips by all respondents						
Variable	**Locations**	**Ratio**	**Concentration**	**Clustering**	**Ellipse area**	**Kernel: Cells**	**Kernel: Volume**	**SPN not weighted**	**SPN weighted**	**Locations**	**Ratio**	**Concentration**	**Clustering**	**Ellipse area**	**Kernel: Cells**	**Kernel: Volume**	**Locations**	**Ratio**	**Concentration**	**Clustering**	**Ellipse area**	**Kernel: Cells**	**Kernel: Volume**
Gender		+	+										+								+	+	+
Age	+	+		+		+			+	+	+	+		+			+		+			+	+
Household type		+		+						+					+								
Working status								+	+					+				+					+
Income		+	+			+	+		+						+								
Car use	+	+	+		+	+		+	+	+	+	+		+	+	+		+	+		+	+	
Urban																							
Density												+	+	+	+	+							
Car use X urban																							
Car use X density											+	+	+	+									
Urban X density																							
N	316	316	309	316	316	316	316	158	158	229	229	229	229	228	229	229	143	143	143	143	143	143	143
R2	0.12	0.15	0.12	0.05	0.14	0.16	0.07	0.16	0.21	0.14	0.26	0.26	0.11	0.35	0.29	NS	0.12	0.17	0.08	0.10	0.12	0.24	0.16

Table 11.16 *continued*

Survey	Borlänge survey: Car trips									Copenhagen survey: Car trips							Atlanta survey: Car trips			
Variable	**Locations**	**Ratio**	**Concentration**	**Clustering**	**Ellipse area**	**Kernel: Cells**	**Kernel: Volume**	**SPN not weighted**	**SPN weighted**	**Locations**	**Ratio**	**Concentration**	**Clustering**	**Ellipse area**	**Kernel: Cells**	**Kernel: Volume**	**Locations**	**Ratio**	**Concentration**	**Clustering**
Gender																			+	
Age		+																+		
Household type																	+			
Working status																	+		+	
Income		+								+								+	+	
Car use	+																+			
Urban																				
Density														+						
Car use X urban																				
Car use X density																				
Urban X density																				
N	44	44	44	44	44	44	44	44	44	197	197	197	197	197	197	197	404	404	404	404
R2	Models not significant as such (NS)													0.06	NS		0.08	0.04	0.10	NS

+ Significance level <0.05, RSS is weighted by the number of reported weeks; type I sum of squares is relevant for the significance test.

In summary, some detectable explanatory trends are worth considering, given the limited number of covariates and the small sample sizes of data on regular car drivers and the GPS observations. One consistent pattern is the effect of car use on most of the given activity-space characteristics. The impact of age and therefore life-cycle group membership is another clearly observable trend. Where urban density (with its potentially better conditions for organizing daily life more efficiently and avoiding car use) is a covariate, as in the Thurgau survey, interactions with the activity-space size become evident. Car use combined with density may even amplify effects. Further significant effects were found for gender (Uppsala survey) and income (Mobidrive survey).

As expected, life-cycle group membership shaped the size and structure of human activity space due to differences in activity-demand structures and commitments at different stages of life. The most important results, however, were the effects of mobility-tool ownership and the location of the household. Activity space was unquestionably influenced by the possibility of travelling fast, comfortably and without the constraint of timetables–all of which were strongly positive, as shown at the bottom of Table 11.16. Car use based on car access and availability was a definite determinant of destination choice. Finally, travellers tended to (or rather: were forced to) increase their activity space if their home environment did not offer enough opportunities to satisfy activity demand for various purposes.

PART IV
Conclusions

Chapter 12
Concluding Remarks

Our analysis of the longitudinal data sets has generated interesting new findings about the structures of daily travel and their determinants. This is particularly true for the analysis of human activity spaces, which had never been investigated in such detail before. We believe our findings will support the development of better behavioural models of destination choice – a field which still attracts a lot of attention in transportation research (see Bekhor and Prashker 2007 for a recent discussion).

Before discussing the relevance of our analyses for the research community as well as for policy and planning, we shall provide a compact summary of the key results along with some methodological conclusions. The findings are grouped into the categories *data issues, temporal rhythms of activity demand* and *representing and measuring human activity spaces*.

Summary of key findings and methodological implications

The results confirm the theoretical model outlined in Chapter 2, which suggests that day-to-day travel behaviour is partially shaped by routinization ("risk-aversion") and variety seeking, as well as by the will to minimize generalized costs. Furthermore, our findings underpin the notion of strong dynamics within daily mobility patterns which differ according to a traveller's particular social context and access to mobility tools.

Data issues

The use of longitudinal travel data to reveal the dynamics of activity demand and spatial choice has shown promising results. Our analysis included a wide range of variables which allowed us to study the fundamental patterns of the temporal and spatial structures of travel. In addition, important motives based on travellers' socio-economic attributes could be identified. The highly exact georeferencing of trip destinations was vital to developing approaches to measuring human activity spaces for the first time. The combination of travel-diary data and GPS observations shows potential for future work, as the results based on the extremely long GPS monitoring periods confirmed the trends revealed in the diary data and extended the scope of earlier analyses (such as e.g., by Schlich [2004], using Mobidrive data only). Interestingly, the different regional contexts of the data sets do not seem to have had a significant impact on the temporal and spatial patterns of long-term trip making and activity demand. Whereas travel volumes, durations and distances differed, the underlying temporal demand structures were not much affected by the travellers' national or regional contexts.

Clearly, some features of the data sets diminished the significance of the results: for example, the small sample sizes. The low number of respondents – especially in the Borlänge and Copenhagen data, which also lacked important socioeconomic information about the drivers due to the original purpose of the data collection – had implications for the stratification of the samples. Group sizes became rather small, which might make it difficult to achieve the necessary depth of analysis.

Furthermore, the GPS data structure and processing level must be taken into account when interpreting the outcomes (see also Chapter 6). There might be biases in the results due the initial character of post-processing with the rough threshold approach to eliminate suspect trips and activities, or the identification of the actual drivers might be missing.

Despite these constraints, we found that the quality level of the GPS data was more than sufficient for our analytical needs. The major objective of the investigation in this book was to detect the fundamental patterns of long-term travel demand and "urban rhythms".

Temporal rhythms of activity demand

Our analysis of the intrapersonal variability of activity demand showed that rhythmic structures differ significantly for different trip purposes, which was to be expected. The (relatively) fine categorization of activity types in the Mobidrive and Thurgau surveys helped to detect underlying demand structures in more detail. Interestingly, non-obligatory activities, in particular "leisure", showed strong rhythmic structures too (see, e.g., "stroll"), which clearly has implications for future activity- and travel-demand forecasting in this growing segment of daily mobility.

Using survival analysis techniques to model the intervals of activity demand did not yield an entirely uniform picture for the two surveys analysed. Therefore, it is likely that the chosen covariates represented only some of the determinants of regularity in travel. However, important trends could be identified in our analysis: Occupational status and car availability and usage were found to be predominant factors for the periodicity of daily life. This finding is in line with a range of earlier disaggregated models of human behaviour (see the list of studies given in Chapter 4) and indicates (a) the strong dominance of the main activity of the different socio-economic groups (especially work) and (b) the restrictions or the degree of freedom which are imposed by a traveller's precommitment to a certain mobility tool (see also Axhausen 2005).

Household size and household structures are other strong attributes controlling travel behaviour over time. This is especially true for the temporal structures of leisure travel and shopping. Other lifestyle precommitments such as club membership or dog ownership shape the temporal structures of activity demand as well. Long-term decisions such as community or club commitments tend to have strong implications for short-term choices in time and space (e.g., departure time or destination choices). Future survey designs need to put a strong focus on querying for this information.

Representing and measuring human activity space

The enumeration, mapping and transformed representation of observed trips and locations gives a better insight into the structures of spatial choice. Our analysis has widely confirmed existing conceptual approaches of human and transport geography (see, e.g., Golledge and Stimson 1997). Our findings made clear that:

- the structure of daily destination choices is dominated by a few locations;
- there is a permanent process of discovery of "new" locations and a constant innovation rate;
- the size of the activity space is relatively stable over longer periods; and
- travellers tend to spatially cluster their activities in order to minimize the cost of travel.

Our major finding is clearly the ambiguity between strong habits and variety seeking in spatial behaviour. On the one hand, trips were greatly concentrated on a few predominant destinations; on the other hand, the innovation or discovery rate of "new" places remained stable even after many months of monitoring. Furthermore, while the activity-space size in total remained stable due to the general constraints of given time budgets and speeds, new places were regularly sought out beyond the boundaries of the travellers' daily "home range".

The continuous representation of activity spaces turned out to be visually impressive. However, predicting individual activity spaces beyond the obvious relationship between the amount of travel and their sizes remains difficult. This is because the measurement approaches are models of human behaviour and are therefore simplifications of environmental perception and actual decision processes. Looking at the simplifying features of the proposed measurements in more detail, there are some critical issues to discuss, including:

- the over-representation of actually used urban space, especially with the confidence-ellipse measurement ("Is the area covered by the geometries actually used or perceived by the travellers?");
- the restricted range of shapes and the fact that the resultant figures of the activity spaces (confidence ellipses) are necessarily symmetrical;
- the assumption of the continuousness of space usage and knowledge indicated by the geometric shapes of the measurements ("Do we really perceive, know and use urban areas in a continuous way? Should we not rather represent spatial behaviour by indicators of contact with single

features of the environment, such as activity locations, landmarks, network sections or important junctions?");
- missing information about what "happens" in and between the subcentres of daily life (mode choice, share of duration, etc.) and about interactions between the accessibility of locations and the behavioural outcome;
- the strong impact of the frequency of travel on the measurement results, especially on kernel densities and shortest-path networks ("If there is such a high correlation between the size of the activity space and the individual amount of travel, what new information is gained by an investigation of activity spaces and their determinants?"); and
- the sensitivity of threshold values and its implications for the magnitude of the results, e.g., the bin range, the cell size and the threshold for the consideration of densities for the kernel-density measurement.

Taking these points into account, our development of measurements of activity space is a substantial contribution to the analysis of multiday travel behaviour. Similar to other analysis tasks based on longitudinal data sets, few existing indicators were available to measure the stability and variability of travel behaviour. The techniques applied should not only be judged by their technical shortcomings or benefits, but also by what can be learned for the practice of human geography and transport research. As Raine pointed out:

> the calculation of ellipses as a means of summarizing the point distributions did allow the analysis to reach beyond the purely descriptive level of terms such as 'random' or 'clustered' and to say something more about their key spatial properties (Raine 1978, 331).

Moreover, activity-space measurements are certainly helpful for comparative purposes, i.e., for investigating differences in spatial behaviour between respondents. Finally, the application of activity-space measurements will help to generate and test new hypotheses about point patterns and to summarize data.

Implications for travel behaviour analysis and further work

We are confident that our results will have an impact on future research in travel behaviour analysis. The following issues are a (doubtlessly incomplete) listing of potential areas of methodological development in behavioural analysis.

First, there is the need to rethink concepts of the spatial organization of human activities. There is some evidence that the often-supposed bipolar structure of daily travel, which is believed to extend between home and work or home and school, is vanishing. Whereas home is for many an undoubted peg or anchor of most activity spaces, the workplace appears to be more isolated in terms of activity clustering than previously assumed. In addition, one could question whether other (minor) activities are spatially organized between work and home as authors have argued in the past (Holzapfel 1980). Investigations into activity distribution in urban areas indicate that locational choice is less organized away from the travellers' home area.

A second interesting issue for further research will be the potential for predicting spatial choice and activity spaces. Will we be able to make reliable assumptions about the socio-economic impact of various factors on personal activity space? And will it be possible to "reconstruct" human activity spaces based on the observed equilibrium of the perceived choice set, individual innovation rates and individual propensity for variety seeking in general? We have shown so far that the amount of travel directly affects the number of unique locations. Even if the latter number does not necessarily lead to a greater dispersion of visited places and thus to a larger activity space, the same determinants which control the amount of mobility will have a great impact on the perception, knowledge and acquisition of urban space as well as on a personal's innovation rate in spatial choice. Furthermore, if the structure of activity space is a function of the places known and the observed extent and consolidation of an individual's innovation rate, then the size and structure of activity spaces may be predicted to a certain extent.

On the subject of travel-survey design, the question often arises as to whether there is an "ideal" length for longitudinal surveys such as Mobidrive or the Thurgau survey. In other words, what might be the ideal length for a consecutive-days (-weeks) panel survey which should capture a maximum of intrapersonal behavioural variability? This question was also addressed by Schlich (2004), who used the six-week Mobidrive data to identify homogenous groups of behaviour based on longitudinal observation.

The analysis in this book, which has focused on the level of stability in individual travel and deviation from widely routinized day-to-day behaviour, may help. Empirical results about destination choice over time, especially the development of typical repertoires of regularly frequented locations, indicate that about two to four weeks of reporting seem to be an acceptable (minimum) duration. Schlich proposed a similar length for travel-diary surveys to allow for temporal variations in travel. However, an ideal length of longitudinal surveys remains subject to the analyst's need for certainty about the individual level of routines. For example, would capturing 75 per cent of intrapersonal variability explain human behaviour over time well or insufficiently?

Another field for further investigation is the interaction between the aspirations shown for variety seeking in destination choice and the dynamics of the (travel) environment. Although stable in the short term, spatial properties of the built environment do change, whether – in the best case – due to innovation and development or to a deterioration of facilities and public space. Without a doubt, innovation in behaviour is affected by such spatial trends, for example when "search spaces" for new locations to be discovered have been altered. A combination of data sources which cover long-term behavioural data and land-use information and their dynamics (e.g., GPS observations plus point-of-interest data) might reveal interesting findings about the balance, synchronization or time delays between these two phenomena. In travel behaviour research, the investigation of long-term dynamics and the impact of external factors on behaviour are still rare. One area of exploration of such dynamics is car ownership using panel data, such as by Landsman (1991). Landsman developed a dynamic model which associates deviations in household travel patterns from mean travel patterns with changes in car ownership over prolonged periods. The development of similar analysis and modelling approaches which take the changing travel environment into account seems promising.

A related direction of analytical interest is the relationship between supply and demand structures of spatial choice: i.e., the effect of individually perceived and/or actually existing accessibility of places. The enumeration of daily activity locations and the analysis of the distribution of such places (the "activity space") have revealed demand structures which may be seen as a joint consequence of:

- individual choice preferences,
- mobility tool ownership, and
- the spatial supply of activity opportunities.

In this book, the latter aspect and its impact on destination choice over time was not addressed explicitly. Travel behaviour research has already started to investigate how the accessibility of places shapes the size and structure of activity spaces (see, e.g., Miller 1991; Kim and Kwan 2003). However, an examination of that relationship which takes a long-term perspective (i.e., by using longitudinal data) is still missing (see also the next section of this chapter for the implications for planning).

Finally, our results on location choice have the potential to influence current practice in transport modelling. This investigation will deepen the discussion of the size and structure of individual choice sets in destination choice. Modelling widely assumes that all spatial alternatives are known to the traveller, which allows the researcher to create an arbitrarily composed choice set for estimation. This assumption goes back more than one hundred years to Lill's (1889) paper on the "*Grundgesetze des Personenverkehrs*" ("Basic Laws of Personal Travel"). Our analysis of longitudinal data sets has shown that this practice eventually leads to biased parameter estimates, as the alternatives of which the traveller is aware are limited, clustered and unevenly known. Observed spatial behaviour is a trade-off which can not be replicated by a random sample of alternatives. The results imply that choice sets are likely to be more condensed than thus far assumed. The concentration of a large share of trips in a few locations supports the notion of spatially stable behaviour over time (see also Buliung and Roorda 2005). The application of activity-space measurements has, for example, shown that we can define a (fixed) area for each individual which contains 90 to 95 per cent of all potential places of interest. This might help to better define the probability of locations as potential alternatives and to characterize choice sets more efficiently.

However, our analysis has also shown that the challenge of defining appropriate choice sets lies in travellers' desires and need for variety seeking in spatial choice.

Implications for society, policy and planning

Our analysis has shown that travel is a function of needs and commitments which have a more or less regular character. Travel behaviour is also determined by habitual temporal and spatial choices, a legitimate means of avoiding decision situations which demand additional (new) search efforts. This could be shown for the timing of activities as well as for destination-choice structures. From the perspective of the individual, habits appear to be efficient, controllable and target oriented, which is more attractive than having to constantly make new decisions.

The differences between a behavioural routine and a deliberate action or choice are manifold (see, e.g., Fishbein and Ajzen 1975). Whereas a deliberate action requires a certain motivation for making a decision, for example when an outcome appears to give extra benefit, a routinized choice is made when the decision is inconsequential or trivial. In addition, deliberate actions are usually taken when there is enough time to decide and the decision maker has sufficient cognitive capacity to evaluate the pros and cons of her or his choice.

Habitual choices often also signify a lack of awareness of better alternatives or of the real costs connected with those which have been chosen instead. This leads to unfavourable situations such as congestion, which not only have negative effects on the individual but on other travellers as well. Hence, travellers' habits and routines often contradict the behavioural changes which are favoured by transport policy and which would be necessary for a more efficient transport system.

As a consequence, better knowledge and a better understanding of habitual behaviour and the determinants of routines in trip making and activity demand are crucial to public planning and regulation. Travel behaviour analysis, environmental psychology and related research fields need to analyse:

- the characteristics and structures of habitual behaviour,
- the fundamental principles of decision-making processes which lead to habitual travel choices, and
- the best strategies for influencing unfavourable behaviour and breaking routines (Gärling and Axhausen 2003).

Interestingly, habitual behaviour is often independent of and conflicts with a person's own attitudes and convictions. From a planning perspective, this makes it very difficult to mediate policy measures successfully. Recent attitude surveys show the existence of persistent positive public attitudes, for example towards the economical use of natural resources or reducing greenhouse gas emissions (e.g.,

DEFRA 2007). Respondents even felt that using the car less often – which might be difficult in practice for many travellers – would greatly benefit the environment.

The question then arises: Why does a positive attitude towards environmental protection not lead to a consequent change in travel behaviour, such as reducing the use of travel modes which considerably contribute to local or global emissions problems and climate change?

This discussion has found its way into studies of environmental psychology, which identified mechanisms of the "Normative Decision Making (NDM)" theory (Schwartz 1977) as one of the obstacles for behavioural change. In brief, NDM is a concept which tries to describe decision making as a multistage process which consists of the following steps:

- (the signal/stimulus/problem emerges);
- problem realization (attention stage);
- build up of motivation for action;
- assessing potential consequences of behaviour;
- if assessment in the last step is positive, behaviour is invoked.

Psychologists discuss two ways in which routines negatively affect this logical order of steps (Klöckner and Matthies 2004). First, habits block the decision-making process as certain signals automatically provoke (routinized) actions. In other words, there is a direct link between stimulus and response which bypasses the attention stage as well as the motivation build-up stage and the evaluation of a potential action. Second, habits might affect the assessment or evaluation stage and in particular the assessment of so-called non-moral consequences such as potential time losses or expenditure. Individuals apparently rate the time saved by not searching for additional information more positively than a new choice with uncertain consequences or costs.

Hence, planning may influence "bad" routines only if a few preconditions are met:

- initializing a more conscious process of decision making which consists of the steps: "stop old behaviour", "store the good intention", "a multiple testing of the new solution" and "the repeated choice of the new solution";
- supporting the formulation of an individual intention for change;
- altering the decision context, i.e., jettisoning old (bad) attitudes and individual targets, modifying rewards and penalizing available ("bad") options.

In principle, successful strategies need to differentiate between choice situations in which deliberate action is feasible and those in which habitual choices are predominant and potentially avoidable. Existing studies with a focus on mode choice show that measures which take this into account are more successful than those which neglect the above preconditions (Bamberg 2000; Fuji, Gärling, and Kitamura 1999).

Having reached the very end of this book, the issue of a more sustainable, fairer and healthier transportation system should be raised. By enumerating daily activity locations and analysing their distribution, we have revealed both the supply structure of activity-space opportunities and the destination-choice behaviour of travellers given their perceived supply. This invites transport planning and research to once again evaluate present and imaginable future urban structures from the perspective of sustainable transport policy. Sustainable planning would include, for example, measures to increase the amount of opportunities (i.e., potential destinations) to satisfy activity demand in the households' neighbourhoods. Such a measure might successfully reduce individual (hidden) travel costs, congestion and emissions. There is strong evidence that local, accessibility-oriented land-use planning matters (Banister 2000; Simma 2000). However, the complexity of and nonlinearities within the interaction between location supply and actual destination choices must be taken into consideration.

Furthermore, the activity-space issue has to be put on the agenda when discussing the relationship between poverty, the deprivation of urban areas and transport. Kenyon, Lyons, and Rafferty (2002) have argued that important determinants of activity space such as insufficient or unavailable transport (e.g., car ownership) as well as reduced accessibility to facilities, goods and services are dimensions and factors of social exclusion (see also Casas 2007 for an empirical analysis). The size and structure of activity space may therefore act as a – highly political – indicator of social justice, of the efficiency of an infrastructure supply policy and of whether it is meeting societal needs. Our analysis of the samples revealed systematic differences between different categories of certain variables, but did not reveal clear classes of travellers with unusually small activity spaces (see also Schönfelder and Axhausen 2003). This study and the samples used were not designed to address this issue in the first place, but a dedicated attempt to construct a sample with respondents who can be considered to be at risk might lead to different conclusions.

Finally, the activity-space approach could receive more attention in the wider context of physical-activity analysis. Since the relationship between physical activity (or the lack thereof) and health has been identified as one of the key challenges to people in the developed world (WHO 2004), suitable indicators of activity and movement will be needed to identify necessary strategies to support physical exercise. Transport and urban planning are key actors in providing walkable and cyclable environments. The discussion has already encouraged researchers to apply activity-space measurements to investigations of related health issues such as functional assessment, level of disability assessment or health-care accessibility (Kopec 1995; Sherman et al. 2005). This is a field of promising cooperation between the public-health research and travel behaviour analysis communities. Our discipline's expertise in data collection and management as well as in the analysis of the relationship between the built environment, infrastructures, the supply of transport services and human movement patterns might support the design and implementation of policy-relevant studies in this area.

Appendix

A1 City:mobil activity purpose categorisation (see Götz et al. 1997)

1	Work
2	Work related
3	School/Education
4	Further education/courses
5	Serve passenger
6	Daily shopping/Grocery
7	Long-term shopping
8	Window shopping
9	Private business
10	Meet family
11	Meet friends
12	Club, church etc.
13	Doctor, dentist, hair cut
14	Car service/cleaning
15	Active sports
16	Excursion into nature
17	Stroll
18	Excursion over weekend
19	Garden/cottage
20	Sightseeing
21	Going out (bar, restaurant, cinema etc.)
22	Home
23	Other
24	Graveyard
25	Voluntary work
26	Family related (e.g., parents' meeting at school)

A2 Hazard model estimation results for the selected activity categories (LIMDEP output for Chapter 9)

Dependent variable is INTERVAL (duration between two activities of same type).
Model type: Ordered probability model (Han and Hausman 1990).

Abbreviations of explanatory variables used:

MALE	Is male
AGE	Age
AGE2	Age squared
MARRIED / COHABITING	Is married/lives in fixed partnership
PARENT	Is parent
CLUB	Is club member
FULLTIME	Works fulltime
DOGGY	Is dog owner
N_O_HHM	Number of household members
INCOME3	High income (appr. >1,000 Euro or 3,000 CHF p.m. p.p.)
N_O_PV	Number of personal vehicles (cars)
CAR_AVAI	Is main car user
CITYCODE	Karlsruhe subsample (Mobidrive only)
AGGLO	Lives in Frauenfeld (Thurgau only)

Mobidrive results

	Daily shopping				Long-term shopping				Private business				Meet family of friends			
Variable	**β**		**SE**	**Mean**	**β**		**SE**	**Mean**	**β**		**SE**	**Mean**	**β**		**SE**	**Mean**
MALE	-0.02		0.08	0.41	0.17		0.13	0.41	0.00		0.09	0.49	0.10		0.10	0.49
AGE	0.00		0.01	45.63	0.02		0.01	43.41	0.01		0.01	45.51	0.00		0.01	33.07
AGE2	0.00		0.00	2367.70	0.00		0.00	2,179.44	0.00		0.00	2,366.50	0.00	*	0.00	1,436.82
MARRIED	-0.19	*	0.09	0.62	-0.09		0.15	0.59	-0.11		0.10	0.61	-0.20		0.13	0.40
PARENT	-0.54	**	0.09	0.39	-0.35	*	0.16	0.35	-0.82	**	0.11	0.38	0.48	**	0.15	0.20
CLUB	0.19	*	0.09	0.20	-0.02		0.13	0.26	0.03		0.09	0.23	0.10		0.10	0.30
FULLTIME	0.71	**	0.09	0.30	0.41	*	0.15	0.30	0.18		0.10	0.35	0.22		0.12	0.27
DOGGY	-0.26	*	0.10	0.15	0.13		0.18	0.11	0.43	**	0.13	0.11	0.27		0.17	0.08
N_O_HHM	0.18	**	0.04	2.64	0.16	*	0.06	2.76	0.26	**	0.04	2.62	-0.05		0.05	2.80
INCOME3	-0.27	**	0.09	0.27	-0.17		0.15	0.27	-0.40	**	0.10	0.32	0.23		0.13	0.26
N_O_PV	0.08		0.07	1.10	0.36	**	0.11	1.09	0.07		0.07	1.14	0.11		0.09	1.21
CAR_AVAI	0.03		0.08	0.43	-0.01		0.13	0.41	0.10		0.09	0.46	-0.29	*	0.11	0.40
CITYCODE	-0.02		0.07	0.52	0.03		0.11	0.51	-0.10		0.08	0.57	0.03		0.09	0.58
Number of observations				3,019				1,031				2,346				1,670
Log likelihood β				-5,351.51				-2,469.14				-4,640.71				-3,386.85
Log likelihood constant				-5,409.23				-2,480.58				-4,696.99				-3,450.67
-2 Log likelihood				115.42				22.87				112.55				127.64
Degrees of freedom				12				12				12				12
Prob chi-squared				0.00				0.03				0.00				0.00

* Statistically significant at the 0.05 level; ** statistically significant at the 0.01 level.

Mobidrive results *continued*

	Club meeting				Active sports				Excursion into nature				Stroll				Going out (bar, restaurant etc.)			
Variable	β		SE	Mean	β		SE	Mean	β		SE	Mean	β		SE	Mean	β		SE	Mean
MALE	0.43	*	0.20	0.47	-0.22		0.14	0.57	1.45	*	0.72	0.57	-0.22		0.19	0.47	-0.09		0.15	0.51
AGE	0.04		0.02	37.33	0.01		0.02	32.25	-0.22	*	0.10	42.83	0.05	*	0.02	39.6	0.05	**	0.01	38.33
AGE2	0.00		0.00	1,825.23	0.00		0.00	1,438.79	0.00	*	0.00	2,312.57	0.00		0.00	1,856.44	0.00	*	0.00	1,774.74
MARRIED	-0.01		0.29	0.47	-0.23		0.21	0.42	0.86		0.75	0.38	-0.19		0.25	0.66	-0.44	*	0.18	0.46
PARENT	1.02	**	0.33	0.29	0.13		0.20	0.29	1.77		0.93	0.27	-1.10	**	0.27	0.47	-0.37	*	0.19	0.29
CLUB	-0.03		0.21	0.40	-0.73	**	0.15	0.70	-0.09		0.61	0.38	0.29		0.27	0.11	-0.19		0.14	0.36
FULLTIME	-0.81	*	0.30	0.26	0.00		0.19	0.30	-2.48	*	1.01	0.23	0.47	*	0.21	0.38	-0.23		0.18	0.46
DOGGY	0.56		0.32	0.13	0.24		0.26	0.07	2.31		1.43	0.05	-2.25	**	0.17	0.71	0.57		0.31	0.05
N_O_HHM	-0.05		0.10	3.30	0.17	*	0.07	3.29	1.19	**	0.41	2.78	0.10		0.09	2.98	0.21	**	0.07	2.54
INCOME3	0.67		0.34	0.23	0.86	**	0.17	0.21	3.19	**	0.84	0.38	-1.16	**	0.27	0.21	-0.05		0.18	0.38
N_O_PV	0.16		0.17	1.23	0.30	*	0.12	1.39	-0.68		0.76	1.08	-0.03		0.19	1.12	0.06		0.11	1.28
CAR_AVAI	-1.02	**	0.24	0.31	-0.43	*	0.16	0.39	0.57		0.84	0.43	0.10		0.22	0.35	-0.71	**	0.15	0.55
CITYCODE	0.04		0.22	0.70	-0.21		0.13	0.68	-0.09		0.76	0.80	0.89	**	0.20	0.2	-0.17		0.15	0.71
Number of observations				448				900				320				883				800
Log likelihood β				-921.30				-1,789.28				-601.17				-1,104.40				-1,765.66
Log likelihood constant				-935.81				-1,841.85				-611.72				-1,259.69				-1,799.56
-2 Log likelihood				29.01				105.15				21.09				310.58				67.81
Degrees of freedom				12				12				12				12				12
Prob chi-squared				0.39				0.00				0.05				0.00				0.00

Thurgau results

	Daily shopping				Long-term shopping				Private business				Meet family of friends			
Variable	***β***		**SE**	**Mean**	***β***		**SE**	**Mean**	***β***		**SE**	**Mean**	***β***		**SE**	**Mean**
MALE	0.43	**	0.11	0.35	0.12		0.18	0.35	0.06		0.14	0.47	0.17		0.13	0.42
AGE	-0.02		0.01	47.8	0.05	**	0.02	42.84	0.00		0.01	49.19	0.03		0.02	36.80
AGE2	0.00		0.00	2,503.89	0.00	**	0.00	2,086.12	0.00		0.00	2,597.46	0.00		0.00	1,698.42
COHABITING	0.05		0.13	0.75	-0.57	*	0.23	0.79	0.10		0.15	0.76	0.11		0.15	0.58
PARENT	-0.81	**	0.16	0.25	-0.95	**	0.22	0.38	-0.28		0.21	0.28	0.30		0.20	0.14
CLUB	-0.30	**	0.10	0.45	0.00		0.16	0.49	-0.47	**	0.12	0.49	-0.16		0.12	0.52
FULLTIME	0.75	**	0.12	0.40	0.41	*	0.18	0.51	0.40	*	0.15	0.48	0.02		0.15	0.58
DOGGY	-0.01		0.14	0.15	0.32		0.24	0.13	-0.15		0.16	0.15	0.14		0.19	0.11
N_O_HHM	0.31	**	0.06	2.57	0.28	**	0.08	3.11	0.07		0.08	2.51	0.19	**	0.05	2.81
INCOME3	-0.32	**	0.11	0.69	-0.31		0.19	0.59	-0.35	*	0.14	0.69	-0.01		0.14	0.59
N_O_PV	-0.01		0.04	1.75	-0.05	*	0.06	2.02	0.02		0.05	1.76	-0.12	*	0.05	2.02
CAR_AVAI	0.41	*	0.16	0.85	0.11		0.30	0.86	0.55	*	0.23	0.92	-0.62	*	0.24	0.74
AGGLO	-0.09		0.11	0.59	0.13		0.16	0.45	0.06		0.12	0.51	0.40	**	0.13	0.43
Number of observations				1,526				561				1,135				1,035
Log likelihood *β*				-2,936.59				-1,368.47				-2,251.22				-2,267.69
Log likelihood constant				-2,987.44				-1,381.14				-2,273.86				-2,302.52
-2 Log likelihood				101.70				25.33				45.30				69.66
Degrees of freedom				12				12				12				12
Prob chi-squared				0.00				0.01				0.00				0.00

* Statistically significant at the 0.05 level; ** statistically significant at the 0.01 level.

Thurgau results *continued*

	Club meeting			Active sports			Excursion into nature			Stroll			Going out (bar, restaurant etc.)		
Variable	**β**	**SE**	**Mean**	**β**	**SE**	**Mean**	**β**	**SE**	**Mean**	**β**	**SE**	**Mean**	**β**	**SE**	**Mean**
MALE	0.10	0.15	0.48	0.11	0.14	0.51	0.16	0.26	0.64	0.23	0.20	0.48	-0.30 *	0.14	0.59
AGE	0.03	0.03	35.33	-0.01	0.02	37.07	0.05	0.03	49.48	0.07 *	0.03	45.59	-0.01	0.02	40.96
AGE2	0.00	0.00	1,620.75	0.00	0.00	1,779.07	0.00	0.00	2,770.8	0.00 **	0.00	2,326.69	0.00	0.00	1,915.14
COHABITING	-1.00 **	0.34	0.59	0.58 **	0.20	0.54	-1.48 **	0.47	0.79	-0.81 **	0.26	0.79	-0.13	0.15	0.72
PARENT	-0.22	0.24	0.20	-0.41 *	0.19	0.20	0.14	0.35	0.21	0.07	0.24	0.27	0.25	0.18	0.23
CLUB	-0.44 *	0.20	0.74	0.52 **	0.15	0.63	-0.25	0.25	0.44	-0.44 *	0.17	0.43	0.20	0.12	0.55
FULLTIME	0.16	0.17	0.51	0.18	0.14	0.49	-0.06	0.27	0.49	0.13	0.20	0.47	-0.04	0.16	0.68
DOGGY	0.80 *	0.31	0.06	1.26 **	0.25	0.07	0.14	0.32	0.13	-2.46 **	0.17	0.70	0.43 *	0.21	0.08
N_O_HHM	0.34 **	0.09	3.46	0.10	0.06	3.37	0.11	0.14	2.72	0.32 **	0.08	2.96	0.33 **	0.06	2.63
INCOME3	-0.24	0.17	0.58	-0.29	0.18	0.62	-0.36	0.25	0.69	-0.07	0.18	0.72	0.45 **	0.15	0.64
N_O_PV	-0.08	0.06	2.39	0.08	0.05	2.07	-0.24	0.14	1.33	-0.02	0.08	2.03	-0.05	0.07	1.75
CAR_AVAI	0.69	0.45	0.65	0.30	0.23	0.65	0.51	0.39	0.73	-0.11	0.42	0.89	-0.83 **	0.23	0.87
AGGLO	-0.21	0.16	0.45	-0.10	0.16	0.55	-0.03	0.33	0.73	0.42 *	0.17	0.36	0.28	0.13	0.47
Number of observations			609			859			320			781			1,102
Log likelihood β			-1,313.43			-1,717.62			-601.16			-1,119.07			-2,079.17
Log likelihood constant			-1,323.12			-1,757.77			-611.71			-1,261.17			-2,138.66
-2 Log likelihood			19.38			80.30			21.09			284.19			118.98
Degrees of freedom			12			12			12			12			12
Prob chi-squared			0.08			0.00			0.049			0.00			0.00

Bibliography

Abdel-Aty, M., Kitamura, R., and Jovanis, P. (1995), 'Exploring Route Choice Behavior Using Geographic Information System-Based Alternative Routes and Hypothetical Travel Time Information Input', *Transportation Research Record 1493, 74–80.*

Amlaner, C. J. and MacDonald, D. W. (eds) (1980), *A Handbook on Biotelemetry and Radio Tracking: Proceedings of an International Conference on Telemetry and Radio Tracking in Biology and Medicine, Oxford, 20–22 March 1979* (Oxford: Pergamon Press).

Ampt, E. S., Richardson, A. J., and Brög, W. (eds) (1985), *New Survey Methods in Transport: 2nd International Conference, Hungerford Hill, Australia, 12-16 September 1983* (Utrecht: VNU Science Press).

Anderberg, M. R. (1973), *Cluster Analysis for Applications* (New York: Academic Press).

Anderson, D. J. (1982), 'The Home Range: A New Nonparametric Estimation Technique', *Ecology* 63:1, 103–12.

Anderson, J. R. (2000), *Learning and Memory: An Integrated Approach* (New York: Wiley).

Arentze, T. A. and Timmermans, H. J. P. (2005), 'Information Gain, Novelty Seeking and Travel: A Model of Dynamic Activity-Travel Behavior under Conditions of Uncertainty', *Transportation Research Part A: Policy and Practice* 39:2–3, 125–45.

— et al. (2000), 'ALBATROSS: Multiagent, Rule-Based Model of Activity Pattern Decisions', *Transportation Research Record* 1706, 136–44.

Arnold, S. J., Oum, T. H., and Tigert, D. J. (1983), 'Determinant Attributes in Retail Patronage: Seasonal, Temporal, Regional, and International Comparisons', *Journal of Marketing Research* 20:1, 149–57.

Ås, D. (1978), 'Studies of Time-Use: Problems and Prospects', *Acta Sociologica* 21:2, 125–41.

Axhausen, K. W. (1995), *Travel Diaries: An Annotated Catalogue*, 2nd Edition. Working paper (Innsbruck: Institut für Straßenbau und Verkehrsplanung, Leopold-Franzens-Universität, Innsbruck) <http://ntl.bts.gov/lib/6000/6900/6973/td.pdf>, last accessed May 2009.

— (1996), 'The Design of Environmentally Aware Travel Diaries', *Transportation Planning and Technology* 19:3–4, 275–90.

— (2005), 'A Dynamic Understanding of Travel Demand: A Sketch', in M. E. H. Lee-Gosselin and S. T. Doherty (eds), 1–20.

— (2007a), 'Activity Spaces, Biographies, Social Networks and their Welfare Gains and Externalities: Some Hypotheses and Empirical Results', *Mobilities* 2:1, 15-36.

— (2007b), Predicting Response Rate: A Natural Experiment, (*Arbeitsberichte Verkehrs- und Raumplanung,* 434; Zürich: IVT, ETH Zürich).

— et al. (2002), 'Observing the Rhythms of Daily Life: A Six-Week Travel Diary', *Transportation* 29:2, 95–124.

— et al. (2007), 'Fatigue in Long-Duration Travel Diaries', *Transportation* 34:2, 143–60.

— et al. (2008), 'State-of-the-Art Estimates of the Swiss Value of Travel Time Savings', *Transport Policy* 15:3, 173–85.

Bamberg, S. (2000), 'The Promotion of New Behavior by Forming an Implementation Intention: Results of a Field Experiment in the Domain of Travel Mode Choice', *Journal of Applied Social Psychology* 30:9, 1903–22.

Banister, D. (2000), 'Sustainable Urban Development and Transport – a Eurovision for 2020', *Transport Reviews* 20:1, 113–30.

Barro, R. J. (2001), 'Human Capital and Growth', *American Economic Review* 91:2, 12–17.

— and Lee, J.-W. (2001), 'International Data on Educational Attainment: Updates and Implications', *Oxford Economics Papers* 53:3, 541–63.

Bates, J. J. (1987), 'Measuring Travel Time Values with a Discrete Choice Model: A Note', *Economic Journal* 97:386, 493–98.

Battelle Transportation Division (1997), *Global Positioning Systems for Personal Travel Surveys: Lexington Area Travel Data Collection Test.* Final Report to Office of Highway Information Management (Washington, DC: Federal Highway Administration).

Baumeister, R. (1876), *Stadterweiterungen in technischer, baupolizeilicher und wirtschaftlicher Beziehung* (Berlin: Ernst & Korn).

Becker, G. S. (1962), 'Investment in Human Capital: A Theoretical Analysis', *Journal of Political Economy* 70:S5, 9–49.

— (1965), 'A Theory of the Allocation of Time', *Economic Journal* 75:299, 493–517.

— (1978), *The Economic Approach to Human Behavior* (Chicago: University of Chicago Press).

Beckman, R. J., Baggerly, K. A., and McKay, M. D. (1996), 'Creating Synthetic Baseline Populations', *Transportation Research Part A: Policy and Practice* 30:6, 415–29.

Beckmann, K. J. (1983), 'Untersuchung kleinräumiger Raum-Zeit-Verhaltensweisen als Grundlage für Infrastrukturplanung in Innenstadtbereichen' (Veröffentlichungen des Instituts für Stadtbauwesen 36; Braunschweig: Technische Universität Braunschweig).

Beckmann, M. J., Golob, T. F., and Zahavi, Y. (1983a), 'Travel Probability Fields and Urban Spatial Structure: 1. Theory', *Environment and Planning A* 15:5, 593–606.

— (1983b), 'Travel Probability Fields and Urban Spatial Structure: 2. Empirical Tests', *Environment and Planning A* 15:6, 727–38.

Bekhor, S. and Prashker, J. N. (2007), GEV-based Destination Choice Models that Account for Unobserved Similarities among Alternatives, *Transportation Research B* 42:3, 243-62.

Bell, C. and Newby, H. (1976), 'Communion, Communalism, Class and Community Action: The Sources of New Urban Politics', in D. T. Herbert and R. J. Johnston (eds), 283–301.

Ben-Akiva, M. and Lerman, S. R. (1985), *Discrete Choice Analysis: Theory and Application to Travel Demand* (Cambridge: MIT Press).

Berkson, J. and Gage, R. P. (1950), 'Calculation of Survival Rates for Cancer', *Proceedings of Staff Meetings of the Mayo Clinic* 25:11, 270–86.

Berkowitz, L. (ed.) (1977), *Advances in Experimental Social Psychology*, Volume 10 (New York: Academic Press).

Bhat, C. R. (1996a), 'A Hazard-Based Duration Model of Shopping Activity with Nonparametric Baseline Specification and Nonparametric Control for Unobserved Heterogeneity', *Transportation Research Part B: Methodological* 30:3, 189–207.

— (1996b), 'A Generalized Multiple Durations Proportional Hazard Model with an Application to Activity Behavior during the Evening Work-to-Home Commute', *Transportation Research Part B: Methodological* 30:6, 465–80.

— (1997), 'Work Travel Mode Choice and Number of Non-Work Commute Stops', *Transportation Research Part B: Methodological* 31:1, 41–54.

— (1998), 'Analysis of Travel Mode and Departure Time Choice for Urban Shopping Trips', *Transportation Research Part B: Methodological* 32:6, 361–71.

— (1999), 'An Analysis of Evening Commute Stop-Making Behavior Using Repeated Choice Observations from a Multi-Day Survey', *Transportation Research Part B: Methodological* 33:7 495–510.

— (2000a), 'A Multi-Level Cross-Classified Model for Discrete Response Variables', *Transportation Research Part B: Methodological* 34:7, 567–82.

— (2000b), 'Duration Modeling', in D. A. Hensher and K. J. Button (eds), *Handbook of Transport Modelling* (Amsterdam: Pergamon Press), 91–111.

— (2001), 'Modeling the Commute Activity-Travel Pattern of Workers: Formulation and Empirical Analysis', *Transportation Science* 35:1, 61–79.

— and Koppelman, F. S. (1999), 'A Retrospective and Prospective Survey of Time-Use Research', *Transportation* 26:2, 119–39.

— and Steed, J. L. (2002), 'A Continuous-Time Model of Departure Time Choice for Urban Shopping Trips', *Transportation Research Part B: Methodological* 36:3, 207–24.

— and Zhao, H. (2002), 'The Spatial Analysis of Activity Stop Generation', *Transportation Research Part B: Methodological* 36:6, 557–75.

— Sivakumar, A. and Axhausen, K. W. (2003), 'An Analysis of the Impact of Information and Communication Technologies on Non-Maintenance Shopping Activities', *Transport Research Part B: Methodological* 37:10, 857–81.

— Srinivasan, S. and Axhausen, K. W. (2005), 'An Analysis of Multiple Interepisode Durations Using a Unifying Multivariate Hazard Model', *Transportation Research Part B: Methodological* 39:9, 797–823.

— et al. (2004a), 'Intershopping Duration: An Analysis Using Multiweek Data', *Transportation Research Part B: Methodological* 38:1, 39–60.

— et al. (2004b), 'A Comprehensive Econometric Microsimulator for Daily Activity-Travel Patterns (CEMDAP)', *Transportation Research Record* 1894, 57–66.

Biddle, B. J. (1979), *Role Theory: Expectations, Identities, and Behaviors* (New York: Academic Press).

Bieger, T., Laesser, C., and Maggi, R. (eds) (2008), *Jahrbuch der Schweizerische Verkehrswirtschaft 2005/2006* (St. Gallen: IDT-HSG).

Biding, T. and Lind, G.: (2002), *Intelligent Speed Adaptation(ISA): Results of Large-Scale Trials in Borlänge, Lidköping, Lund and Umeå during the Period 1999–2002.* Publication 2002:89E (Borlänge: Vägverket [Swedish National Road Administration]).Van Selm, M. and Jankowski, N. W. (2006), 'Conducting Online Surveys', *Quality and Quantity* 40:3, 435–56.

Black, W. C. (1984), 'Choice-Set Definition in Patronage Modeling', *Journal of Retailing* 60:2, 63–85.

Blum, A., Goldstein, H., and Guérin-Pace, F. (2001), 'International Adult Literacy Survey (IALS): An Analysis of International Comparisons of Adult Literacy', *Assessment in Education: Principles, Policy and Practice* 8:2, 225–46.

Booth, C. (1889), *Life and Labour of the People of London* (London: Williams and Norgate).

Borgers, A. W. J., van der Heijden, R. E. C. M., and Timmermans, H. J. P. (1989), 'A Variety Seeking Model of Spatial Choice-Behaviour', *Environment and Planning A* 21:8, 1037–48.

Boudard, E. and Jones, S. (2003), 'The IALS Approach to Defining and Measuring Literacy Skills', *International Journal of Educational Research* 39:3 191–204.

Bovy, P. H. L. (1996), 'Stochastic Traffic Assignment Technique Enhancements for Congested Networks', in P. H. L Bovy (ed.), *Transportation Modelling for Tomorrow: Rudimental Contributions* (Delft: Delft University Press), 129–145.

Bowman, J. L. (1995), 'Activity Based Travel Demand Model System with Daily Activity Schedules', M.S. thesis (Dept. of Civil and Environmental Engineering, Massachusetts Institute of Technology).

— et al. (1999), 'Demonstration of an Activity-Based Model for Portland', *World Transport Research: Proceedings* iii, 171–84.

Bradley, M. A. and Bowman, J. L. (2006), 'A Summary of Design Features of Activity-Based Micro-Simulation Models for U.S. MPOs', paper presented at the TRB Conference on Innovations in Travel Demand Modeling, Austin, May 2006.

Bricka, S. and Bhat, C. R. (2006), 'Comparative Analysis of Global Positioning System-Based and Travel Survey-Based Data', *Transportation Research Record* 1972, 9–20.

Brög, W. and Meyburg, A. H. (1980), 'Nonresponse Problem in Travel Surveys: An Empirical Investigation', *Transportation Research Record* 775, 34–38.

— — (1981), 'Consideration of Nonresponse Effects in Large-Scale Mobility Surveys', *Transportation Research Record* 807, 39–46.

Buhl, T. and Widmer, P. (2004), 'Stabilität des Verkehrsverhaltens', Feldbericht, *SVI Forschungsarbeit* 2001:514 (Frauenfeld and Zürich: Büro Widmer and IVT, ETH Zürich).

Buliung, R. N. (2001), 'Spatiotemporal Patterns of Employment and Non-Work Activities in Portland, Oregon', *Proceedings of the 2001 ESRI International User Conference*, San Diego, July 2001.

— and Roorda, M. J. (2005), 'Exploring the Spatial Stability of Activity-Travel Behaviour: Initial Results from the Toronto Travel-Activity Panel Survey', paper presented at the PROCESSUS 2nd International Colloquium on the Behavioural Foundations of Integrated Land-Use and Transportation Models, Toronto, June 2005.

Burnett, P. and Hanson, S. (1982), 'An Analysis of Travel as an Example of Complex Human Behavior in Spatially Constrained Situations', *Transportation Research Part A: General* 16:2, 87–102.

Buttimer, A. (1972), 'Social Space and the Planning of Residential Areas', *Environment and Behaviour* 4:3, 279–318.

Campbell, J. P. (1970), *A Stochastic Model of Human Movement* (Iowa City: Department of Geography, University of Iowa).

Carlstein, T., Parkes, D., and Thrift, N. J. (eds) (1978), *Timing Space and Spacing Time ii: Human Activity and Time Geography* (London: Arnold).

Carpenter, S. M. and Jones, P. M. (eds) (1983), *Recent Advances in Travel Demand Analysis* (Aldershot: Gower Publishing).

Casas, I. (2007), 'Social Exclusion and the Disabled: An Accessibility Approach', *The Professional Geographer* 59:4, 463-77.

Cascetta, E., Pagliara, F., and Papola, A. (2007), 'Alternative Approaches to Trip Distribution Modelling: A Retrospective Review and Suggestions for Combining Different Approaches', *Papers in Regional Science* 86:4, 597-620.

Chang, G.-L. and Mahmassani, H. S. (1989), 'The Dynamics of Commuting Decision Behaviour in Urban Transportation Networks', in Bernard G. (ed.), 15–26.

Chapin, F. S. (1965), *Urban Land Use Planning* (Urbana: University of Illinois Press).

— (1974), *Human Activity Patterns in the City: Things People Do in Time and in Space* (New York: Wiley).

— (1978), 'Human Time Allocation in the City', in T. Carlstein, D. Parkes, and N. J. Thrift (eds), 13–26.

Chikaraishi, M., Fujiwara, A., Zhang, J. and Axhausen, K. (forthcoming) 'Exploring Variation Properties of Departure Time Choice Behavior Using Multilevel Analysis Approach', *Transportation Research Record.*

Chung, E.-H. and Shalaby, A. (2005), 'A Trip Reconstruction Tool for GPS-Based Personal Travel Surveys', *Journal of Transportation Planning and Technology* 28:5, 381–401.

Cox, D. R. (1972), 'Regression Models and Life-Tables', *Journal of the Royal Statistical Society, Series B: Methodologica* 34:2, 187–220.

— and Oakes, D. (1984), *Analysis of Survival Data* (Monographs on Statistics and Applied Probability 21; London: Chapman and Hall).

Cullen, I. G. (1978), 'The Treatment of Time in the Explanation of Spatial Behaviour', in T. Carlstein, D. Parkes, and N. J. Thrift (eds), 27–38.

Damm, D. (1983), 'Theory and Empirical Results: A Comparison of Recent Activity-Based Research', in S. Carpenter and P. M. Jones (eds), 3–33.

Dangschat, J. et al. (1982), *Aktionsräume von Stadtbewohnern: Eine empirische Untersuchung in der Region Hamburg* (Beiträge zur sozialwissenschaftlichen Forschung 36; Opladen: Westdeutscher Verlag).

Deci, E. L. and Ryan, R. M. (2000), 'The "What" and "Why" of Goal Pursuits: Human Needs and the Self-Determination of Behavior', *Psychological Inquiry* 11:4, 227–68.

Department for Environment, Food and Rural Affairs (DEFRA) (2007), *Report, Questionnaire and Data Tables Following Survey of Public Attitudes and Behaviours toward the Environment: 2007* (London: DEFRA).

DeSerpa, A. C. (1971), 'A Theory of the Economics of Time', *Economic Journal* 81:324, 828–46.

Diggle, P. J., Liang, K.-Y., and Zeger, S. L. (1994), *Analysis of Longitudinal Data* (Oxford: Oxford University Press).

Dijkstra, E. W. (1959), 'A Note on Two Problems in Connexion with Graphs', *Numerische Mathematik* 1, 269–71.

Dijst, M. (1999), 'Two-Earner Families and Their Action Spaces: A Case Study of Two Dutch Communities', *GeoJournal* 48:3, 195–206.

Dillman, D. A. (2000), *Mail and Internet Surveys: The Tailored Design Method*, 2nd Edition. (New York: Wiley).

Dixon, K. R. and Chapman, J. A.(1980), 'Harmonic Mean Measure of Animal Activity Areas', *Ecology* 61:5, 1040–4.

Doherty, S. T. (2002), 'Interactive Methods for Activity Scheduling Processes', in K. G. Goulias (ed.), 7.1–7.25.

— (2005), 'How Far in Advance are Activities Planned? Measurement Challenges and Analysis', *Transportation Research Record* 1926, 41–9.

— and Miller, E. J. (2000), 'A Computerized Household Activity Scheduling Survey', *Transportation* 27:1, 75–97.

— et al. (2004), 'Computerized Household Activity-Scheduling Survey for Toronto, Canada, Area: Design and Assessment', *Transportation Research Record* 1894, 140–9.

Domencich, T. A. and McFadden, D. (1975), *Urban Travel Demand: A Behavioral Analysis* (Contributions to Economic Analysis 93; Amsterdam: North-Holland Publishing).

Downs, R. M. and Stea, D. (1977), *Maps in Mind: Reflections on Cognitive Mapping* (New York: Harper & Row).

Draijer, G., Kalfs, N., and Perdok, J. (2000), 'Global Positioning System as Data Collection Method for Travel Research', *Transportation Research Record* 1719, 147–53.

Du, J. and Aultman-Hall, L. (2007), 'Increasing the Accuracy of Trip Rate Information from Passive Multi-Day GPS Travel Datasets: Automatic Trip End Identification Issues', *Transportation Research Part A: Policy and Practice* 41:3, 220–32.

Dürr, H. (1979), *Planungsbezogene Aktionsraumforschung: Theoretische Aspekte und eine empirische Pilotstudie* (Veröffentlichungen der Akademie für Raumforschung und Landesplanung, Hannover: Beiträge 34; Hannover: Schroedel).

Edwards, P. et al. (2002), 'Increasing Response Rates to Postal Questionnaires: Systematic Review' *BMJ* 324 (7347):1183, 1–9.

Ellegård, K. and Vilhelmson, B. (2004), 'Home as a Pocket of Local Order: Everyday Activities and the Friction of Distance', *Geografiska Annaler, Series B: Human Geography* 86:4, 281–96.

Emmerink, R. H. M. and Van Beek, P. (1997), 'Empirical Analysis of Work Schedule Flexibility: Implications for Road Pricing and Driver Information Systems', *Urban Studies* 34:2, 217–34.

Ettema, D., Borgers, A. W. J., and Timmermans, H. J. P. (1995), 'Competing Risk Hazard Model of Activity Choice, Timing, Sequencing, and Duration', *Transportation Research Record* 1493, 101–9.

Fischer, M. M., Nijkamp, P., and Papageorgiou, Y. Y. (eds) (1990), *Spatial Choices and Processes* (Studies in Regional Science and Urban Economics, 21; Oxford: Elsevier Science).

Fishbein, M. and Ajzen, I. (1975), *Belief, Attitude, Intention, and Behavior: An Introduction to Theory and Research* (Reading: Addison-Wesley).

Fosgerau, M. (2005), 'Unit Income Elasticity of the Value of Travel Time Savings', paper presented at the 8th NECTAR Conference, Las Palmas, June 2005.

Fotheringham, A. S. (1983), 'A New Set of Spatial-Interaction Models: The Theory of Competing Destinations', *Environment and Planning A* 15:1, 15–36.

— and O'Kelly, M. E. (1989), *Spatial Interaction Models: Formulations and Applications* (Dordrecht: Kluwer Academic).

— Brunsdon, C., and Charlton, M. (2000), *Quantitative Geography: Perspectives on Spatial Data Analysis* (London: Sage).

Fraschini, E. M. and Axhausen, K. W. (2001), *Day on Day Dependencies in Travel: First Results Using ARIMA Modelling* (*Arbeitsberichte Verkehrs- und Raumplanung,* 63; Zürich: IVT, ETH Zürich).

Frees, E. W. (2004), *Longitudinal and Panel Data: Analysis and Applications in the Social Sciences* (Cambridge: Cambridge University Press).

Frey, B. S. (2008), *Happiness: A Revolution in Economics* (Munich Lectures in Economics; Cambridge: MIT Press).

Fuji, S., Gärling, T., and Kitamura, R. (1999), 'Changing Habitual Drivers' Attitudes toward Public Transport: Triggering Cooperation in a Real-World Social Dilemma', working paper (Gothenburg: University of Gothenburg).

Gärling, T. and Axhausen, K. W. (2003), 'Introduction: Habitual Travel Choice', *Transportation* 30:1, 1–11.

Garrison, W. L. et al. (1959), *Studies of Highway Development and Geographic Change* (Seattle: University of Washington Press).

Garvill, J., Marell, A., and Nordlund, A. M. (2003), 'Effects of Increased Awareness on Choice of Travel Mode', *Transportation* 30:1, 63–79.

Giddens, A. (1984), *The Constitution of Society: Outline of the Theory of Structuration* (Berkeley: University of California Press).

Glaeser, E. L., Laibson, D., and Sacerdote, B. (2002), 'An Economic Approach to Social Capital', *Economic Journal* 112:11, 437–58.

Gliebe, J. P. and Koppelman, F. S. (2002), 'A Model of Joint Activity Participation Between Household Members', *Transportation* 29:1, 49–72.

— — (2005), 'Modeling Household Activity-Travel Interactions as Parallel Constrained Choices', *Transportation* 32:5, 449–71.

Goldin, C. and King, L. (2008), 'The Race between Education and Technology' (Cambridge: Harvard University Press).

Golob, T. F., Kitamura, R., and Long, L. (eds) (1997), *Panels for Transportation Planning: Methods and Applications* (Transportation Research, Economics and Policy v; Boston: Kluwer Academic).

Golledge, R. G. (1999), 'Human Wayfinding and Cognitive Maps', in R. G. Golledge (ed.), 5–45.

Golledge, R. G. (ed.) (1999), *Wayfinding Behavior: Cognitive Mapping and Other Spatial Processes* (Baltimore: Johns Hopkins University Press).

Golledge, R. G. and Stimson, R. J. (1997), *Spatial Behavior: A Geographic Perspective* (New York: Guilford Press).

Golledge, R. G. and Timmermans, H. J. P. (eds) (1988), *Behavioural Modelling in Geography and Planning* (London: Croom Helm).

Goodwin, P. B., Kitamura, R., and Meurs, H. (1990), 'Some Principles of Dynamic Analysis of Travel Behaviour', in P. M. Jones (ed.), 56–72.

Götz, K., Jahn, T., and Schultz, I. (1997), *Mobilitätsstile: Ein sozial-ökologischer Untersuchungsansatz* (Forschungsberichte Stadtverträgliche Mobilität vii; Frankfurt am Main: Institut für sozial-ökologische Forschung).

Gould, P. R. and White, R. R. (1986), *Mental Maps*, 2nd Edition (London: Routledge).

Goulias, K. G. (1999), 'Longitudinal Analysis of Activity and Travel Pattern Dynamics Using Generalized Mixed Markov Latent Class Models', *Transportation Research Part B: Methodological* 33:8, 535–58.

Goulias, K. G. (ed.) (2002), *Transportation Systems Planning: Methods and Applications* (New York: CRC Press).

Greene, W. H. (1998), *LIMDEP User's Manual: Version 7.0* (Plainview: Econometric Software).

Grieco, M. S. (1987), *Keeping it in the Family: Social Networks and Employment Chance* (London: Tavistock Publications).

— (1996), *Workers' Dilemmas: Recruitment, Reliability and Repeated Exchange: An Analysis of Urban Social Networks and Labour Circulation* (London: Routledge).

Guensler, R. L., Ogle, J., and Li, H. (2006), 'Variability in 2004 Commute Atlanta Instrumented Vehicle Travel Activity', paper presented at the 85th Annual Meeting of Transportation Research Board, Washington, DC, January 2006.

Hägerstrand, T. (1953), *Innovationsförloppet ur Korologisk Synpunkt* (Lund: Gleerupska Univ.-Bokhandeln).

— (1970), 'What about People in Regional Science?', *Papers in Regional Science* 24:1, 6–21.

Hamed, M. M. and Mannering, F. L. (1993), 'Modeling Travelers' Postwork Activity Involvement: Toward a New Methodology', *Transportation Science* 27:4, 381–94.

— Kim, S.-G., and Mannering, F. (1993), 'A Note on Travelers' Home-Stay Duration and the Efficiency of Proportional Hazard Models', working paper (Seattle: University of Washington).

Han, A. and Hausman, J. A. (1990), 'Flexible Parametric Estimation of Duration and Competing Risk Models', *Journal of Applied Econometrics* 5:1, 1–28.

Hanson, S. and Burnett, K. P. (1981), 'Understanding Complex Travel Behavior: Measurement Issues', in P. R. Stopher, A. H. Meyburg, and W. Brög (eds), 207–30.

— and Huff, J. O. (1982), 'Assessing Day-to-Day Variability in Complex Travel Patterns', *Transportation Research Record* 891, 18–23.

— — (1986), 'Classification Issues in the Analysis of Complex Travel Behavior', *Transportation* 13:3, 271–93.

— — (1988a), 'Systematic Variability in Repetitious Travel', *Transportation* 15:1–2, 111–35.

— — (1988b), 'Repetition and Day-to-Day Variability in Individual Travel Patterns: Implications for Classification', in R. G. Golledge and H. J. P. Timmermans (eds), 368–98.

Harvey, A. S. (1982), 'Role and Context: Shapers of Behaviour', *Studies of Broadcasting* 18, 69–92.

— et al. (1997), *24-Hour Society and Passenger Travel*. Final Report (Halifax, Canada: St. Mary's University).

Hatcher, S. G. and Mahmassani, H. S. (1992), 'Daily Variability of Route and Trip Scheduling Decisions for the Evening Commute', *Transportation Research Record* 1357, 72–81.

Hatton, T. J. and Williamson, J. G. (2005), *Global Migration and the World Economy: Two Centuries of Policy and Performance* (Cambridge: MIT Press).

Haynes, K. E. and Fotheringham, A. S. (1990), 'The Impact of Space on the Application of Discrete Choice Models', *The Review of Regional Studies* 20:2, 39–49.

Heckman, J. J., Lochner, L. J., and Todd, P. E. (2003), 'Fifty Years of Mincer Earnings Regressions' (IZA Discussion Paper, 775; Bonn: Institute for the Study of Labor [IZA]).

Heidemann, C. (1981), 'Spatial Behaviour Studies: Concepts and Contexts', in P. R. Stopher, A. H. Meyburg, and W. Brög (eds), 289–315.

Hensher, D. A. (1997), 'The Timing of Change: Discrete and Continuous Time Panels in Transportation', in T. F. Golob, R. Kitamura, and L. Long (eds), 305–20.

— and Button, K. J. (eds) (2000), *Handbook of Transport Modelling* (Handbooks in Transport, i; Amsterdam: Pergamon Press).

— and Johnson, L. W. (1981), *Applied Discrete-Choice Modelling* (London: Croom Helm).

— and Mannering, F. L. (1994), 'Hazard-Based Duration Models and Their Application to Transport Analysis', *Transport Reviews* 14:1, 63–82.

— et al. (eds) (2004), *Handbook of Transport Geography and Spatial Systems* (Handbooks in Transport v; Oxford: Elsevier Science).

Herbert, D. T. and Johnston, R. J. (eds) (1976), *Social Areas in Cities, ii: Spatial Perspectives on Problems and Policies* (Chichester: Wiley).

Herbert, D. T. and Raine, J. W. (1976), 'Defining Communities within Urban Areas: An Analysis of Alternative Approaches', *Town Planning Review* 47:4, 325–38.

Herz, R. (1983), 'Stability, Variability and Flexibility in Everyday Behaviour', in S. M. Carpenter and P. M. Jones (eds), 385–400.

Hess, S., Erath, A. and Axhausen, K. W. (2008), 'Estimated Value of Savings in Travel Time in Switzerland: Analysis of Pooled Data', *Transportation Research Record* 2082, 43-55.

Holzapfel, H. (1980), *Verkehrsbeziehungen in Städten* (Schriftenreihe des Instituts für Verkehrsplanung und Verkehrswegebau v; Berlin: Technische Universität).

Horton, F. E. (ed.) (1968), *Geographical Studies of Urban Transportation and Network Analysis* (Studies in Geography 16; Evanston: Northwestern University).

Horton, F. E. and Reynolds, D. R. (1971), 'Effects of Urban Spatial Structure on Individual Behavior', *Economic Geography* 47:1, 36–48.

Hosmer, D. W. and Lemeshow, S. (1999), *Applied Survival Analysis: Regression Modeling of Time to Event Data* (New York: Wiley).
Hubert, J.-P., Armoogum, J., Axhausen, K. W. and Madre, J.-L. (2008), 'Immobility and Mobility Seen Through Trip Based Versus Time Use Surveys', *Transport Reviews* 28:5, 641-58.
Huff, J. O. and Hanson, S. (1986), 'Repetition and Variability in Urban Travel', *Geographical Analysis* 18:2, 97–114.
— — (1990), 'Measurement of Habitual Behaviour: Examining Systematic Variability in Repetitive Travel', in P. M. Jones (ed.), 229–49.
Hunt, L. M., Boots, B., and Kanaroglou, P. S. (2004), 'Spatial Choice Modelling: New Opportunities to Incorporate Space into Substitution Patterns', *Progress In Human Geography* 28:6, 746–66.
Hutchinson, B. G. (1974), *Principles of Urban Transports Systems Planning* (Washington: Scripta Book).
Hutchinson, B., Nijkamp, P. and Batty, M. (eds) (1983), *Optimization and Discrete Choice in Urban Systems, Lecture Notes in Economics and Mathematical Systems* (New York: Springer).
Hyland, G. A. (1970), 'A Social Interaction Analysis of the Appalachian In-Migrant', M.A. thesis (University of Cincinnati).
Isard, W. (1956), *Location and Space-Economy: A General Theory Relating to Industrial Location, Market Areas, Land Use, Trade and Urban Structure* (Cambridge: Technology Press of MIT; New York: Wiley).
Jakle, J. A., Brunn, S., and Roseman, C. C. (1976), *Human Spatial Behaviour: A Social Geography* (North Scituate: Duxbury Press).
Jennrich, R. I. and Turner, F. B. (1969), 'Measurement of Non-Circular Home Range', *Journal of Theoretical Biology* 22:2, 227–37.
Jones, P. M. (1981), 'Activity Approaches to Understanding Travel Behavior', in P. R. Stopher, A. H. Meyburg, and W. Brög (eds), 253–66.
Jones, P. M. (ed.) (1990), *Developments in Dynamic and Activity-Based Approaches to Travel Analysis* (Oxford Studies in Transport; Aldershot: Avebury Publishing).
Jones, P. M. and Clarke, M. I. (1988), 'The Significance and Measurement of Variability in Travel Behaviour', *Transportation* 15:1–2, 65–87.
— Koppelman, F. S. and Orfeuil, J.-P. (1990), 'Activity Analysis: State-of-the-Art and Future Directions', in P. M. Jones (ed.), 34–55.
— et al. (1983), *Understanding Travel Behaviour* (Oxford Studies in Transport; Aldershot: Gower Publishing).
Jou, R.-C. and Mahmassani, H. S. (1996), 'Comparability and Transferability of Commuter Behavior Characteristics between Cities: Departure Time and Route-Switching Decisions', *Transportation Research Record* 1556, 119–30.
— (1997), 'Comparative Analysis of Day-to-Day Trip-Chaining Behavior of Urban Commuters in Two Cities', *Transportation Research Record* 1607, 163–70.

Juster, F. T. and Stafford, F. P. (1991), 'The Allocation of Time: Empirical Findings, Behavioral Models, and Problems of Measurement', *Journal of Economic Literature* 29:2, 471–522.

Kahneman, D., Slovic, P., and Tversky, A. (eds) (1982), *Judgment under Uncertainty: Heuristics and Biases* (Cambridge: Cambridge University Press).

Kalbfleisch, J. D. and Prentice, R. L. (1980), *The Statistical Analysis of Failure Time Data* (New York: Wiley).

Kang, H. and Scott, D. M. (2008), 'An Integrated Spatio-Temporal GIS Toolkit for Exploring Intra-Household Interactions', *Transportation* 35:2, 253–68.

Kaplan, E. L. and Meier, P. (1958), 'Nonparametric Estimation from Incomplete Observations', *Journal of the American Statistical Association* 53:282, 457–81.

Kaspar, C., Laesser, C., and Bieger, T. (eds) (2001), *Jahrbuch 2000/2001 Schweizerische Verkehrswirtschaft* (St. Gallen: SVWG).

Kempermann, A. D. A. M., Borgers, A. W. J., and Timmermans, H. J. P. (2002), 'Incorporating Variety Seeking and Seasonality in Stated Preference Modeling of Leisure Trip Destination Choice: Test of External Validity', *Transportation Research Record* 1807, 67–76.

— et al. (2000), 'Consumer Choice of Theme Parks: A Conjoint Choice Model of Seasonality Effects and Variety Seeking Behavior', *Leisure Sciences* 22:1, 1–18.

Kenyon, S., Lyons, G., and Rafferty, J. (2002), 'Transport and Social Exclusion: Investigating the Possibility of Promoting Inclusion through Virtual Mobility', *Journal of Transport Geography* 10:3, 207–19.

Keßler, C., 'The Revival of Time-Geography' <http://www.gisblog.net/research/the-revival-of-time-geography>, accessed 29 August 2008.

Kim, H.-M. and Kwan, M.-P. (2003), 'Space-Time Accessibility Measures: A Geocomputational Algorithm with a Focus on the Feasible Opportunity Set and Possible Activity Duration', *Journal of Geographical Systems* 5:1, 71–91.

Kirkby, C. A. (2001), 'Estimation of Home Range, Core Area and Habitat Utilisation of Urban Foxes (Vulpes Vulpes) Using a Fixed Kernel Technique in a GIS Environment'. The University of York. <http://www.geocities.com/chris_kirkby/foxes.htm>, accessed 8 August 2004.

Kitamura, R. (1988), 'An Evaluation of Activity-Based Travel Analysis', *Transportation* 15:1–2, 9–34.

— and van der Hoorn, T. (1987), 'Regularity and Irreversibility of Weekly Travel Behavior', *Transportation* 14:3, 227–51.

Kleinbaum, D. G. (1996), *Survival Analysis: A Self-Learning Text* (New York: Springer).

Klöckner, C. A. and Matthies, E. (2004), 'How Habits Interfere with Norm-Directed Behaviour: A Normative Decision-Making Model for Travel Mode Choice', *Journal of Environmental Psychology* 24:3, 319–27.

Koll-Schretzenmayr, M., Keiner, M., and Nussbaumer, G. (eds) (2004), *The Real and Virtual Worlds of Spatial Planning* (Heidelberg: Springer).

Kopec, J. A. (1995), 'Concepts of Disability: The Activity Space Model', *Social Science and Medicine* 40:5, 649–56.

Koppelman, F. S. and Pas, E. I. (1984), 'Estimation of Disaggregate Regression Models of Person Trip Generation with Multiday Data', in J. Volmuller and R. Hamerslag (eds), 513–31.

Kruskal, J. B. (1956), 'On the Shortest Spanning Subtree of a Graph and the Traveling Salesman Problem', *Proceedings of the American Mathematical Society* 7:1 48–50.

Kutter, E. (1972), *Demographische Determinanten des städtischen Personenverkehrs* (Veröffentlichungen des Instituts für Stadtbauwesen der TU Braunschweig, 9; Braunschweig: TU Braunschweig).

— (1973), 'A Model for Individual Travel Behaviour', *Urban Studies* 10:2, 235–58.

Kwan, M.-P. (1999), 'Gender and Individual Access to Urban Opportunities: A Study Using Space-Time Measures', *Professional Geographer* 51:2, 210–27.

— (2000), 'Interactive Geovisualization of Activity-Travel Patterns Using Three-Dimensional Geographical Information Systems: A Methodological Exploration with a Large Data Set', *Transportation Research Part C: Emerging Technologies* 8:1–6, 185–203.

— (2006), 'From oral histories to visual narratives: re-presenting the post-September 11 experiences of the Muslim women in the USA', *Social and Cultural Geography* 9:6, 653–59.

Lammers, G. and Herz, R. (1979), 'Aktivitätenmuster für die Stadtplanung', *Seminarberichte* (Karlsruhe: Institut für Städtebau und Landesplanung, Universität Karlsruhe).

Landsman, J. K. (1991), 'Dynamic Travel Environment Change as an Outcome of Travel Related Stresses' (MS Engineering thesis, University of California, Irvine).

Larsen, J., Urry, J. and Axhausen, K. W. (2006), *Mobilities, Networks, Geographies* (Aldershot: Ashgate).

Law, A. M. and Kelton, W. D. (1991), *Simulation Modeling and Analysis*, 2nd Edition (New York: McGraw Hill).

Lee-Gosselin, M. E. H. (2002), 'Some Reflections on GPS-Supported Travel Survey Methods in an Increasingly ICT-Rich Environment', paper presented at the workshop 'ICT, Innovation and the Transport System', Arlington, January 2002.

Lees, L., Slater, T. and Wyly, E. (2007), *Gentrification* (London: Routledge).

Leibbrand, K. (1957), *Verkehrsingenieurwesen* (Basel: Birkhäuser).

Lenntorp, B. (1976), *Paths in Space-Time Environments: A Time-Geographic Study of Movement Possibilities of Individuals* (Lund Studies in Geography B: Human Geography 44; Lund: Department of Geography, Royal University of Lund).

Lerman, S. R. (1983), 'Random Utility Models of Spatial Choice', in B. G. Hutchinson, P. Nijkamp, and M. Batty (eds), *Optimization and Discrete Choice in Urban Systems: Proceedings of the International Symposium on New Directions in Urban Systems Modelling Held at the University of Waterloo, Canada, July 1983* (Lecture Notes in Economics and Mathematical Systems 247; Berlin: Springer), 200–17.

Levine, N. (2004), *CrimeStat: A Spatial Statistics Program for the Analysis of Crime Incidents Locations* (version 3.0), (Houston: Ned Levine and Associates; Washington, DC: National Institute of Justice).

Lill, E. (1889), 'Die Grundgesetze des Personenverkehrs: Eine Studie', *Zeitschrift für Eisenbahnen und Dampfschiffahrt der Österreichisch-Ungarischen Monarchie* 35, 697–706; 36, 713–25.

Lilley, K. D. (2002), *Urban Life in the Middle Ages: 1000-1450* (London and New York: Palgrave Macmillan).

Little, R. J. A. and Rubin, D. B. (1987), *Statistical Analysis with Missing Data* (New York: Wiley).

Löchl, M. et al. (2005), *Stabilität des Verkehrsverhaltens*. Final Report for SVI 2001/514 (*Schriftenreihe* 1120; Bern: Bundesamt für Strassen, UVEK).

Long, L. (1997), 'Panels for Transportation Planning: Theoretical Issues and Empirical Challenges', in T. F. Golob, R. Kitamura, and L. Long (eds), xv–xxiii.

Lynch, K. (1960), *The Image of the City* (Cambridge: MIT Press).

Machguth, H. and Löchl, M. (2004), *Geokodierung 6-Wochenbefragung Thurgau 2003* (*Arbeitsberichte Verkehrs- und Raumplanung* 219; Zürich: IVT, ETH Zürich).

Madre, J.-L., Axhausen, K. W., and Brög, W. (2007), 'Immobility in Travel Diary Surveys', *Transportation* 34:1, 107–28.

Mahmassani, H. S. (1988), 'Some Comments on Activity-Based Approaches to the Analysis and Prediction of Travel Behavior', *Transportation* 15:1–2, 35–40.

— (1997), 'Dynamics of Commuter Behaviour: Recent Research and Continuing Challenges', in P. R. Stopher and M. E. H. Lee-Gosselin (eds), 279–313.

— (2001), 'Dynamic Network Traffic Assignment and Simulation Methodology for Advanced System Management Applications', *Networks and Spatial Economics* 1:3–4, 267–92.

— and Liu, Y.-H. (1999), 'Dynamics of Commuting Decision Behaviour under Advanced Traveller Information Systems', *Transportation Research Part C: Emerging Technologies* 7: 2–3, 91–107.

— Hatcher, S. C., and Caplice, C. G. (1997), 'Daily Variation of Trip Chaining, Scheduling and Path Selection Behaviour of Work Commuters', in P. R. Stopher and M. E. H. Lee-Gosselin (eds), 351–79.

Mannering, F. L. (1989), 'Poisson Analysis of Commuter Flexibility in Changing Routes and Departure Times', *Transportation Research Part B: Methodological* 23:1, 53–60.

— and Hamed, M. M. (1990), 'Occurrence, Frequency, and Duration of Commuters' Work-to-Home Departure Delay', *Transportation Research Part B: Methodological* 24:2, 99–109.
— Murakami, E., and Kim, S.-G. (1992), 'Models of Travelers' Activity Choice and Home-Stay Duration: Analysis of Functional Form and Temporal Stability', working paper (Seattle: University of Washington).
——— (1994), 'Temporal Stability of Travelers' Activity Choice and Home-Stay Duration: Some Empirical Evidence', *Transportation* 21:4, 371–92.
Manski, C. F. (1977), 'The Structure of Random Utility Models', *Theory and Decision* 8:3, 229–54.
Marble, D. F. and Bowlby, S. R. (1968), 'Shopping Alternatives and Recurrent Travel Patterns', in F. E. Horton (ed.), 42–75.
— and Nystuen, J. D. (1963), 'An Approach to the Direct Measurement of Community Mean Information Fields', *Papers in Regional Science* 11:1, 99–109.
— Hanson, P. O., and Hanson, S. E. (1972), *Household Travel Behavior Study Report No. 1: Field Operations and Questionnaires* (Evanston: The Transportation Center at Northwestern University).
Martin, B. V., Memmott, F. W., and Bone, A. J. (1961), *Principles and Techniques of Predicting Future Demand for Urban Area Transportation* (Cambridge: MIT Press).
McAlister, L. and Pessemier, E. (1982), 'Variety Seeking Behaviour: An Interdisciplinary Review', *Journal of Consumer Research* 9:3, 311–22.
McNally, M. G. (2000), 'The Activity-Based Approach'. Paper UCI-ITS-AS-WP-00-4 (Irvine: Center for Activity Systems Analysis, University of California) <http://repositories.cdlib.org/itsirvine/casa/UCI-ITS-AS-WP-00-4>, last accessed May 2009.
Meyer, B. D. (1987), 'Semiparametric Estimation of Duration Models', Ph.D thesis (Massachusetts Institute of Technology).
Meyer, R. J. (1980), 'Theory of Destination Choice-Set Formation under Informational Constraint', *Transportation Research Record* 750, 6–12.
Michelson, W. M. (2005) *Time Use: Expanding Explanation in the Social Sciences* (Boulder: Paradigm Publishers).
Miller, E. J. (1999), *Panels and Other Survey Extensions to the Transportation Tomorrow Survey*, report to the Data Management Group, Joint Program in Transportation (Toronto: University of Toronto).
— and O'Kelly, M. (2005), 'Estimating Shopping Destination Choice Models from Travel Diary Data', *The Professional Geographer* 35:4, 440-9
— and Roorda, M. J. (2003), 'Prototype Model of Household Activity-Travel Scheduling', *Transportation Research Record* 1831, 114–21.
Miller, H. J. (1991), 'Modelling Accessibility Using Space-Time Prism Concepts within Geographical Information Systems', *International Journal of Geographical Information Systems* 5:3, 287–301.
— (2004), 'Activities in Space and Time', in D. A. Hensher et al. (eds), 647–60.

— and Wu, Y.-H. (2000), 'GIS Software for Measuring Space-Time Accessibility in Transportation Planning and Analysis', *GeoInformatica* 4:2, 141–59.
Mitchell, A. (1999), *The ESRI Guide to GIS Analysis, i: Geographic Patterns and Relationships* (Redlands: ESRI Press).
Mokhtarian, P. L. and Salomon, I. (2001), 'How Derived is the Demand for Travel? Some Conceptual and Measurement Considerations', *Transportation Research Part A: Policy and Practice* 35:8, 695–719.
Moore, E. (1970), 'Some Spatial Properties of Urban Contact Fields', *Geographical Analysis* 2, 376-86.
Mumford, L. (1961), *The City in History* (London: Penguin Books).
Muthyalagari, G. R., Parashar, A., and Pendyala, R. M. (2001), 'Measuring Day-to-Day Variability in Travel Characteristics Using GPS Data', paper presented at the 80th Annual Meeting of the Transportation Research Board, Washington, DC, January 2001.
Nagel, K., Beckman, R. J., and Barrett, C. L. (1998), 'TRANSIMS for Transportation Planning', Manuscript 244, *InterJournal Complex Systems* <http://www.interjournal.org/manuscript_abstract.php?49912>, last accessed May 2009.
Newsome, T. H., Walcott, W. A., and Smith, P. D. (1998), 'Urban Activity Spaces: Illustrations and Application of a Conceptual Model for Integrating the Time and Space Dimensions', *Transportation* 25:4, 357–77.
Nielsen, O. A. (2004), 'Behavioral Responses to Road Pricing Schemes: Description of the Danish AKTA Experiment', *Journal of Intelligent Transportation Systems* 8:4, 233–51.
— and Jovicic, G. (2003), 'The AKTA Road Pricing Experiment in Copenhagen', paper presented at the 10th International Conference on Travel Behaviour Research, Lucerne, August 2003.
Niemeier, D. A. and Morita, J. G. (1996), 'Duration of Trip-Making Activities by Men and Women: A Survival Analysis' *Transportation* 23:4, 353–71.
Nuttin, J. M., Jr. (1984), *Motivation, Planning, and Action: A Relational Theory of Behavior Dynamics* (Leuven: Leuven University Press).
Ogle, J., Guensler, R, and Elango, V. (2005), 'Georgia's Commute Atlanta Value Pricing Program: Recruitment Methods and Travel Diary Response Rates', *Transportation Research Record* 1931, 28–37.
— et al. (2006), 'Analysis of Under-Reporting and Other Errors in Commute Atlanta Travel Diaries Using Instrumented Vehicle Data', paper presented at the 85th Annual Meeting of the Transportation Research Board, Washington, DC, January 2006.
Oh, L. (2000), 'Identification of the Causal Factors of Activity Dynamics Using Hazard-Based Duration Models', working paper (London: Centre for Transport Studies, Imperial College of Science, Technology and Medicine).
Oi, W. Y. and Shuldiner, P. W. (1962), *An Analysis of Urban Travel Demands* (Evanston: Northwestern University Press).

Organisation for Economic Co-operation and Development (OECD) and Statistics Canada (eds) (2000), *Literacy in the Information Age: Final Report of the International Adult Literacy Survey* (Paris: OECD Publications).

— Human Resources Development Canada (eds) (1997), Literacy Skills for the Knowledge Society: Further Results from the International Adult Literacy Survey (Paris and Ottawa, ON: OECD and HRDC).

Ortúzar, J. de D. and Willumsen, L. G. (2001), *Modelling Transport*, 3rd Edition (Chichester: Wiley).

Pahl, R. E. (1970), *Patterns of Urban Life* (London and Harlow: Longmans, Green and Co.).

Parsons, G. R. and Hauber, A. B. (1998), 'Spatial Boundaries and Choice Set Definition in a Random Utility Model of Recreation Demand', *Land Economics* 74:1, 32–48.

Pas, E. I. (1980), 'Towards the Understanding of Urban Travel Behavior through the Classification of Daily Urban Travel/Activity Patterns', Ph.D. thesis (Northwestern University).

— (1983), 'A Flexible and Integrated Methodology for Analytical Classification of Daily Travel-Activity Behavior', *Transportation Science* 17:4, 405–29.

— (1986), 'Multiday Samples, Parameter Estimation Precision, and Data Collection Costs for Least Squares Regression Trip-Generation Models', *Environment and Planning A* 18:1, 73–87.

— (1987), 'Intrapersonal Variability and Model Goodness-of-Fit', *Transportation Research Part A: General* 21:6, 431–8.

— (1988), 'Weekly Travel-Activity Behavior', *Transportation* 15:1–2, 89–109.

— (1990), 'Is Travel Demand Analysis and Modeling in the Doldrums?', in P. M. Jones (ed.), 3–33.

— and Harvey, A. S. (1997), 'Time Use Research and Travel Demand Analysis Modelling', in P. R. Stopher and M. E. H. Lee-Gosselin (eds), 315–38.

— and Koppelman, F. S. (1986), 'An Examination of the Determinants of Day-to-Day Variability in Individuals' Urban Travel Behavior', *Transportation* 13:2, 183–200.

— and Sundar, S. (1995), 'Intrapersonal Variability in Daily Urban Travel Behavior: Some Additional Evidence', *Transportation* 22:2, 135–50.

Pearson, D. F. (2001), 'Global Positioning System (GPS) and Travel Surveys: Results from the 1997 Austin Household Survey', paper presented at the 8th Conference on the Application of Transportation Planning Methods, Corpus Christi, Texas, April 2001.

Pendyala, R. M. (1999), *Day-to-Day Variability in Travel Using Lexington, KY GPS-Based Data Set: Measuring Day-to-Day Variability in Travel Behavior Using GPS Data*. Final Report (Washington, DC: FHWA) <http://www.fhwa.dot.gov/ohim/gps/>

— Yamamoto, T., and Kitamura, R. (2002), 'On the Formulation of Time-Space Prisms to Model Constraints on Personal Activity-Travel Engagement', *Transportation* 29:1, 73–94.

Polak, J. W. and Han, X. L. (1997), 'Iterative Imputation Based Methods for Unit and Item Nonresponse in Travel Diary Surveys', paper presented at the 8th Meeting of the International Association for Travel Behaviour Research, Austin, September 1997.
Pollak, R. A. (1999), 'Notes on Time Use', *Monthly Labor Review* 122:8, 7–11.
Prentice, R. L. (1976), 'A Generalization of the Probit and Logit Methods for Dose Response Curves', *Biometrics* 32:4, 761–8.
— and Gloeckler, L. A. (1978), 'Regression Analysis of Grouped Survival Data with Application to Breast Cancer Data', *Biometrics* 34:1, 57–67.
Prim, R. C. (1957), 'Shortest Connection Networks and Some Generalizations', *Bell Systems Technical Journal* 36, 1389–1401.
Psacharopoulos, G. and Patrinos, H. A. (2004), 'Returns to Investment in Education: A Further Update', *Education Economics* 12:2, 111–34.
Putnam, R. D. (2000), *Bowling Alone: The Collapse and Revival of American Community* (New York: Simon & Schuster).
Raine, J. W. (1978), 'Summarizing Point Patterns with the Standard Deviational Ellipse', *Area* 10:5, 328–33.
Reader, S. and McNeill, F. R. (1999), 'Hazard-Rate Modelling of Store-Switching Behaviour', *Environment and Planning A* 31:8, 1353–70.
Recker, W. W. and Kitamura, R. (1985), 'Activity-Based Travel Analysis', in G. R. M. Jansen, P. Nijkamp, and C. J. Ruijgrok (eds), *Transportation and Mobility in an Era of Transition* (Studies in Regional Science and Urban Economics, 13; Amsterdam: North-Holland Publishing), 157–83.
Reilly, W. J. (1931), *The Law of Retail Gravitation* (New York: Knickerbocker Press).
Richardson, A. J. (2003a), 'Behavioral Mechanisms of Nonresponse in Mail-Back Travel Surveys', *Transportation Research Record* 1855, 191–9.
— (2003b), 'Temporal Variability of Car Usage as an Input for the Design of Before and After Studies', *Transportation Research Record* 1855, 112-20.
Rindsfüser, G., Perian, T., and Schönfelder, S. (2001), 'Raum-Zeit-Analyse individueller Tätigkeitsprofile: Erste Annäherung auf der Basis einer Längsschnitterhebung (Mobidrive)', *Stadt Region Land* 71, 89–106.
Rubin, D. B. (1987), *Multiple Imputation for Nonresponse in Surveys* (Wiley Series in Probability and Statistics; New York: Wiley).
Rubin, D. B. (2004), *Multiple Imputation for Nonresponse in Surveys* (Wiley Classics Library, i; New York: Wiley).
Ruiter, E. R. (1967), 'Improvements in Understanding, Calibrating, and Applying the Opportunity Model', *Highway Research Record* 165, 1–21.
Saleh, W. and Farrell, S. (2005), 'Implications of Congestion Charging for Departure Time Choice: Work and Non-Work Schedule Flexibility' *Transportation Research Part A: Policy and Practice* 39:7–9, 773–91.
Saxena, S. and Mokhtarian, P. L. (1997), 'The Impact of Telecommuting on the Activity Spaces of Participants', *Geographical Analysis* 29:2, 124–44.

Scheiner, J. (2001), 'Berlin – noch immer geteilt? Untersuchungen zur Mobilität zwischen dem West- und Ostteil der deutschen Hauptstadt', *Geographische Rundschau* 53:3, 17–23.

Schlich, R. (2004), 'Verhaltenshomogene Gruppen in Längsschnitterhebungen', Diss. (ETH Zürich).

— and Axhausen, K. W. (2003), 'Habitual Travel Behaviour: Evidence from a Six-Week Travel Diary', *Transportation* 30:1, 13–36.

— König, A., and Axhausen, K. W. (2000), 'Stabilität und Variabilität im Verkehrsverhalten', *Straßenverkehrstechnik* 44:9, 431–40.

— et al. (2002*a*), 'Durchführung einer 12-wöchigen Langzeitbefragung', *Stadt Region Land* 73, 141–54.

— et al. (2002*b*), *Entwicklung eines Tagebuchs zur Erhebung von Freizeitverhalten* (Arbeitsberichte Verkehrs- und Raumplanung, 121; Zürich: IVT, ETH Zürich).

Schmiedel, R. (1978), *Methoden zur Analyse periodischer Komponenten von Zeitreihen: Theoretische Grundlagen, Interpretationshilfen und EDV-Programme zur harmonischen Analyse und Spektralanalyse* (Karlsruhe: Institut für Städtebau und Landesplanung, Universität Karlsruhe).

Schnabel, W. and Lohse, D. (1997), *Grundlagen der Strassenverkehrstechnik und der Verkehrsplanung*, ii: *Verkehrsplanung* (Berlin: Verlag für Bauwesen).

Schneider, H. (1991), *Verweildaueranalyse mit GAUSS* (Frankfurt: Campus).

Schnittger, S. and Zumkeller, D. (2004), 'Longitudinal Microsimulation as a Tool to Merge Transport Planning and Traffic Engineering Models: The MobiTopp Model', paper presented at the European Transport Conference, Strasbourg, October 2004.

Schofer, J., Khattak, A., and Koppelman, F. S. (1993), 'Behavioural Issues in the Design and Evaluation of Advanced Traveler Information Systems', *Transportation Research Part C: Emerging Technologies* 1:2, 107–17.

Schönfelder, S. (2003), 'Between Routines and Variety Seeking: The Characteristics of Locational Choice in Daily Travel', paper presented at the 10th International Conference on Travel Behaviour Research, Lucerne, August 2003.

— and Axhausen, K. W. (2000), 'Periodizität im Verkehrsverhalten: Erste Ergebnisse mit Überlebenszeitmodellen', *Stadt Region Land* 69, 131–44.

— (2001a), 'Modelling the Rhythms of Travel Using Survival Analysis', in C. Kaspar, C. Laesser, and T. Bieger (eds), 137–62.

— (2001b), 'Mobi*drive* – Längsschnitterhebungen zum individuellen Verkehrsverhalten: Perspektiven für raum-zeitliche Analysen', in M. Schrenk (ed.), 315–21.

— (2002), *Measuring the Size and Structure of Human Activity Spaces: The Longitudinal Perspective* (Arbeitsberichte Verkehrs- und Raumplanung, 135; Zürich: IVT, ETH Zürich).

— (2003), 'Activity Spaces: Measures of Social Exclusion?' *Transport Policy* 10:4, 273–286.

— (2004a), 'On the Variability of Human Activity Spaces', in M. Koll-Schretzenmayr, M. Keiner, and G. Nussbaumer (eds), 237–62.

— (2004b), *Structure and Innovation of Human Activity Spaces* (*Arbeitsberichte Verkehrs- und Raumplanung,* 258; Zürich: IVT, ETH Zürich).

— and Samaga, U. (2003), 'Where do you Want to Go Today? More Observations on Daily Mobility', paper presented at the 3rd Swiss Transport Research Conference, Ascona, March 2003.

Schrenk, M. (ed.) (2001), *CORP 2001 Geo Multimedia: Computergestützte Raumplanung. Beiträge zum 6. Symposion zur Rolle der Informationstechnologie in der und für die Raumplanung, Wien, Februar 2001* ii (Wien: Technische Universität Wien).

Schüssler, N. and Axhausen, K. W. (2008), *Identifying Trips and Activities and Their Characteristics from GPS Raw Data without Further Information* (Arbeitsberichte Verkehrs- und Raumplanung, 502; Zürich: IVT, ETH Zürich).

Schwanen, T. and Dijst, M. (2003), 'Time Windows in Workers' Activity Patterns: Empirical Evidence from the Netherlands', *Transportation* 30:3, 261–83.

Schwartz, S. (1977), 'Normative Influences on Altruism', in Berkowitz (ed.).

Schwesig, R. (1988), 'Räumliche Strukturen von Ausserhausaktivitäten: Ein Konzept zur Analyse räumlichen Verhaltens und empirische Überprüfung am Beispiel der Aktionsräume von Bewohnern der Stadtregion Hamburg', Diss. (Universität Hamburg).

Scott, D. M. (2003), 'Comparison of Two GIS-Based Algorithms for Generating Potential Path Areas', paper presented at the 50th Annual Northern American Meeting of the Regional Science Association International, Philadelphia, November 2003.

Scott, J. (2000), *Social Network Analysis: A Handbook*, 2nd Edition. (London: SAGE Publications).

Shapcott, M. and Steadman, P. (1978), 'Rhythms of Urban Activity', in T. Carlstein, D. Parkes, and N. J. Thrift (eds), *Timing Space and Spacing Time, ii: Human Activity and Time Geography* (London: Arnold), 49–74.

Sheffi, Y. (1985), *Urban Transportation Networks: Equilibrium Analysis with Mathematical Programming Methods* (Englewood Cliffs: Prentice-Hall).

Sheller, M. and Urry, J. (2006), 'The New Mobilities Paradigm', *Environment and Planning A* 38:2, 207–26.

Sherman, J. E. et al. (2005), 'A Suite of Methods for Representing Activity Space in a Healthcare Accessibility Study', *International Journal of Health Geographics* 4:24, 1–21.

Silverman, B. W. (1986), *Density Estimation for Statistics and Data Analysis* (Monographs on Statistics and Applied Probability, 26; London: Chapman & Hall / CRC Press).

Simma, A. (2000), 'Verkehrsverhalten als eine Funktion soziodemografischer und räumlicher Faktoren', Diss. (Leopold-Franzens-Universität, Innsbruck).

Simon, H. A. (1957), *Models of Man: Social and Rational; Mathematical Essays on Rational Human Behavior* (New York: Wiley).

Singhi, P. (2001), *Creation of Vehicle Diaries Using C++ (*Arbeitsberichte Verkehrs- und Raumplanung, 90; Zürich: IVT, ETH Zürich).

Smith, N. (1996), *The New Urban Frontier: Gentrification and the Revanchist City* (London: Routledge).

Srinivasan, S. and Bhat, C. R. (2005), 'Modeling Household Interactions in Daily In-Home and Out-of-Home Maintenance Activity Participation', *Transportation* 32:5, 523–44.

— — (2006), 'A Multiple Discrete-Continuous Model for Independent- and Joint-Discretionary-Activity Participation Decisions', *Transportation* 33:5, 497–515.

Srivastava, G. and Schönfelder, S. (2003), *On the Temporal Variation of Human Activity Spaces* (Arbeitsberichte Verkehrs- und Raumplanung, 196; Zürich: IVT, ETH Zürich).

Steed, J. L. and Bhat, C. R. (2000), 'On Modeling Departure-Time Choice for Home-Based Social/Recreational and Shopping Trips', *Transportation Research Record* 1706, 152–9.

Stewart, J. Q. (1948), 'Demographic Gravitation: Evidence and Applications', *Sociometry* 11:1–2, 31–58.

Stopher, P. and Greaves, S. P. (2007), 'Guidelines for Samplers: Measuring a Change in Behaviour from before and after Surveys', *Transportation* 34:1, 35–51.

— Lee-Gosselin, M. E. H. (eds) (1997), *Understanding Travel Behaviour in an Era of Change* (Oxford: Pergamon Press).

— — and Brög, W. (eds) (1981), *New Horizons in Travel-Behavior Research* (Lexington: Lexington Books).

— et al. (2008), 'Reducing Burden and Sample Sizes in Multiday Household Travel Surveys', *Transportation Research Record* 2064, 12–18.

Stouffer, S. A. (1940), 'Intervening Opportunities: A Theory Relating Mobility and Distance', *American Sociological Review* 5:6, 845–67.

Sueyoshi, G. T. (1992), 'Semiparametric Proportional Hazards Estimation of Competing Risks Models with Time-Varying Covariates', *Journal of Econometrics* 51:1–2, 25–58.

Szalai., A. (ed.) (1972), *The Use of Time: Daily Activities of Urban and Suburban Populations in Twelve Countries* (The Hague: Mouton).

Thill, J.-C. (1992), 'Choice Set Formation for Destination Choice Modelling', *Progress in Human Geography* 16:3, 361–82.

Timmermans, H. J. P. (1990), 'Theoretical Aspects of Variety-Seeking Choice Behaviour', in M. M. Fischer, P. Nijkamp, and Y. Y. Papageorgiou (eds), 101–15.

TRANSIMS Open-Source (2009), Transportation Analysis and Simulation System (open source project site) <http://transims.tsasa.lanl.gov/>, last accessed May 2009.

Tschopp, M., Fröhlich, P., and Axhausen, K. W. (2006), *Verkehrsinfrastruktur und räumliche Entwicklung: Eine ökonometrische Analyse* (Arbeitsberichte Verkehrs- und Raumplanung, 352; Zürich: IVT, ETH Zürich).

Tsui, S. Y. A. and Shalaby, A. S. (2006), 'Enhanced System for Link and Mode Identification for Personal Travel Surveys Based on Global Positioning Systems', *Transportation Research Record* 1972, 38–45.

Urry, J. (2004), 'Small Worlds and the New 'Social Physics'', *Global Networks* 4:2, 109–30.

Venkatesh, S. A. (2006), *Off the Books: The Underground Economy of the Urban Poor* (Cambridge: Harvard University Press).

Voigt, D. R. and Tinline, R. R. (1980), 'Strategies for Analyzing Radio Tracking Data', in C. J. Amlaner and D. W. MacDonald (eds), 387–404.

Völker, B., Flap, H., and Lindenberg, S. (2007), 'When Are Neighbourhoods Communities? Community in Dutch Neighbourhoods', *European Sociological Review* 23:1, 99–114.

Volkmar, H. F. (1984), *Räumliche und zeitliche Aktivitätschancen: Kriterien für die Beurteilung von Erreichbarkeitsverhältnissen in der Verkehrsplanung* (Schriftenreihe des Instituts für Verkehrsplanung und Verkehrswegebau, 14; Berlin: Universitätsbibliothek der Technischen Universität Berlin).

Volmuller, J. and Hamerslag, R. (eds) (1984), *Proceedings of the Ninth International Symposium on Transportation and Traffic Theory* (Utrecht: VNU Science Press).

Vovsha, P., Petersen, E., and Donnelly, R. (2002), 'Microsimulation in Travel Demand Modeling: Lessons Learned from the New York Best Practice Model', *Transportation Research Record* 1805, 68–77.

Wardman, M. (2001), 'A Review of British Evidence on Time and Service Quality Valuations', *Transportation Research E* 37:2–3, 107–28.

Webber, M. J. (1978), *Urban Spatial Structure: An Information Theoretic Approach*, Report to SSHRC on project 410-7-0582 (Hamilton: Department of Geography, McMaster University).

Weiner, E. (2008), *Urban Transportation Planning in the United States: An Historical Overview* (Berlin: Springer).

Weis, C. et al. (2008), 'Vergleich zwischen web-basierten und schriftlichen Befragungen zum Verkehrsverhalten im Zürcher Hochschulquartier', in T. Bieger et al. (eds), 9–30.

Wermuth, M. J. (1985), 'Non-Sampling Errors Due to Non-Response in Written Household Travel Surveys', in E. S. Ampt, A. J. Richardson, and W. Brög (eds), 349–65.

White, E. H. and Company, Inc. (1991), *1990 Bay Area Travel Survey: Final Report* (Oakland: Metropolitan Transportation Commission).

Wilson, A. G. (1967), 'A Statistical Theory of Spatial Distribution Models', *Transportation Research* 1, 253–69.

Winston, G. C. (1982), *The Timing of Economic Activities: Firms, Households, and Markets in Time-Specific Analysis* (Cambridge: Cambridge University Press).

Wiswede, G. (1977), *Rollentheorie* (Urban Taschenbücher, 259; Stuttgart: Kohlhammer).

Wolf, J. (2000), 'Using GPS Data Loggers to Replace Travel Diaries in the Collection of Travel Data', PhD diss. (Georgia Institute of Technology, School of Civil and Environmental Engineering).

— (2003), 'Tracing People and Cars with GPS and Diaries: Current Experience and Tools', paper presented at IVT seminar, Zürich, February 2003.

— Guensler, R., and Bachman, W. (2001), 'Elimination of the Travel Diary: An Experiment to Derive Trip Purpose from GPS Travel Data', paper presented at the 80th Annual Meeting of the Transportation Research Board, Washington, DC, January 2001.

— Oliveira, M., and Thompson, M. (2003), 'The Impact of Trip Underreporting on VMT and Travel Time Estimates: Preliminary Findings from the California Statewide Household Travel Survey GPS Study', *Transportation Research Record* 1854, 189–98.

— et al. (2004), 'Eighty Weeks of Global Positioning System Traces: Approaches to Enriching Trip Information', *Transportation Research Record* 1870, 46–54.

Wolpert, J. (1965), 'Behavioral Aspects of the Decision to Migrate', *Papers in Regional Science* 15:1, 159–69.

World Health Organization (WHO) (2004), 'WHA57.17: Global Strategy on Diet, Physical Activity and Health', in *Fifty-Seventh World Health Assembly: Resolutions and Decisions. Eighth Plenary Meeting, 22 May 2004; Committee A, Third Report* (Geneva: WHO), 38–55 <http://www.who.int/gb/ebwha/pdf_files/WHA57/A57_R17-en.pdf> (last accessed May 2009).

Worton, B. J. (1987), 'A Review of Models of Home Range for Animal Movement', *Ecological Modelling* 38:3–4, 277–98.

Wu, Y. and Miller, H. J. (2001), 'Computational Tools for Measuring Space-Time Accessibility within Dynamic Flow Transportation Networks', *Journal of Transportation and Statistics* 4:2/3, 1–14.

— Hung, M.-C. (2001), 'A GIS-Based Decision Support System for Analysis of Route Choice in Congested Urban Road Networks', *Journal of Geographical Systems* 3:1, 3–24.

Wyatt, J. C. (2000), 'When to Use Web-Based Surveys', *Journal of the American Medical Informatics Association* 7:4, 426–29.

Yun, D. and O'Kelly, M. E. (1997), 'Modeling the Day-of-the-Week Shopping Activity and Travel Patterns', *Socio-Economic Planning Sciences* 31:4, 307-19.

Zahavi, Y. (1974), *Travel Time Budgets and Mobility in Urban Areas*. FHWA PL 8183, Final Report (Washington, DC: US Department of Transportation, Federal Highway Administration).

— (1979), *The 'UMOT' Project*. DOT-RSPA-DPB-20-79-3: Final Report (Washington, DC: US Department of Transportation, Research and Special Programs Administration).

Zanetti, M., Vodoz, A., and Oberli, R. (2008), *Lösungsansätze zur Erfassung der Routenwahl mittels Geokodierung während CATI Befragungen* (Bern: Bundesamt für Raumentwicklung [ARE], Bundesamt für Statistik [BFS]), <http://www.bfs.admin.ch/bfs/portal/de/index/themen/11/07/01/02/05.Document.111163.pdf>.

Zängler, T. W. and Karg, G. (2002), 'Zielorte in der Freizeit', *Stadt Region Land* 73, 155–61.

Zhang, J., Fujiwara, A., and Kusakabe, T. (2004), 'A New Discrete Choice Model with Endogenous Generation of Choice Set Based on the Principle of Relative Utility Maximization', paper presented at the 84th Annual Meeting of the Transportation Research Board, Washington DC, January 2004.

Zhou, J. and Golledge, R. (2000), 'An Analysis of Household Travel Behavior Based on GPS', paper presented at the 9th International Conference on Travel Behaviour Research, Gold Coast, July 2000.

Zimmermann, A. et al. (2001), *Mobidrive: Dynamik und Routinen im Verkehrsverhalten: Pilotstudie Rhythmik*. Bericht an das Bundesministerium für Forschung und Technologie (Karlsruhe, Zürich and Aachen: PTV AG, Institut für Verkehrsplanung, Transporttechnik, Strassen- und Eisenbahnbau [IVT], ETH Zürich und Institut für Stadtbauwesen, RWTH Aachen).

Zimowski, M. et al. (1997) *Nonresponse in Household Travel Surveys*. Prepared for the Federal Highway Administration (Chicago: NORC) <http://tmip.fhwa.dot.gov/resources/clearinghouse/docs/surveys/nonresponse/non.pdf>, last accessed May 2009.

Index

Note: *italic* page numbers denote references to figures/tables.